Calvert's Powers of Arres

Calvert's Powers of Arrest and Charges

Ninth edition

Lewis Heavens LLB

Formerly Chief Inspector and an Assistant Director of
the Inspectors Course, Police Staff College, Bramshill
and currently Tutor in Law,
Norfolk Adult Education Service

Butterworths
London, Dublin, Edinburgh
1995

United Kingdom	Butterworths, a Division of Reed Elsevier (UK) Ltd, Halsbury House, 35 Chancery Lane, LONDON WC2A 1EL and 4 Hill Street, EDINBURGH EH2 3JZ
Australia	Butterworths, SYDNEY, MELBOURNE, BRISBANE, ADELAIDE, PERTH, CANBERRA and HOBART
Canada	Butterworths Canada Ltd, TORONTO and VANCOUVER
Ireland	Butterworth (Ireland) Ltd, DUBLIN
Malaysia	Malayan Law Journal Sdn Bhd, KUALA LUMPUR
New Zealand	Butterworths of New Zealand Ltd, WELLINGTON and AUCKLAND
Puerto Rico	Butterworth of Puerto Rico, Inc, SAN JUAN
Singapore	Butterworths Asia, SINGAPORE
South Africa	Butterworths Publishers (Pty) Ltd, DURBAN
USA	Butterworth Legal Publishers, CARLSBAD, California and SALEM, New Hampshire

A CIP Catalogue record for this book is available from the British Library.

ISBN 0 406 02477 4

Printed and bound by Mackays of Chatham plc, Chatham, Kent

Preface

It was fifty years ago when the late Chief Superintendent Fred Calvert MBE, QPM drafted the *Constable's Pocket Guide to Powers of Arrest and Charges* with the first edition being published in 1945. Since that time and through eight editions it has stood the test of time; succeeding generations of police officers have used it as a companion and practical guide in one of the most difficult areas of their work. This ninth edition brings with it a change in format both in relation to size and the arrangement of materials into four specific parts. Contemporary means of mobility and speed of communications in today's police service coupled with the need for quick reference has necessitated a change from the pocket book format to a larger scale reference work which can be readily available in police stations and carried in police vehicles.

The first part deals with powers of arrest, search and seizure under the Police and Criminal Evidence Act 1984. Part two concentrates on powers and charges under the general criminal law whilst part three is concerned with powers under the Road Traffic Acts. Part four contains the text of the Police and Criminal Evidence Act, Codes of Practice, A, B and C.

The passage of time since the last edition in 1987 has necessitated a substantial review of many significant changes which have taken place. In the field of road traffic there has been increasing public concern in relation to acts of dangerous and careless driving, offences of driving under the influence of drink or drugs and more particularly where death is caused by these acts. Moreover, the unlawful taking and aggravated taking of motor vehicles has involved the police and courts in an ever increasing workload. The new section on road traffic deals with these offences in detail. The Police and Criminal Evidence Act 1984 is the primary source of law, practice and procedure in relation to arrest, search and seizure. This piece of legislation forms the core material for the book.

The text in part two directs officers to their powers in relation to the more common criminal offences. These have been updated since the last edition so as to include the Malicious Communications Act 1988, the Football Spectators Act 1989, the Computer Misuse Act 1990, the Football Offences Act 1991 and the Crossbows Act 1987. Furthermore, during the early course of preparation of this edition, the Criminal Justice and Public Order Bill was introduced into Parliament and it was clear that this book would be incomplete and defective without its provisions. This piece of legislation received a complex and lengthy passage through the House with much external criticism. The new law has necessitated re-writing considerable parts of the text so that the important changes and additions are included.

The Children Act 1989 also deserves special mention as this single piece of legislation has significantly changed the law on police powers relating to children. The text in part two deals with the law and powers on child protection, abduction, and children arrested for criminal offences. The arrest of juveniles also receives special mention in the Codes of Practice.

As before the mode of trial and maximum penalty are given at the head of each offence as follows: IO–triable on indictment only; SO–triable summarily only. Where the offence is triable 'either way', this is stated in full. References to the Police and Criminal Evidence Act are abbreviated throughout to PACE and where an offence is a 'serious arrestable offence' this is referred to as SAO.

The primary object of this edition is to provide quick practical assistance to patrol officers, custody officers, the CID and those more senior officers in a supervisory role. The editor hopes, however, that the book may be of wider use to those working in Magistrates' Clerks Departments and the Crown Prosecution Service. Busy lawyers in these departments often require quick recourse to the law and procedure on arrest and formulation of charges. It is hoped that this book meets the need in the concise nature of the text, ease of reference and the fact that it is not bulky and is easily portable. Members of the public and all those who have a practical and academic interest in the powers of the police may also find the book useful and informative.

Lewis Heavens
King's Lynn
January 1995

Contents

PART ONE

Powers of Arrest and Search

PROCEDURE ON ARREST

When a person is arrested it is a statutory requirement under the Police and Criminal Evidence Act 1984 that he shall be informed that he is under arrest. He must also, at the same time, be told of the grounds for the arrest and cautioned. Sometimes a situation will arise where it is not possible to inform the person arrested straight away, for example if he is violent or resisting arrest. If such circumstances do arise, then the information must be given as soon as practicable after the arrest regardless of whether the grounds of arrest are obvious. The foregoing strict requirements do not apply if a person escapes after he is arrested and it was not reasonably practicable to give him the required information.

If a person is requested by the police to attend voluntarily at a police station or any other place for the purpose of assisting them with an investigation, he is not under arrest. The same applies to a situation where a person is requested by an officer to accompany him voluntarily to a police station or any other place, such as a police car in order to assist their enquiries. Where such attendance is purely voluntary, a person is entitled to leave at will unless he is placed under arrest. If a volunteer does decide to leave at will and the constable decides that he should remain, then the constable must inform him straight away that he is no longer a free man and that he is under arrest. He must be given the grounds for the arrest and cautioned. The obligation upon police officers is quite clear: a man is either under arrest or he is not, there is no half-way stage.

When a person is arrested he must be taken by the police officer to a police station as soon as practicable after the arrest. A constable may delay taking the arrested person to the police station if the prisoner is necessarily required elsewhere in order to carry out such investigations as it is reasonable for the police to carry out immediately. For example, a thief may be able to lead officers to valuable property and evidence which might be lost if he was taken to a police station immediately. If an arrested person is not taken to a police station then this fact must be recorded.

Chief officers of police must designate police stations within their area for the purpose of detaining arrested persons. These will generally be divisional or sub-divisional headquarters. The Police and Criminal Evidence Act lays down that prisoners must be taken to these designated stations. There are exceptions to this general rule: an arrested person may be taken to a non-designated station where an officer either makes the arrest himself, or where he has taken a person into custody from a private individual who has made an arrest and in both cases the arrest has been made without the assistance of any other constable and that no other constable was available to assist the arresting officer. In addition, in both cases, it must appear to the officer that he will be unable to take the prisoner to a designated station without the prisoner injuring himself, the constable or some other person. One further exception is where a constable is working in a locality where there is no designated station, for example, in a remote rural area, unless it appears that the prisoner will have to be detained for longer than six hours. Thus if the constable considers that the prisoner is likely to be kept in custody overnight (over six hours) for court appearance the next morning, then he will have to take the prisoner to a designated station no matter how remote his beat locality unless the first two exceptions mentioned above apply. If a person is taken to a non-designated police station he must be transferred to a designated station not more than six hours after his arrival at the former station unless he has been released previously.

Where an officer makes an arrest whilst on patrol and then makes further enquiries before reaching the station, then if such enquiries reveal that there are no grounds for keeping the person under arrest, the officer must release him and record the fact as soon as practicable afterwards.

SEARCH UPON ARREST

The arrest of a suspect usually takes place at a location other than a police station. In such circumstances s 32 of the Police and Criminal Evidence Act directs that a constable may search the arrested person where he has reasonable grounds for believing the prisoner may present a danger to himself or others. For all practical purposes an officer may seize and retain anything he finds. An officer may also effect a search if he has reasonable grounds for believing that the prisoner may have concealed on him articles which he might use to assist him to escape from lawful custody or which might be evidence relating to an offence. These powers of search do not authorise the constable to remove any of the suspect's clothing in public other than an outer coat jacket or gloves. When s 54, Criminal Justice and Public Act 1994 comes into force it will authorise the search of the suspect's mouth.

Furthermore, in addition to searching the prisoner personally, a constable has power to enter and search premises in which the prisoner was arrested, or immediately before he was arrested, for evidence relating to the offence for which he has been arrested. Where the search is in relation to two or more separate dwellings, the power is limited to searching any dwelling in which the arrest took place or in which the person was immediately before his arrest. The constable may also search any parts of the premises commonly shared with other occupiers. Before making the search of premises a constable must have reasonable grounds for believing that there is evidence on the premises for which a search is permitted. In both personal searches and searches of premises, a constable may only search to the extent that is reasonably required for discovering the means of escape or the evidence.

Powers additional to s 32 are provided in s 18 which states that a constable may enter and search any premises occupied or controlled by a person who is under arrest for an arrestable offence, if he has reasonable grounds for suspecting that there is on the premises evidence which relates to the arrestable offence concerned, or to some other arrestable offence which is connected with, or similar to that offence. The constable has power to seize and retain items found by virtue of this section. The constable before exercising his power of search under s 18 must obtain authority to do so in writing from an officer of the rank of inspector or above. It will often happen that an officer may wish to conduct a search of premises under the control of the person arrested before taking him to the police station. In such circumstances the constable need not obtain written authorisation, provided that the presence of the arrested person is necessary at the place to be searched for the effective investigation of the offence. If a constable conducts a search without written authorisation, he is obliged to inform an officer of inspector rank or above that he has made such a search as soon as reasonably practicable after he has made it. The officer who authorises a search or who is informed of the search where there is no written authorisation, shall record in writing the grounds for the search and the nature of the evidence which was sought.

SEARCH SUBSEQUENT TO ARREST

By virtue of s 54 of the Police and Criminal Evidence Act, the custody officer at the police station must record everything a person possesses when at a police station following his arrest. For this purpose he may make the necessary personal searches. Clothes and personal effects may only be seized if the custody officer believes that the person from whom they are seized may use them to cause physical injury to himself or others, damage property, interfere with evidence or assist him to escape. The custody officer may also seize clothes and personal effects where he has reasonable grounds for believing that they may be evidence relating to an offence. Thus clothing may be taken for forensic analysis in appropriate cases to establish the evidence necessary to prove the crime to be charged. The prisoner must be told the reason for the seizure unless he is violent or likely to become violent or he is incapable of understanding what is said to him. Intimate searches may not be carried out under s 54, they must be carried out under s 55 (see below).

BODY SEARCHES AND SAMPLES

Section 55 of the Police and Criminal Evidence Act directs that intimate searches may be carried out and relevant items seized where a prisoner may have concealed on him anything which he could use to cause physical injury to himself or others while he is in police detention or in the custody of the court. Such searches may also be made for certain drugs (see page 71). Authority for intimate searches can only be made by an officer of at least superintendent rank and then only where he has reasonable grounds for believing the above circumstances exist. Such authority can be given orally or in writing, but if made orally the officer must confirm it in writing as soon as practicable. Intimate searches can only be made at a police station (except for drugs cases), hospital, doctor's surgery or some other place used for medical purposes. The search must be by way of examination by a registered medical practitioner or a registered nurse. However, except in drug offence searches, a search by a constable may be made provided that an officer of the rank of superintendent considers that it is not practicable for the examination to be made by the above qualified persons. In such instances, a constable must not carry out an intimate search of a person of the opposite sex.

Where an intimate search is made this must be entered in the custody record as soon as practicable after the search, details relating to the part of the body searched and why they were searched. If any item is seized, the prisoner must be told the reason for the seizures, unless he is violent or likely to become violent or is incapable of understanding what is said to him. An 'intimate search' means a search consisting of the physical examination of a person's body orifices other than the mouth.

Quite apart from the power provided for intimate searches, s 62(1), authorises the taking of intimate samples from persons in police detention. Once again, an officer of the rank of superintendent or above must authorise it and the prisoner must consent in writing. In the case of young persons aged between 14 and 17, there must in addition be the consent of parent or guardian. With regard to children under 14, only the consent of parent or guardian is required. Authorisation by the police may only be given if there are reasonable grounds for suspecting the person from whom the sample is to be taken is involved in a 'serious arrestable offence' (see pages 16–17). (Note: This will be extended to a person's involvement in a 'recordable offence' when s 54, Criminal Justice and Public Order Act 1994 comes into force. For this purpose a recordable offence will be one of those designated as such by the Secretary of State. Separate regulations will specify the offences concerned.) The police authorisation may be given orally or in writing but if given orally it must be recorded in writing as soon as practicable. The person from whom the sample is to be taken must be informed of the giving of the police authorisation and the grounds for giving it (which must include a statement of the nature of the offence involved). Appropriate entries as set out in s 62(7) and (8) must be entered in the prisoner custody record. Intimate samples may only be taken by a medical practitioner except where the sample is one of urine or saliva.

When the Criminal Justice and Public Order Act 1994 comes into force a dental impression can be taken as an intimate sample but only by a registered dentist.

Where a prisoner does not consent to the taking of intimate samples without good cause, the court or jury may draw such inferences from the refusal as appear proper. Such refusal may be treated as amounting to corroboration of the material evidence.

When s 54(1), Criminal Justice and Public Order Act 1994 comes into force, the above powers will be extended so that intimate samples may be taken from persons who are not in police detention but from whom in the course of investigation of an offence two or more non-intimate samples suitable for the same means of analysis have been taken which have proved insufficient.

Section 63, Police and Criminal Evidence Act 1984, directs that a person must give consent in writing for non-intimate samples to be taken. Consent is not required for taking such samples if the person is in police detention or is being held in custody on the authority of the court and an officer of at least superintendent rank authorises it. When s 55, Criminal Justice and Public Order Act 1994 comes into force the power to take non-intimate samples without consent will be extended to include persons who have been charged with a recordable offence (for meaning see page 6) or have been informed they will be reported for such an offence (and the conditions set out in sub-section (3A)(b) are satisfied) or where a person has been convicted of such an offence.

An 'intimate sample' is defined in the Police and Criminal Evidence Act (as amended by the Criminal Justice and Public Order Act 1994) as being:

(a) a sample of blood, semen, any other tissue fluid, urine, or pubic hair;
(b) a dental impression;
(c) a swab taken from a person's body orifice other than the mouth. A 'non-intimate sample' means–

(a) a sample of hair other than pubic hair;
(b) a sample taken from a nail or under a nail;
(c) a swab taken from any part of a person's body including the mouth but not any other body orifice;
(d) saliva;
(e) a footprint or similar impression of any part of a persons body other than part of his hand.

When s 168(2) and Schedule 10, paragraphs 57 and 58, Criminal Justice and Public Order Act 1994 comes into force, police officers must inform the prisoner before a sample (intimate and non-intimate) is taken that it may be the subject of a 'speculative search' and that fact must be recorded in the custody record as soon as practicable after the sample has been taken. Similar provisions will apply to the taking of fingerprints (see below). A 'speculative search' in relation to a person's samples or fingerprints means a check against other samples or fingerprints or against information derived from other samples.

FINGERPRINTING

Section 61, Police and Criminal Evidence Act 1994, directs that no person's fingerprints may be taken without consent. However, fingerprints of a person detained at a police station may be taken without such consent if an officer of superintendent rank or above authorises it or where the person has been charged with or reported for a 'recordable offence' (for meaning see page 6 above) and has not had his fingerprints taken in the course of investigation of the offence. Such authorisation may only be given if the officer concerned has reasonable grounds for suspecting involvement in a criminal offence and he believes fingerprints will tend to confirm or disprove such involvement. When s 168(2) and Schedule 10, paragraph 56, Criminal Justice and Public Order Act 1994 comes into force, officers must inform the prisoner before fingerprints are taken that such prints may be the subject of a 'speculative search' (for meaning see page   above). This fact shall be recorded as soon as practicable after the fingerprints have been taken. (See also page 18 for powers in relation to fingerprinting of certain offenders under s 27, PACE).

THE RIGHTS OF PRISONERS

The Police and Criminal Evidence Act provides in s 56 that where a person has been arrested and is being held in custody in a police station or other premises he shall be entitled, if he so requests, to have one friend or relative or other person who is known to him or who is likely to take an interest in his welfare, told, as soon as practicable, that he has been arrested. Exceptionally, delay is permitted where a person is in custody for a serious arrestable offence (for meaning–see pages 16–17) and provided an officer of at least superintendent rank authorises it under the special provisions of the section. In any event the right must be exercised within 36 hours of the relevant time as outlined in s 41(2) of the Act.

If there is to be a delay in allowing a detainee to exercise the above right then the superintendent should be informed immediately so that he can exercise his responsibilities under the Act.

With regard to access to legal advice, a prisoner must be entitled, if he so requests, to consult a solicitor privately at any time. He must be allowed to consult as soon as practicable after arrest but delay is permitted under the same criteria mentioned in the foregoing paragraphs.

The Code of Practice directs that the custody officer must inform the prisoner of the above rights and in addition the right to consult the codes of practice. The prisoner must be given written notice setting out the rights and the right to a copy of the custody record and the caution administered to him (see Codes of Practice, Part four).

THE RIGHT OF SILENCE

A person who is questioned by the police, whether he is under arrest or not, has the right to remain silent. The wording of the caution makes the right of silence quite clear. Under the law at the time of publication, the rules are that the prosecution may not comment on the fact of silence and a judge must not suggest to a jury that silence may be evidence of guilt. Changes will, however, take place once ss 34–39 of the Criminal Justice and Public Order Act 1994 come into force. Section 34 provides that where in any proceedings against a person for an offence, evidence is given that the accused was questioned by the police prior to charge and the accused failed to mention certain facts, the court or jury may draw such inferences as appear proper. For the section to apply, the investigating officer must be questioning the accused with a view to discovering whether or by whom the offence had been committed. In addition the fact which the accused failed to mention must relate to a fact which he is relying on in his defence of the proceedings concerned. The court must also be satisfied that the fact which the accused failed to mention was one which in the circumstances existing at the time, the accused could reasonably have been expected to mention when being questioned. The same criteria applies where an accused on being charged with the offence or is officially informed that he might be prosecuted fails to mention a fact relied upon in his defence. The ramifications of this change are quite enormous. It is clear that the statutory caution given by officers to the accused prior to questioning or on being charged will need to reflect the implications of remaining silent. At the time of publication, the Secretary of State has not decided upon the wording of a new caution.

THE ACCUSED'S FAILURE OR REFUSAL TO ACCOUNT FOR OBJECTS ETC

Section 36, Criminal Justice and Public Order Act 1994 provides for the effect of an accused's failure or refusal to account for objects, substances or marks. For the section to become operative, the following must apply:

(a)   The accused must be under arrest.
(b)   There must be found an object, substance or mark, or a mark on any such object.
(c)   The object etc must be on the accused's person or on his clothing or footware or otherwise in his possession or in any place in which he was at the time of his arrest.
(d)   The constable must reasonably believe that the object etc may be attributable to the participation of the person under arrest in the commission of an offence specified by the constable.
(e)   The constable must inform the detainee of his belief and request him to account for the presence of the object etc.

If the accused fails or refuses to provide an account in (e) above, then in any proceedings for the offence specified, where evidence of those matters is given, then a court or jury may draw such inferences from the failure or refusal as appear proper.

In (c) above, a 'place' will include any building or part of a building, any vehicle, vessel, aircraft or hovercraft and any other place whatsoever.

THE ACCUSED'S FAILURE OR REFUSAL TO ACCOUNT FOR HIS PRESENCE AT A PARTICULAR PLACE

In section 37 of the above legislation, there are provisions similar to s 36 in relation to the effect of an accused's failure or refusal to account for his presence at a particular place. The following criteria must apply:

(a)   A person must be under arrest.
(b)   The detainee must have been found by the officer at a place at or about the time the offence for which he was arrested is alleged to have been committed.
(c)   A constable (or investigating officer) must reasonably believe that the presence of the person at that place and time may be attributable to his participation in the commission of the offence.
(d)   The constable must inform the detainee of his belief and request him to account for his presence.

Failure or refusal by the accused to account as above will allow the court or Jury to draw such inferences as appear proper.

The definition of 'place' is the same as in s 36 above.

THE POWER TO STOP AND SEARCH GENERALLY

Quite apart from the powers in relation to arrest, any officer may search any person or vehicle or thing which is in or on the vehicle. In order to accomplish the search the police may detain the person or vehicle concerned provided he has reasonable grounds for suspecting that he will find stolen or prohibited articles or any article in which a person has committed or is committing, or is going to commit an offence under s 139, Criminal Justice Act 1988. There is no power to stop or detain a person against his will in order to find grounds for a search.

The Police and Criminal Evidence Act defines a prohibited article as either an offensive weapon or an article made or adapted for use in the course of or in connection with the offences specified below or intended by the person having such an article with him for such use either by him or some other person. The offences specified in the Act are burglary (see page 38), theft (see page 140), taking a motor vehicle or other conveyance without authority (see page 169) and obtaining property by deception (see page 66).

With regard to offensive weapons, the definition in the Act covers an extremely wide range of instruments. An article will be an offensive weapon if it is made or adapted for use for causing injury to persons or is intended by the person having it with him for such use by him or some other person (s 1(9), PACE).

The power to search may be exercised in any place to which the public have access, whether on payment or otherwise, at the time the officer proposes to make the search. In addition, the power exists in any other place to which people have ready access but which is not a dwelling. Thus searches may lawfully take place, for example, on the street, in car parks, football grounds, pop festivals, public dances and discos and public houses.

Special care must be taken with regard to searches in dwellings and their surrounds. The power to search before an arrest is prohibited inside a dwelling unless it is specifically permitted by law. However, once an arrest has been made inside a dwelling then clearly the power to search then exists by virtue of s 32 of the Act (see page 4). If a suspect is in a garden, yard or other place occupied with and used for the purpose of a dwelling, an officer may not effect a search prior to arrest unless the officer has reasonable grounds for believing that the suspect or person in charge of the vehicle does not reside in the dwelling and that he is not in the place in question with the express or implied permission of the person who resides in the dwelling.

Where an officer stops and makes a search, the code of practice states that the officer may question the person about his behaviour or his presence in circumstances which give rise to suspicion. Such questioning will enable the officer to determine whether a search is necessary. The person being questioned may have a satisfactory explanation thus eliminating the element of reasonable suspicion, in which case no search should take place.

Before any search of a detained person or vehicle takes place, the officer must give the suspect the following information:

(a)   the officer's name and the name of the police station to which he is attached;

(b)   the object of the search; and

(c)   the grounds for making the search.

An officer who is not in uniform must show his warrant card. The police have a statutory duty to record specific details of searches carried out under the Act. The person to be searched or the person in charge of the vehicle to be searched should be told he is entitled to a copy of the record of the search if he asks for it within one year. If the person wishes to have a copy and is not given one on the spot, he should be advised to which police station he should apply for a copy.

With regard to searches of unattended vehicles or anything in or on such a vehicle, the constable must leave a notice inside the vehicle (unless it is not reasonably practicable to do so without damage) stating that a search has been made and the name of the officer making it. The notice must also give the name of the police station to which he is attached and the fact that application for compensation for any damage caused by the search may be made to the officer's police station and the effect of s 3(8) of the Act relating to the provision of copies of the record of search to those entitled to it.

The vehicle searched must if practicable be left secure. The powers of stop and search under s 1, does not authorise an officer to require a person to remove any of his clothing in public other than an outer coat, jacket or gloves. Neither is there any power authorising a constable who is not in uniform to stop a vehicle.

Officers should remember that the stop and search provisions in s 1 will invariably be used where sufficient and reasonable suspicion has been aroused in the officer with regard to an individual's demeanour and his activities prior to arrest. Once an arrest has been made then the officer should apply his wide powers under s 32 of the Act. Finally, officers should become conversant with the code of practice in relation to stop and search and in particular to annex 'B' of the code which provides the criteria for what amounts to the concept of 'reasonable suspicion'.

When in force s 60, Criminal Justice and Public Order Act 1994 will provide officers with extended powers to stop and search where violence is anticipated. The full powers and charges arising thereunder are given at page 114.

ENTRY AND SEARCH OF PREMISES FOR THE PURPOSE OF ARREST

Under s 17 of the Police and Criminal Evidence Act 1984, a constable may enter and search any premises for the purpose of executing:

(a) A warrant of arrest issued in connection with or arising out of criminal proceedings.

(b) A warrant of commitment issued under s 76 of the Magistrates' Courts Act 1980.

(c) Arresting a person for an arrestable offence (see page 14).

(d) Arresting a person under s 1 of the Public Order Act 1936 (prohibition of uniforms in connection with political objects).

(e) Arresting a person under s 4 of the Public Order Act 1986 (fear or provocation of violence) (see page 116).

(f) Arresting a person for an offence under ss 6 to 8 or 10 of the Criminal Law Act 1977 (see page 104).

(g) Recapturing a person who is unlawfully at large and whom he is pursuing.

(h) Saving life or limb or preventing serious injury to property.

Except for (viii) above, the powers of entry and search thus conferred are only exercisable if the constable has reasonable grounds for believing that the person whom he is seeking is on the premises. In addition, where premises contain two or more dwellings (eg flats), the power is limited to entry and search of parts of the premises commonly used by the occupiers and any dwellings in which the constable has reasonable grounds for believing the person whom he is seeking may be.

Nothing in s 17 affects any power of entry of a constable to deal with or prevent a breach of the peace.

ARREST OF JUVENILES

All powers of arrest may be exercised in respect of persons under the age of seventeen in the same way as adults. The same foregoing provisions will apply to such juveniles but officers should remember that in law a child under ten years of age cannot commit any crime. Such children can, however, be dealt with under s 46, Children Act 1989 where it is considered they are in need of police protection (see page 48).

When considering whether to exercise a power of arrest in respect of a juvenile, officers should consider the age of the child or young person together with the circumstances of the offence and the offender. Very often the use of summons procedure will be the more appropriate way to deal with such offenders rather than the exercise of powers of arrest.

The Codes of Practice (see Part four) direct that generally a juvenile must not be interviewed or asked to provide or sign a statement in the absence of his parent or guardian or if he is in care, the care authority or a social worker.

Juveniles may only be interviewed at their place of education in exceptional circumstances and then only when the principal or his nominee agrees and is present.

A juvenile should not be arrested at his place of education unless this is unavoidable. If an arrest is made at school or college, the principal or his nominee must be informed.

Juveniles have not only the rights of an arrested adult, they have additional rights prescribed by s 57 of the Police and Criminal Evidence Act and s 34 of the Children and Young Persons Act 1933. Under these sections the police must take such steps as are practicable to ascertain the identity of the person responsible for the juvenile. The responsible person should be told that the child or young person has been arrested, why he has been arrested and where he is being detained. Such information should be given as soon as it is practicable to do so. In addition, where the juvenile is the subject of a supervision order, the person responsible for his supervision must also be informed and also the local authority if they are providing accommodation under s 20 of the Children Act 1989.

The Criminal Justice and Public Order Act 1994 inserts a new section 23(A) into the Children and Young Persons Act 1969. Under this section (when in force) a child or young person who has been committed to local authority accommodation and conditions have been imposed upon him, then if any of those conditions are broken an officer may arrest without warrant. The arresting officer must have reasonable grounds for suspecting that the person is in breach. Where such an arrest is made, the detainee must be brought before a JP for the area where arrested as soon as practicable and in any event within 24 hours after his arrest. If the arrest is made within 24 hours of the time he was due to appear in court, the detainee should be taken before the court where he was due to appear. In reckoning the period of 24 hours, no account shall be taken of Christmas day, Good Friday or any Sunday.

ARRESTABLE OFFENCES
(Police and Criminal Evidence Act 1984, s 24)

An 'arrestable offence' is:

(a)   any offence for which the sentence is fixed by law (ie murder and treason);

(b)   any offence for which a person of 21 years of age or over (not previously convicted) may be sentenced to imprisonment for a term of five years (or might be so sentenced but for the restrictions imposed by s 33, Magistrates' Courts Act 1980);

(c)   any attempt or conspiracy or incitement to commit any of the offences mentioned at (i) and (ii) above;

(d)   offences for which a person may be arrested under the Customs and Excise Acts, as defined in s 1(1), Customs and Excise Management Act 1979;

(e)   offences under the Official Secrets Act 1920 that are not arrestable offences by virtue of the term of imprisonment for which a person may be sentenced in respect of them;

(f)   offences under any provision of the Official Secrets Act 1989 except s 8(1), (4) or (5);

(g)   an offence of causing prostitution of women (s 22, Sexual Offences Act 1956);

(h)   an offence of procuration of a girl under 21 (s 23, Sexual Offences Act 1956);

(i)   an offence of taking and driving a motor vehicle or other conveyance without the consent of the owner or other lawful authority or allowing himself to be carried in or on it (s 12(1),Theft Act 1968);

(j)   an offence of going equipped for stealing (s 25(1),Theft Act 1968);

(k)   any offence under the Football (Offences) Act 1991;

(l)   conspiring, attempting, inciting, aiding, abetting, counselling or procuring the commission of any of the offences in (iv) to (xi) above.

(Note: the following offences will be added when the relevant commencement order under the Criminal Justice and Public Order Act 1994 comes into force:

(m)   an offence of publication of an obscene matter (s 2, Obscene Publications Act 1959);

(n)   an offence under s 1, Protection of Children Act 1978 (indecent photographs etc of children). The offences (m) and (n) will also become 'serious arrestable offences' (see page 46).

POWERS TO ARREST FOR ARRESTABLE OFFENCES

1. Any person

Any person may arrest without warrant:

(a)   anyone who is in the act of committing an arrestable offence;

(b)   anyone whom he has reasonable grounds for suspecting to be committing such an offence.

Where an arrestable offence has been committed any person may arrest without warrant:

(a)   Anyone who is guilty of the offence;
(b)   Anyone whom he has reasonable grounds for suspecting to be guilty of it.

2. Constables

(a)   Where a constable has reasonable grounds for suspecting that an arrestable offence has been committed, he may arrest without warrant anyone whom he has reasonable grounds for suspecting to be guilty of the offence.
(b)   A constable may arrest without warrant:

    (i)   anyone who is about to commit an arrestable offence;
    (ii)   anyone whom he has reasonable grounds for suspecting to be about to commit an arrestable offence.

Mere suspicion is not sufficient to justify an arrest. A reasonable amount of evidence must be available in every case.

Section 117 of the Police and Criminal Evidence Act 1984 permits police officers to use reasonable force, if necessary, to effect his powers of arrest either for arrestable offences or generally. Under the same section such reasonable force may also be used to enter and search premises to execute a search warrant, to make an arrest, to search persons on arrest, to search a person detained at a police station, to make intimate searches and take samples, to take fingerprints and to search premises following an arrest for an arrestable offence.

Moreover, by virtue of s 3 of the Criminal Law Act 1967, **any person** may use such force as is reasonable in the circumstances:

(a)   to effect a lawful arrest;
(b)   to assist a lawful arrest;
(c)   to prevent crime.

SERIOUS ARRESTABLE OFFENCES

Throughout the Police and Criminal Evidence Act 1984, the police are given special powers in relation to 'serious arrestable offences'. Section 116 and Sch 5 of the Act define and list such offences. Arrestable offences which under the Act are *always* to be regarded as serious are marked throughout this book with the letters 'SAO'.

Other arrestable offences may be serious only if their commission or the threat to commit has led to or is intended to lead to or in the case of threats is likely to lead to the following consequences:

(a)   serious harm to the security of the state or to public order;
(b)   serious interference with the administration of justice or the investigation of offences;
(c)   the death of a person;
(d)   serious injury to a person;
(e)   substantial financial gain to any person;
(f)   serious financial loss to any person.

The more important powers given to the police by virtue of the arrestable offence being serious arise in s 4 (road checks), s 42 (authority to detain without charge for up to 36 hours), ss 43 and 44 (magistrates' warrants for further detention), s 56 (delay in notification of a person's arrest) and s 58 (delay in allowing access to legal advice).

THE GENERAL POWERS OF ARREST
(Police and Criminal Evidence Act 1984, s 25)

Where a constable has reasonable grounds for suspecting that **any offence which is not an arrestable offence** has been committed, or attempted, or is being committed or attempted, he may arrest any person (the relevant person), whom he has reasonable grounds to suspect of:

(a)   having committed; or
(b)   having attempted to commit; or
(c)   being in the course of committing or attempting to commit

the offence concerned and it appears to him that the service of a summons is impracticable or inappropriate because the following general arrest conditions are satisfied:

(a)   that the name of the relevant person is unknown to, and cannot be readily ascertained by the constable;
(b)   that the constable has reasonable grounds for doubting whether a name furnished by the relevant person as his name is his real name;
(c)   that:

    (i)   the relevant person has failed to furnish a satisfactory address for service; or
    (ii)   the constable has reasonable grounds for doubting whether an address furnished by the relevant person is a satisfactory address for service;

(d)   that the constable has reasonable grounds for believing that arrest is necessary to prevent the relevant person:

    (i)   causing physical harm to himself or any other person;
    (ii)   suffering physical injury;

      (iii)   causing loss or damage to property;
      (iv)   committing an offence against public decency; or
      (v)   causing an unlawful obstruction of the highway;

(e)   that the constable has reasonable grounds for believing that arrest is necessary to protect a child or other vulnerable person from the relevant person.

With regard to paragraph (d)(iv) above the arrest is not authorised except where members of the public going about their normal business cannot reasonably be expected to avoid the person to be arrested.

For the purpose of the general arrest conditions an address is a satisfactory address for service if it appears to the constable:

(a)   that the relevant person will be at it for a sufficiently long period for it to be possible to serve him with a summons; or

(b)   That some other person specified by the relevant person will accept service of a summons for the relevant person at it.

The effect of s 25 is that it removes all statutory powers of arrest without warrant except those preserved by Sch 2 which are set out in detail in the various sections of this book.

FINGERPRINTING OF CERTAIN OFFENDERS

Section 27 of the Police and Criminal Evidence Act 1984 directs that if a person:

(a)   has been convicted of a recordable offence as set down by the Secretary of State;

(b)   has not at any time been in police detention for the offence; and

(c)   has not had his fingerprints taken:

      (i)   in the course of the investigation of the offence by the police; or
      (ii)   since the conviction;

any constable may at any time not later than one month after the date of the conviction require him to attend a police station in order that his fingerprints may be taken.

The above requirement must give the person at least seven days within which he must attend the police station and in addition may direct the person to attend at a specified time.

Any person who fails to comply with the above requirement may be arrested without warrant by any constable.

ASSISTING PERSONS WHO HAVE COMMITTED ARRESTABLE OFFENCES

If anyone knows or believes a person to have committed an arrestable offence and then, or subsequently, unlawfully and without reasonable excuse, does any act with the intention of impeding the offender's arrest or prosecution, he commits an offence himself (Criminal Law Act 1967, s 4(1)). The consent of the Director of Public Prosecutions is necessary to any resulting court proceedings. Should an immediate arrest without warrant be imperative, however, the 'arrestable offence' powers apply (see page 16); but only if the offender who was assisted is himself liable to ten years' imprisonment or more for his offence. In all other cases the general power of arrest under s 20, PACE will apply.

AIDERS AND ABETTORS

Indictable offences

Any person who aids, abets, counsels or procures the commission of an indictable offence (ie *an offence which if committed by an adult, is triable on indictment, whether it is exclusively so triable or triable either way on indictment or summarily–Criminal Law Act 1977 s 64, as amended by the Interpretation Act 1978, Sch 3, and the Magistrates' Courts Act 1980, Sch 7*), either at common law or by virtue of any statute law, may be tried and punished in the same way as a principal (Accessories and Abettors Act 1861 s 8). Such offences consequently become **'arrestable offences'** (see pages 14–15) **if the principal offence carries a five years' prison sentence** or longer. (See 'max pen' shown at heading of each offence.)

Summary offences

Persons who aid, abet, counsel or procure the commission of a purely summary offence may be arrested under the general power of arrest contained in s 25, PACE (see page 17).

PART TWO

**The Criminal Law
Specific Powers of Arrest and Charges**

ABORTION, BY FEMALE UPON HERSELF
(IO, max pen life imp)

Powers of arrest

Full powers for 'arrestable offences', see pages 14–15.

Charge

Being then with child, did unlawfully administer to herself certain poison (or a certain noxious thing) called . . . (or did unlawfully use a certain instrument (or certain means), namely . . . (or certain means unknown)), with intent to procure her own miscarriage, contrary to s 58, Offences Against the Person Act 1861.

Comments

With this offence officers should ensure that nothing which might have any bearing on the crime is tampered with, and immediately notify a superior officer or the CID. It must be proved that the female was pregnant at the time and this will need to be shown by medical and forensic evidence.

'Intent' is discussed under 'Wounding, etc, with intent'(see page 149).

ABORTION BY SOME PERSON UPON A FEMALE
(IO, max pen life imp)

Powers of arrest

Full powers for 'arrestable offences', see pages 14–15.

Charge

With intent to procure the miscarriage of a certain woman, named . . ., did:

(a) *unlawfully administer to (or cause to be taken by) the said . . . a certain poison (or noxious thing) called . . . (or the name and description whereof are unknown), or*

(b) *unlawfully use a certain instrument called a . . . (or a certain instrument or certain means unknown) contrary to s 58, Offences against the Person Act 1861.*

Comments

The remarks made under 'Abortion by female upon herself' apply equally here; however, in this case the abortionist will be liable even if the woman is not in fact pregnant. Professional abortionists fully appreciate the gravity of the crime which they commit and they are often well prepared for the possibility of detection. In view of this, it is essential to invoke the immediate help of the expert CID or senior uniformed officer in every case.

A registered medical practitioner can lawfully terminate a female's pregnancy in particular circumstances laid down in the Abortion Act 1967– ie risk to the life or mental or physical health of the woman, or substantial risk that if the child were born it would be seriously handicapped by physical or mental abnormality. **Two practitioners** must hold this view unless termination is immediately necessary to save the life, or to prevent grave permanent injury to the physical or mental health of, the woman. The termination procedure is strictly controlled by the Ministry of Health Regulations.

ABORTION, SUPPLYING OR PROCURING MEANS FOR (IO, max pen 5 yrs imp)

Powers of arrest

Full powers 'arrestable offences', see pages 14–15.

Charge

Did supply (or procure) a certain poison (or a certain noxious thing) called . . .(or a certain instrument or thing, called . . .) knowing that the same was intended to be unlawfully used or employed with intent to procure the miscarriage of a certain woman named . . . contrary to s 59, Offences Against the Person Act 1861.

Comments

As in cases of abortion, expert assistance should be obtained as soon as possible.

ABSTRACTING ELECTRICITY (Triable 'either way' max pen 5 yrs imp)

Powers of arrest

Full powers for 'arrestable offences', see pages 14–15.

Charges

(a)   *Dishonestly used certain electricity without due authority; or*

(b)   *dishonestly caused certain electricity to be wasted; or*
(c)   *dishonestly caused certain electricity to be diverted by (give particulars).*

Contrary to s 13, Theft Act 1968.

Comments

Those parts of Sch 3 (para 29) of the Gas Act 1948, which relate to the fraudulent abstracting, consumption or use of gas of the Gas Authority, are revoked by the Theft Act. This offence becomes 'theft', see page 140.

ANIMALS, CRUELTY TO OR ABANDONING OR CAUSING SAME
(SO, max pen 6 mths imp)

Powers of arrest

Any constable may arrest any person whom he has reason to believe is guilty of such an offence in respect of any domestic or captive animal, whether in his own view or upon complaint and information of any person who gives his name and address.

By virtue of s 1(2) of the Act a person may be found guilty of permitting cruelty where he fails to exercise reasonable care and supervision in respect of an animal. Where there is such a conviction, the offender shall not be liable to imprisonment without the option of a fine. The above power of arrest does not extend to cases where the offence is one of permitting cruelty by failure to provide reasonable care and supervision. (Note: a constable also has power to take charge of any animal or vehicle until the termination of court proceedings, etc–s 12, Protection of Animals Act 1911).

Charge

Cruelly did beat (or *kick*, or *ill-treat*, or *override*, or *overdrive*, or *overload*, or *torture*, or *infuriate*, or *terrify*) *a certain animal, namely . . . by* (here describe the ill-treatment, etc) *contrary to s 1, Protection of Animals Act 1911, or did cause, or procure, or being the owner, permit a certain animal, namely . . . to be beaten, or kicked, or ill-treated*, etc (as above) *contrary to s 1, Protection of Animals Act 1911.*

–or, in a case of abandonment–

Being the owner (or *having charge or control*) *of a certain animal, namely, a dog* (or as the case may be) *did abandon it* or *did cause* (or procure) (or *being the owner did permit*) *a certain animal, namely a . . . to be abandoned without reasonable cause or excuse in circumstances likely to cause that animal unnecessary suffering, contrary to s 1(1), Protection of Animals Act 1911 as applied by the Abandonment of Animals Act 1960, s 1.*

Comments

The power of arrest in this case is not generally used, summons procedure being the more common method of bringing the offender to justice. In spite of this, it is well to remember the power of arrest for use in cases where the offender's identity is in question, or where the cruelty is likely to be persisted in unless arrest is made, or the offender is likely to abscond.

'Animal' means any domestic or captive animal. A 'domestic animal' is any sort of animal (including a fowl, etc) which has been or is being sufficiently tamed to serve some purpose for the use of man. A captive animal is any sort of animal (including a bird, fish or reptile) which is either captive or confined or maimed or pinioned or subjected to any appliance, etc intended to hinder or prevent its escape (see s 15(a), (b) and (c), Protection of Animals Act 1911).

Under s 5A, Protection of Animals Act 1911 it is an offence to be present without reasonable excuse when animals are placed together for the purpose of their fighting each other. It is also an offence under the Protection Against Cruel Tethering Act 1988 to tether any horse, ass, or mule under such conditions or in such a manner as to cause unnecessary suffering.

There are a number of statutes which protect specific animals from cruelty or poaching eg Badgers Act, Deer Act etc.

ARSON
(Triable 'either way', max pen life imp)

Powers of arrest

Full powers for 'arrestable offences', see pages 14–15.

Charge

Use charge under 'Damaging or destroying property', page 60, or 'Damaging or destroying property with intent, etc', page 61 as appropriate but with the words '*by fire*' at the point marked with the asterisk*.

Comments

See headings referred to under 'charge', above. An offence committed by destroying or damaging property by fire shall be charged as arson ((s 1(3), Criminal Damage Act 1971).

ASSAULT, COMMON
(SO only)

Powers of arrest

Any person has power to arrest if (a) a breach of the public peace occurs in his presence; or (b) such a breach has occurred and is likely to begin if no arrest is made; or (c) a breach of the public peace is seriously threatened (common law).

See also powers relative to 'Wounding, etc' pages 149–151 and 'Assault occasioning bodily harm', below.

Charge

Did assault and beat (or assault) one . . . contrary to common law and triable pursuant to s 42, Offences Against the Person Act 1861.

Comments

Generally, if the injury inflicted is not serious and no weapon has been used, the person assaulted is left to take action by way of summons. The police only take action where the circumstances are more serious. A police officer as such is not entitled to appear in court as informant on a charge of 'common assault' under s 42 on behalf of the person assaulted. Section 47 provides for the arrestable offence of assault occasioning actual bodily harm (see next heading). It is good policy to make a report of every complaint of assault received–injuries originally appearing unimportant have later resulted in homicide charges. Section 42 is merely procedural and does not create an offence; accordingly it is wrong to charge a person with assault contrary to s 42 (*R v Harrow Justice ex p Osaseri* [1985] 3 All ER 185).

ASSAULT OCCASIONING ACTUAL BODILY HARM
(Triable 'either way', max pen 5 yrs imp)

Powers of arrest

Full powers for 'arrestable offences', see pages 14–15.

Charge

Did assault . . . thereby occasioning unto the said . . . (name of person assaulted) actual bodily harm. Contrary to s 47, Offences Against the Person Act 1861.

Comments

This offence relates to unlawful assaults which cause actual bodily harm without either the circumstances or the gravity of the injury justifying a more serious charge ie 'Wounding or causing grievous bodily harm' (with, or without, intent), pages 149–151.

ASSAULT ON POLICE (INCLUDING OBSTRUCTING OR RESISTING)
(SO only)

Powers of arrest

A constable may arrest when the assault is committed upon himself or in his presence or if he is physically obstructed or resisted **in the course of his duty** (common law). Police officers may also use the general power of arrest under s 25, PACE (see pages 17–18). See also powers relative to 'Wounding, etc', pages 149–151.

Charges

Did assault ... (or ... *a person assisting* ...) (name of constable) *a constable of the (county) of* ... *in the execution of his duty, contrary to s 51 (1) of the Police Act 1964*; or *did resist* (or *wilfully obstruct*) ... (or ... *a person assisting*) (name of constable) *a constable of the (county) of* ... *in the execution of his duty, contrary to s 51(3), Police Act 1964.*

Comments

Remember that, in law, an assault is 'an attempt or offer of bodily violence to the person of another' (committed, of course, in a hostile manner) and the actual infliction of hurt is not demanded. Generally the constable will not take action unless there is some 'bodily violence' but the case is sometimes met with in which the offender throws articles at the constable without hitting him. Do not wait until he scores a bull's eye!

If you are on duty in civilian dress and suffer an assault, the assailant should be made aware of the fact that you are a police officer when he commits the assault. But see the important House of Lords decision in *Albert v Lavin* [1981] 3 All ER 878 where it was held, inter alia, that where the assailant's belief that an officer in plain clothes was a private citizen and not a constable, it would not have made his resistance to the officer's restraint of him lawful.

Bear in mind that the assault must happen in the course of lawfully performing actual *police duty*. Be especially cautious in this respect when performing 'special duties' at events for which your Police Authority is receiving payment from a private source.

In the case of *Lewis v Cox* [1985] 3 All ER 672, it was held that a person wilfully obstructs a police constable in the execution of his duties if he deliberately does an act which though not necessarily 'aimed at' or 'hostile to' the police, in fact prevents a constable from carrying out his duties or makes it more difficult for him to do so. If he knows and intends that his conduct will have that effect; the motive for which the act is committed is irrelevant unless it constitutes a lawful excuse for the obstruction.

Invariably in cases of assaults on officers the common law power of arrest will be used. In cases of obstruction, the circumstances surrounding the case will need to be considered before deciding whether to arrest. Where there is a physical obstruction it is nearly always better to arrest otherwise a police officer's public duty may be thwarted.

ATTEMPTS TO COMMIT CRIME
(Part I–Criminal Attempts Act 1981)

Powers of arrest

Full powers for 'arrestable offences', see pages 14–15 provided the offence attempted carries a penalty of five years imprisonment or more.

Where the offence attempted carries a sentence of less than five years imprisonment, the general power of arrest under s 25, PACE will apply (see pages 17–18).

Charge

With intent to commit an indictable offence, namely an offence of . . . (specify the indictable offence) *contrary to . . .* (enter either common law or the section and Act creating the indictable offence) *did an act which was more than merely preparatory to the commission of the said indictable offence. Contrary to s 1(1), Criminal Attempts Act 1981.*

Comments

The Criminal Attempts Act 1981 makes important provisions in relation to attempts to commit crime. By virtue of s 6(1), the offence of attempt at common law and any offence at common law of procuring materials for crime are abolished.

The statutory offence of 'attempt' is created by s 1 of the Act but it only applies to attempts to commit **indictable offences**. Section 3, however, ensures that the principles underlying s 1 in the definition of attempt also apply in relation to attempts to commit crime under those existing statutory provisions which are retained and to any which may be created in future.

Both in relation to the offence under s 1 and to any relevant statutory provision referred to in s 3, before a person can be convicted of an attempt to commit a crime he must:

(a)   have an intent to commit the full offence; and
(b)   do an act which is more than merely preparatory to the commission of the offence.

For example, a person intending to commit arson might purchase paraffin, a bale of straw and matches. This may be considered as merely preparatory and would not constitute the offence of attempted arson. If, however, he then places the straw in the premises he intends to burn and he empties the paraffin over it and then ignites a match, at which point he is apprehended, then his acts are far more than preparatory and such a person might justifiably be proceeded against for attempt. The evidence must always reflect the fact that the acts were more than merely preparatory and each case must be treated on its merits. The intent of the person can best be determined by evidence of the extent of his preparatory acts, the time and situation in which he might be found, items found in his possession, his correspondence and conversation with others and his statements immediately following arrest and subsequent interrogation.

Sections 1(2) and (3) and 3(4) and (5) of the Act make it clear that a person may be guilty of attempting to commit either an indictable offence or a relevant statutory offence even though the facts are such that the commission of the offence is impossible. The classic example of the pickpocket who intends to steal money and puts his hand into an empty pocket well illustrates this point. He could never commit the offence of theft in these circumstances but certainly he can be charged with the attempt.

The offence under s 1 (see 'Charge' above) does not apply to attempts to commit the following:

(a)   conspiracy (see page 54);
(b)   aiding, abetting, counselling, procuring or suborning the offence;
(c)   offences under s 4(1) (assisting offenders) or 5(1) (accepting or agreeing to accept consideration for not disclosing information about an arrestable offence) of the Criminal Law Act 1967.

Section 2 states that certain procedural matters under any enactment such as institution of proceedings, power of arrest, search, seizure and detention of property etc, apply to an attempt to commit an offence under s 1 as they apply to the full offence.

Section 4 provides that a person guilty of attempted murder, or any offence for which the penalty is fixed by law, shall be liable to imprisonment for life. Where there is a conviction on indictment for the attempt to commit an indictable offence other than the aforementioned crimes, the offender shall be liable to any penalty to which he would have been liable had he been convicted of the full offence. If the offence attempted under s 1 is triable 'either way' and the offender is convicted summarily he shall be liable to a penalty to which he would have been liable on summary conviction of the full offence.

The Criminal Attempts Act 1981 also makes changes in the law relating to conspiracy (see page 54) and it creates the offence of interference with vehicles (see page 173).

BAIL: ABSCONDING BY PERSON RELEASED ON BAIL
(SO or may be dealt with as criminal contempt of court) (max pen for SO, 3 mths imp or if committed to crown court for sentence, 12 mths imp)

Powers of arrest

A person who has been released on bail in criminal proceedings and is under a duty to surrender into the custody of a court may be arrested without warrant by a constable:

(a)   if he has reasonable grounds for believing that the person is not likely to surrender to custody; or

(b)   if he has reasonable grounds for believing that that person is likely to break any of the conditions of his bail or has reasonable grounds for suspecting that that person has broken any of these conditions; or

(c)   in a case where that person was released on bail with one or more sureties, if a surety notifies a constable in writing that that person is unlikely to surrender to custody and that for that reason the surety wishes to be relieved of his obligations.

When s 29, Criminal Justice and Public Order Act 1994 comes into force the following additional powers of arrest will apply:

(a)   a constable may arrest without a warrant any person who, having been released on bail under Part IV of the Police and Criminal Evidence Act 1984 subject to a duty to attend at a police station, fails to attend at that police station at the time appointed for him to do so.

(b)   a person who has been ordered to surrender to custody under s 5B(5) of the Bail Act 1976 may be arrested without warrant by a constable if he fails without reasonable cause to surrender to custody in accordance with the order.

Charges

(a) *Being a person who having been released on bail in criminal proceedings on . . .* (give date released) *by . . .* (name the court) (or by . . . *a police officer stationed at . . . Police station) did fail without reasonable cause to surrender to the custody of the . . .* (name the court) (or *to custody at . . . police station)* at . . . (give time fixed for surrender) *on . . .* (give date). *Contrary to s 6(1), Bail Act 1976.*

(b) *Being a person who having been released on bail in criminal proceedings on . . .* (give date released) *by . . .* (name the court) (or *by . . . a police officer stationed at . . . police station) and having reasonable cause therefore, failed to surrender to custody at the appointed place, namely . . .* (name the court or police station appointed for surrender) *at the appointed time, namely at . . .* (time) *on . . .* (date), *did fail to surrender to custody of the said court* (or *police station) as soon after the said appointed time as was reasonably practicable. Contrary to s 6(2), Bail Act 1976.*

Comments

Section 6 of the Bail Act 1976, creates two offences in relation to absconding by persons released on bail. The first is self explanatory, the second relates to failing to surrender to custody as soon as possible, after having been unable to do so for reasonable cause (eg through illness). The onus in such cases is on the defendant to prove that failure to surrender was for reasonable cause. Where there is an arrest under s 7(3) of the Bail Act (see 'powers of arrest'), then the prisoner must be brought before a court within 24 hours. The court can be anywhere, unless within 24 hours of the time appointed for his surrender, when it must be the court granting bail. In calculating the 24-hour period, Christmas Day, Good Friday and Sundays do not apply.

Following arrest it is the duty of the custody officer to determine whether bail shall be granted under the provisions of ss 37, 38 and 47 of the Police and Criminal Evidence Act 1984. Before a person is charged the custody officer has a duty to consider whether there is sufficient evidence to justify a charge. If there is not sufficient evidence he must release the prisoner on bail or unconditionally, unless he has reasonable grounds for believing that detention without charge is necessary to secure or preserve evidence relating to an offence for which he is under arrest or to obtain such evidence by questioning him.

Section 38, Police and Criminal Evidence Act 1984 requires that an arrested person charged with an offence be released in specified circumstances. This section will be amended when s 28, Criminal Justice and Public Order Act 1994 comes into force. At that time the custody officer must order release of an adult from police detention either on bail or without bail unless:

(a) his name and address cannot be ascertained or the custody officer has reasonable grounds for doubting he has provided his true name and address;

(b) the custody officer has reasonable grounds for believing that the person arrested will fail to appear in court to answer bail;

(c) in the case of a person arrested for an imprisonable offence, the custody officer has reasonble grounds for believing that the detention of the person arrested is necessary to prevent him from committing an offence;

(d) in the case of a person arrested for an offence which is not an imprisonable offence, the custody officer has reasonable grounds for believing that the detention of the person arrested is necessary to prevent him from causing physical injury to any other person or from causing loss of or damage to property;

(e) the custody officer has reasonable grounds for believing that detention of the person arrested is necessary to prevent him from interfering with the administration of justice or the investigation of offences;

(f) the custody officer has reasonble grounds for believing that the detention of the person arrested is necessary for his own protection.

With regard to an arrested juvenile (under 17), the custody officer must release him on bail after charge unless the above applies or the custody officer has reasonable grounds for believing that he ought to be detained in his own interests. Where such detention is authorised the juvenile should be taken into the care of the local authority and detained by them unless it is impracticable to do so and the custody officer certifies this fact.

Section 47, Police and Criminal Evidence Act 1984, states that a person released on bail subject to a duty to attend at a police station may be re-arrested if new evidence justifying a further arrest comes to light since his release.

When s 25, Criminal Justice and Public Order Act 1994 comes into force, persons charged with or convicted of an offence of murder, attempted murder, manslaughter, rape or attempted rape shall not be granted bail if that person has previously been charged with or convicted of any of these offences. Moreover, when s 26 of the Act comes into force, the court need not grant bail to a person charged with an indictable offence or an offence triable 'either way' and it appears to the court that the person was already on bail in criminal proceedings on the date of the offence.

Under s 27 of the above Act (when in force), the police will be able to impose conditions of bail to ensure the following:

(i)   that the prisoner surrenders to custody;
(ii)   that he does not commit an offence while on bail;
(iii) that he does not interfere with witnesses or otherwise obstruct the
       course of justice whether in relation to himself or any other person.

Furthermore, the police will be able to vary conditions of bail in
appropriate cases and in doing so may impose further conditions or more
onerous conditions.

BLACKMAIL
(IO, max pen 14 yrs imp)

Powers of arrest

Full powers for 'arrestable offences', see pages 14–15.

Charge

*With a view to gain for himself (or . . .); or with intent to cause loss to . . .
made an unwarranted demand with menaces in that he* (give particulars),
contrary to s 21, Theft Act 1968. (See 'Comments' for definitions).

Comments

This crime is very wide in its content. All the essentials are included in
the charge–including the alternatives. The scope of modern 'blackmail'
is shown in the interpretive provisions:

'Gain' and 'loss'–relate **only** to gains or losses in money or other property–
but this can be either temporary or permanent gain or loss–and

'Gain' includes gain by keeping what one **has** as well as by getting what
one has not; and

'Loss' includes a loss by not getting what one might get as well as by
parting with what one has (s 34(2)).

A 'demand with menaces' is 'unwarranted' unless the person making
it believes that he does so on reasonable grounds **and** that the use of the
particular menaces was the proper means of reinforcing his demand. The
menaces made need not be action to be taken by the person making the
demand.

'Intent' is discussed under 'Wounding etc (with intent)', page 149.

The nature of what is asked of the person being blackmailed is
immaterial–it can indeed be either (i) to take some sort of action; or (ii) to
omit to do a particular thing. It is not essential that the person blackmailed
shall meet the 'unwarranted demand' but **he must be menaced** in the terms
described. Words or conduct are menaces if they are **likely** to operate on
the mind of a person of ordinary courage and firmness so as to make him

accede unwillingly to the demand. It is not necessary that the intended victim should be alarmed (*R v Clear*, 1968).

The essence of the offence is that the offender must know either that he has no right to make the demand or that the use of menaces to reinforce it is improper.

Among other things, this provision can go far to beat the 'protection rackets'. Any apparently serious case reported to you should be immediately referred to senior officers for decision and guidance. The feeding-in of criminal sightings and other relevant information to CID and collators can be invaluable here.

This charge can, however, be just as effectively used against the small-time blackmailer.

BOMB HOAXES
(Triable 'either way', max pen 7 yrs imp)

Powers of arrest

Full powers for 'arrestable offences', see pages 14–15.

Charges

(i) *Did place an article namely . . .* (describe the article concerned) *in a place situate at . . .* (name the place or address) (**or** *Did dispatch an article namely . . .* (describe the article) *by post* (or *rail* or *by means of . . .*) (describe the means of dispatch) *being a means of sending things from one place to another) with the intention of inducing in some other person a belief that the said article was likely to explode* (or *ignite*) *and thereby cause personal injury* (*or damage to property*). *Contrary to s 51(1), Criminal Law Act 1977.*

(ii) *Did communicate information which he knew* (*or believed*) *to be false to another person namely . . .* (name the person to whom the information was communicated) *with the intention of inducing in him* [or *with the intention of inducing in some person* (See Comments below)] *a false belief that a bomb* [or *a false belief that a device namely . . .* (name the device) *liable to explode* (*or ignite*)] *as present in a certain place* (*or location*) *situate at . . .* (give the address or location of the place concerned). *Contrary to s 51(2), Criminal Law Act 1977.*

Comments

This section creates two offences to deal with bomb hoaxes. Section 51(3) makes it clear that for a person to be guilty of either of the above offences it is not necessary for him to have any particular person in mind as the person in whom he intends to induce a false belief. Thus an offender may address an article or may make a telephone call to a particular individual with the intention of creating a false belief in the minds of people generally and not necessarily to create the belief solely in the mind of the receiver. Invariably the person creating the hoax has the intention of generally creating disruption, fear or both and does not have any one person or group of persons in mind at the time he puts his scheme into action. The section is therefore wide enough to cover a general as well as a specific intention on the part of the offender.

Officers should bear in mind that all calls or reports relating to bombs should be investigated immediately and should always be treated as genuine. Force instructions should be followed and only if the call or report is confirmed to be a hoax should the investigation commence into the above offence.

Officers should note that s 38, Public Order Act 1986 creates an offence for a person who with the intention of (i) causing public alarm or anxiety or (ii) causing injury to members of the public consuming or using goods or (iii) causing economic loss to any person by reason of goods being shunned by members of the public or (iv) causing economic loss to any person by reason of steps taken to avoid alarm or anxiety, injury or loss, to contaminate or interfere with goods etc. It is also an offence to threaten the foregoing acts, or to have in possession articles with a view to the commission of the offences concerned. Offences are triable 'either way' and on indictment; all carry a maximum of ten years imprisonment. They are therefore arrestable offences thus providing full powers of arrest.

BREACH OF THE PEACE

Powers and procedure

The Police and Criminal Evidence Act 1984 has in s 25(6) preserved the common law powers of arrest for breach of the peace. Thus a constable or any other person may arrest for such a breach which is committed in the presence of the person making the arrest or where the arrestor reasonably believes such a breach will be committed in the immediate future, or where a breach has been committed and it is reasonably believed a renewal is threatened.

In the important House of Lords case of *Albert v Lavin* [1981] 3 All ER 878, it was held that it was the right and duty at common law of every citizen in whose presence an actual or reasonably apprehended breach of the peace was being or about to be committed to make the person who was breaking or threatening to break the peace refrain from so doing and, in appropriate cases, to detain him.

A court may order an offender to enter into a recognisance and find sureties to keep the peace. Imprisonment can follow if there is a default (s 115, Magistrates' Courts Act 1980).

BUGGERY, WITH ANIMAL OR HUMAN BEING
(IO, max pen–

(a) **with a person under the age of 16 or with an animal–life imp (SAO)**

(b) **if the accused is of or over the age of 21 and the other person is under the age of 18–5 years imp;**

(c) **in cases other than (a) or (b) above–2 years imp.**

(Note: Where there is no consent to an act of buggery then this will be rape (see page 124).)

Powers of arrest

Full powers for 'arrestable offences' in respect of (a) and (b). General power of arrest under s 25, PACE in respect of (c).

Charge

Did commit buggery with . . . (name of the person) in a public place namely . . . (name the place) (or did commit buggery with . . . (name of person) a person under the age of 18 years, namely of the age of . . . years) (or did commit buggery with a certain animal namely . . . (name the animal species)), contrary to s 12, Sexual Offences Act 1956, as amended.

Comments–with animal

Arrest the offender whenever the evidence justifies such action. Preserve all possible evidence and, if practicable, segregate the animal concerned. It is of the utmost importance to obtain the assistance of forensic scientists immediately. There is no definition of 'animal' within the act. In *R v Brown* (1889) 24 QBD 357 a domestic fowl was held to be an animal for the purpose of this crime.

Comments–with person under 18 yrs

Arrest as above and preserve all possible evidence. Consider taking any child or young person into police protection under s 46, Children Act 1989 if the circumstances demand it (see page 48).

Comments–the age of consent

See the three categories (a), (b) and (c) shown immediately under the main heading to this offence. Any homosexual act (including gross indecency, see page 88) committed in private between consenting males **both** over the age of 18 years is not an offence unless:

(a)   more than two persons take part or are present; or

(b)   the act is committed in a lavatory to which the public have, or are permitted to have, access–either on payment or otherwise.

(Note: On prosecution your case must **conclusively** prove that the act was **not** done in private, **or** that one of the parties was not 18 years old (see s 1(6), Sexual Offences Act 1967, as amended by s 145, Criminal Justice and Public Order Act 1994)).

BURGLARY
(Max pen–

(i)   where offence was committed in respect of a building or part of a building which is a dwelling–14 yrs imp;

(ii)   in any other case–10 yrs imp.)

(Triable 'either way' unless burglary comprises the commission of, or an intention to commit, an offence triable only on indictment or burglary in a dwelling where persons are subject to violence or threat of violence. In the said excepted cases–triable only on indictment).

Powers of arrest

Full powers for 'arrestable offences', see pages 14–15.

Charges

(a)   *Did enter a certain building (or part of a building or inhabited vehicle or inhabited vessel) situate at . . .* (name of building etc and address) *as a trespasser and with intent to commit an offence of*:

    (i)   *stealing therein;* or

    (ii)   *inflicting on . . . therein certain grievous bodily harm*; or

    (iii)   *raping . . . therein*; or

    (iv)   *doing unlawful damage to the said buildings* (or to property therein) *namely* (state nature of damage);

Contrary to s 9(1)(a), Theft Act 1968.

(b) *Having entered a certain building (or part of a building or inhabited vehicle or inhabited vessel) situate at* . . . (name of building etc and address) *as a trespasser:*

  (i) *did steal* (or *attempt to steal*) . . . (specify property) *therein;* or

  (ii) *did inflict* (or *attempt to inflict*) *on* . . . *therein certain grievous bodily harm.*

Contrary to s 9(1)(b), Theft Act 1968.

BURGLARY–AGGRAVATED
(IO only, max pen life imp)

Was guilty of aggravated burglary in that:

(a) *at a time when he had with him a certain firearm* (or *imitation firearm*, or *weapon of offence*, or *explosive*), *namely* . . . (specify article) *he entered a certain building* (or *part of a building or inhabited vehicle or inhabited vessel) situate at* . . . (name building etc and address) *as a trespasser with intent to commit an offence of*:

  (i) *stealing therein*; or
  (ii) *inflicting on* . . . *therein certain grievous bodily harm*; or
  (iii) *raping* . . . *therein*; or
  (iv) *doing unlawful damage to the said building* (or *to property therein*); or

(b) *having entered a certain building (or part of a building or inhabited vehicle or inhabited vessel) situate at* . . . (name of building etc and address) *as a trespasser he:*

  (i) *did steal* (or *attempt to steal*) . . . (specify property) *therein;* or

  (ii) *did inflict* (or *attempt to inflict*) *on* . . . *therein certain grievous bodily harm,*

and (in either case) *at the time had with him a certain firearm* (or *imitation firearm*, or *weapon of offence*, or *explosive*), *namely* . . . (specify article).

Contrary to s 10, Theft Act 1968.

Comments

Insofar as vehicles and vessels are concerned, burglary can be committed when the lawful inhabitant is absent as well as when he is present (s 9(3)).

Entry must essentially always be as a trespasser (ie without lawful right), but it will suffice if only part of the body enters (arm, hand, etc) or if some instrument, etc under direct physical control from outside, is inserted.

Note from the charges that if a trespasser enters without criminal intent he must commit one of four crimes in the place to be guilty of burglary–ie (i) stealing; (ii) attempting to steal; (iii) inflicting GBH*; or (iv) attempting GBH. If, however, he enters with intent, then four somewhat different crimes apply–(i) stealing in the place (no attempt); (ii) inflicting GBH there (no attempt); (iii) committing rape; or (iv) doing unlawful damage to the place or anything in it. The 'with intent' offence, of course, demands some factual or circumstantial evidence to prove the intention on, or before, entry. For 'Intent', see 'Wounding (with intent)', page 149. For the purpose of this and other relevant sections of the Act, the expressions 'stealing' and 'theft' mean the same (s 1(1)) (see 'Theft', page 140).

It is generally advisable to arrest in all cases of this sort; but in doing so, ensure the minimum disturbance to the place and its contents. Scene of crime officers and the HO Lab experts can do most to assist your case **if conditions are left exactly as you**, and the rightful occupants, etc, find them.

If, while committing burglary, the offender has with him any firearm, imitation firearm, weapon of offence, or explosive, he is guilty of *aggravated burglary* (See 'charge').

'Weapon of offence' means any article made or adapted for use for causing injury to, or incapacitating, a person, or intended by the person having it with him for such use. This definition is somewhat wider than that of 'offensive weapon' for the purpose of s 1, Prevention of Crime Act 1953, see page 100. For definitions of 'firearm', 'imitation firearm' and 'explosive', see s 10(1)(*a*) and (*c*), Theft Act 1968.

*Grievous bodily harm.

CANNABIS–CULTIVATION OF PLANT
(Triable 'either way', max pen 14 yrs imp)

Powers of arrest

Full powers for 'arrestable offences', see pages 14–15.

Charge

Did cultivate a plant of the genus Cannabis (see definition under 'Comments'), *contrary to s 6, Misuse of Drugs Act 1971.*

Comments

'Cannabis' means any plant of the genus *Cannabis* or any part of any such plant (by whatever name designated) except that if it does not include cannabis resin or any of the following products *after separation from the rest of the plant*:

(a)   the mature stalks;
(b)   fibre produced from the mature stalk;
(c)   the seed of any such plant

(Section 52, Criminal Law Act 1977). *This s 6, however, makes cultivation of the entire plant illegal.* The important case of *Taylor v Chief Constable of Kent* (1981) 72 Cr App R 318 held that cultivation of the cannabis plant is synonymous with the production of a controlled drug which is itself an offence under s 4, Misuse of Drugs Act 1971. Cannabis and cannabis resin are Class 'B' drugs; see pages 69–73, 'Drugs–unlawful possession', 'Drugs–unlawful supply'.

Among sources of supply the seed (hemp) is available in certain parrot and other bird seeds. Coarse fishermen will tell you that some of their number are prone to use it as ground-bait. The plant varies in size but can grow to a height of eight feet or more. If you recognise the plant and suspect it is being illegally grown, notify your Drugs Squad and await their guidance. Immediate follow-up enquiries should only be started if the circumstances make this absolutely necessary. While deliberate offenders deserve prosecution, innocent persons who through ignorance or accident have a suspect plant in their garden should not be exposed unnecessarily to the stresses of accusation. See s 28 of the Act for special 'lack of knowledge' defences.

ABANDONING CHILD UNDER 2 YEARS
(Triable 'either way', max pen 5 yrs imp)

Powers of arrest

Full powers for 'arrestable offences', see pages 14–15.

Charge

Did unlawfully abandon (*or expose*) . . . *a child under the age of two years, namely of, the age of* . . . *whereby the life of the said child was endangered* (*or the health of the said child has been* (*or is likely to be*) *permanently injured*) *contrary to s 27, Offences Against the Person Act 1861.*

Comments

This crime is not frequently met with. Under the statute it must be proved that either the life of the child was endangered, or its health had been or was likely to be permanently injured, because of the abandonment. Where this is difficult, it is good policy to include an alternative charge (s 1, Children and Young Persons Act 1933, is recommended). (See 'Children or young persons, cruelty to', pages 44–45.)

CHILD ABDUCTION
(Triable 'either way', max pen 7 yrs imp)

Powers of arrest

Full powers for 'arrestable offences', see pages 14–15.

Charges

1. *Being a person connected with a child named . . .* (name the child) *then being under the age of sixteen years, namely of the age of . . .* (insert the age of the child) *you did take (or send) the said child out of the United Kingdom without the appropriate consent. Contrary to s 1(1), Child Abduction Act 1984.*
2. *Being a person not falling within s 1(2)(a) or (b) of the Child Abduction Act 1984, you did without lawful authority or reasonable excuse take (or detain) a child named . . .* (name the child) *then being under the age of sixteen years, namely of the age of . . .* (insert the age*) *so as to remove him from the lawful control of . . .* (name the person with lawful control), *being a person having lawful control of the said child* (or continue the charge to asterisk* and then add *so as to keep him out of the lawful control of . . .* (name the person with lawful control) *being a person entitled to the lawful control of the said child). Contrary to s 2(1), Child Abduction Act 1984.*

Comments

For the purpose of charge (1), a person is connected with a child if he is the parent; or in the case of a child whose parents were not married to each other at the time of his birth, there are reasonable grounds for believing that he is the father or guardian of the child; or he is a person in whose favour a residence order is in force with respect to the child; or he has custody of the child.

The 'appropriate consent' means the consent of each of the following– the child's mother; the child's father, if he has parental responsibilities for him; any guardian of the child; any person in whose favour a residence order is in force with respect to the child; any person who has custody of the child or the leave of the court was granted under the Children Act 1989.

With regard to the charge under (2) above the persons who do not fall within s 1(2) (*a*) or (*b*) are the father and mother provided they were married at the time of the child's birth; and where they were not married at the time of birth, the child's mother. Others falling outside the sections are guardians, persons in whose favour a residence order is in being and persons having custody under the Children Act 1989.

If an offence of child abduction comes to the notice of a beat officer he should act quickly. Obtain all details in relation to the identity or description of the abductor, vehicle numbers, the child's description and possible locations where the child may be taken. The CID should be informed immediately. Speed is of the essence as the abducted child may well be taken out of the country and jurisdiction of the court within a short space of time. There is a Practice Direction ((1986) 1 All ER 983) which sets out the procedure to be followed with regard to the institution of a 'port alert' where there is a real and imminent danger of the removal of a child from the jurisdiction. Senior officers should have access to this direction at all times. Officers should also have access to the Act itself for the finer details.

CHILD ABDUCTION WHILE IN CARE
(Children Act 1989, s 49)
(SO only)

Powers of arrest

General powers of arrest under s 25, PACE, see pages 17–18.

Charge

You knowingly and without lawful authority or reasonable excuse did take (or *did keep*) (or *did induce* (or *assist*) (or *incite*)) *a child, namely* . . . (name the child) *to whom s 49, Children Act 1989 applies, away from* . . . (name of responsible person) *he being a responsible person under the provisions of the said Act. Contrary to s 49, Children Act 1989.*

Comments

Section 49, Children Act 1989 applies to children who are in care or are the subject of an emergency protection order or are in police protection (see page 48). A 'responsible person' is defined as any person who for the time being has the care of the child by virtue of a care order, emergency protection order or under s 46 of the Act.

Section 50 empowers the court to make a 'recovery order' where it appears that there is reason to believe a child has been unlawfully taken away (or kept away) from the responsible person. A similar order may be made where the child has run away (or kept away) from the responsible person or where the child is simply missing.

The 'recovery order' operates as a direction to any person who is in a position to do so to produce the child on the request of an authorised person. The order may also sanction the removal of the child from where he or she is being kept. Any person who has information as to the child's whereabouts may also be required under the terms of the order to disclose that information if asked to do so by a constable or officer of the court. An order may also authorise the police to enter the premises specified and search for the child and reasonable force may be used for this purpose. Police constables and persons specified by the court will be 'authorised persons' for the purposes of s 50. Officers should refer to page 48 with regard to their powers and duties in relation to child protection.

CHILD DESTRUCTION
(IO, max pen life imp)

Powers of arrest

Full powers for 'arrestable offences', see pages 14–15.

Charge

With intent to destroy the life of the child of . . . then capable of being born alive, by the wilful act of (here specify act done) *did cause the said child to die before it has an existence independent of its mother, contrary to s 1, Infant Life (Preservation) Act 1929.*

Comments

This crime is akin to homicide and may arise through adverse sociological and psychological factors or where the unborn child is illegitimate. Take the same action as applies in the case of murder in regard to preservation of evidence. Be guided by circumstances when deciding whether to make an arrest. Notify the CID or a senior officer as soon as possible.

CHILDREN OR YOUNG PERSONS, CRUELTY TO AND OFFENCES LISTED IN SCH 1, CHILDREN AND YOUNG PERSONS ACT 1933
(Triable 'either way', max pen 10 yrs imp)

Powers of arrest

Full powers for 'arrestable offences', see pages 14–15.

Charge–'Cruelty to children'

Being a person who had attained the age of 16 years and having responsibility for . . . a child (or *young person*) *under the age of 16 wilfully did assault* (and/or *ill-treat* and/or *neglect* and/or *abandon* and/or *expose*) *the said child* (or *young person*) *or cause or procure the said child* (or *young person*) *to be assaulted, etc* (as above) *in a manner likely to cause the said child* (or *young person*) *unnecessary suffering* (and/or *injury to health*) *contrary to s 1, Children and Young Persons Act 1933.*

Comments

From the charge it will be seen that s 1 covers a wide range of incidents involving cruelty to children. It should be noted that the section applies where cruelty etc is inflicted by all those who have responsibility for the child or young person. This definition is very wide and will include all those who are put in a position to care for children even for temporary periods, eg child minders, relatives etc. Injury to health will include loss of sight, hearing or limb, organ of the body or mental derangement. For the purpose of this section a parent or other person legally liable to maintain the child or young person shall be deemed to have neglected him in a manner likely to cause injury to health if he has failed to provide adequate clothing, food, medical care or lodging for him. Furthermore, where it is proved that the death of an infant under three years of age was caused by suffocation (other than through disease or a foreign body in the throat) while the infant was in bed with some other person over 16 years of age, that other person shall, if he was under the influence of drink when he went to bed, be deemed to have neglected the infant in a manner likely to cause injury to its health.

Recent statistics indicate that child abuse is increasing and instances of cruelty may take the form of other substantial crimes such as serious assaults, woundings and sexual offences. If there is evidence of such offences then it is far easier for the constable to charge the more serious offence and use the cruelty charge under s 1 as a back-up.

First and foremost it is of paramount importance that help is given to the stricken juvenile by considering taking him or her into police protection (see page 48). Early advice to your senior officers and the welfare agencies will ensure that the child or young person is adequately cared for.

CHILDREN–INDECENT PHOTOGRAPHS
(Protection of Children Act 1978, s 1)
(Triable 'either way', max pen 3 yrs imp)

Powers of arrest

General power of arrest under s 25, PACE, see pages 17–18. (Note: all of the offences under s 1 (see 'charges' below will become arrestable offences (see pages 14–15) when the relevant commencement order made under the Criminal Justice and Public Order Act 1994 comes into force.

Charges

1. *Did take* (or *did permit to be taken*) (*or did make**) *an indecent photograph (or pseudo-photograph*) of a child under the age of 16 years. Contrary to s 1(1)(a), Protection of Children Act 1978.*
2. *Did distribute* (or *did show*) *an indecent photograph (or pseudo-photograph*)of a child under the age of 16 years. Contrary to s 1(1)(b), Protection of Children Act 1978.*
3. *Did have in his possession certain indecent photographs (or pseudo-photographs*)of a child (or children) under the age of 16 years, with a view to their being distributed* (or *shown*) *by himself* (or *with a view to their being distributed* (or *shown*) *by . . .* (name the person(s)). *Contrary to s 1(1)(c), Protection of Children Act 1978.*
4. *Did publish* (or *did cause to be published*) *an advertisement likely to be understood as conveying that the advertiser distributes* (or *shows*) *indecent photographs (or pseudo-photographs*) of children under the age of 16 years* (or *intends to distribute*) (or *intends to show*) *indecent photographs of children under the age of 16 years. Contrary to s 1(1)(d), Protection of Children Act 1978.*
5. *Did have an indecent photograph (or pseudo-photograph*) of a child under the age of 16 years in his possession. Contrary to s 160, Criminal Justice Act 1988 (SO only).*

*Denotes that words can be used when s 84, Criminal Justice and Public Order Act is in force).

Comments

This legislation is directed against what has come to be called 'kiddy-porn'. Officers should always bear in mind that taking indecent photographs of children could well be associated with more serious offences of a sexual nature, which are dealt with elsewhere in this book. Where there is evidence of such other offences and there is a power of arrest–then use it. Remember the interests of any child found in such lurid circumstances. Powers under s 46, Children Act 1989 described on page 48 should be considered and the help of social and welfare agencies should be brought to bear on the child's problem.

Under s 4 of the 1978 Act, a Justice of the Peace may issue a warrant where there is reasonable grounds for suspecting that in any premises indecent photographs of children may be found. The warrant may authorise a constable to enter (if need be by force) and search the premises and seize and remove any articles which he believes (with reasonable cause) to be, or include, indecent photographs of children taken or shown on the premises or kept there with a view to them being distributed or shown. The search warrant will apply to the search of any stall or vehicle in the same way as they apply to premises. The court may order forfeiture of the photographs as directed in s 5 of the Act.

It is a defence for a person charged under s 1(1)(b) or (c) for him to prove (a) that he had a legitimate reason for distributing or showing the photographs or having them in his possession or (b) that he had not himself seen the photographs and did not know nor had any cause to suspect them to be indecent. Clearly there are certain agencies which might for legitimate reasons possess indecent photographs of children, eg police for training purposes, psychiatrists for clinical purposes.

In any proceedings under the Act a person is to be taken as having been a child at any material time if it appears from the evidence as a whole that he was then under the age of 16.

Under the Act indecent photographs include films, copies of photographs, or films. 'Negative' and 'positive' films are included. Video recordings are also subject to this legislation.

The consent of the DPP is necessary for the prosecution of any offence under the Act.

Officers should note the later additional offence under the CJA 1988 where an offender merely possesses indecent photographs. A person charged with this offence has a defence if he can prove that he had a legitimate reason for having the photograph in his possession or that he had not himself seen the photograph and did not know nor had any cause to suspect it to be indecent or that the photograph was sent to him without any prior request made by him or on his behalf and that he did not keep it for an unreasonable time.

Officers should note that in addition to the offences under s 1 becoming 'arrestable' they will also be deemed to be 'serious arrestable offences' under PACE when the relevant Criminal Justice and Public Order Act 1994 commencement order comes into force. Moreover, under the same legislation, all of the offences under s 1 will in addition include pseudo-photographs. These are defined as an image, whether made by computer-graphics or otherwise, howsoever, which appears to be a photograph.

References to an indecent pseudo-photograph include (a) a copy of the same and (b) data stored on a computer disc or other electronic means.

CHILDREN– POLICE PROTECTION
(Children Act 1989)

Police powers and duties (s 46)

1.   Where a constable has reasonable cause to believe that a child would otherwise be likely to suffer significant harm, he may:

    (a)   remove the child to suitable accommodation and keep him there; or
    (b)   take such steps as are reasonable to ensure that the child's removal from any hospital, or other place in which he is then being accommodated is prevented.

2.   For the purposes of the Children Act 1989, a child with respect to whom a constable has exercised his powers under this section is referred to as having been taken into police protection.

3.   As soon as reasonably practicable after taking the child into police protection, the constable concerned shall:

    (a)   inform the Local Authority within whose area the child was found of the steps that have been and are proposed to be taken under this section with respect to the child and the reasons for taking them;
    (b)   give details to the Authority within whose area the child is ordinarily resident ('the appropriate Authority') of the place at which the child is accommodated;
    (c)   inform the child (if he appears capable of understanding):

        (i)   of the steps that have been taken with respect to him under this section and of the reasons for taking them, and
        (ii)   of the further steps that may be taken with respect to him under this section.

    (d)   take such steps as are reasonably practicable to discover the wishes and feelings of the child;
    (e)   secure that the case is handled by an officer designated for the purpose of this section by the Chief Officer of police of the area concerned; and
    (f)   where the child is taken into police protection by being removed to accommodation which is not provided:

> (i)   by or on behalf of a local authority; or
> (ii)   as a refuge in compliance with the requirements of s 51

> secure that he is moved to accommodation which is so provided.

4.   As soon as is reasonably practicable after taking a child into police protection, the constable concerned shall take such steps as are reasonably practicable to inform:

> (a)   the child's parents;
> (b)   every person who is not a parent of his but who has parental responsibility for him; and
> (c)   any other person with whom the child was living immediately before being taken into police protection,

> of the steps that he has taken under this section with respect to the child, the reasons for taking them and the further steps that may be taken with respect to him under this section.

5.   On completing any enquiry under (3(e)) above, the officer conducting it shall release the child from police protection unless he considers that there is still reasonable cause for believing that the child would be likely to suffer significant harm if released.

6.   No child may be kept in police protection for more than 72 hours.

Comments

Section 46 replaces the 'Place of safety' provisions in s 28, Children and Young Persons Act 1969. It should be noted that the maximum time for holding a child in police protection is 72 hours and in any event the designated officer must release the child when the investigation is completed unless he considers the child would be likely to suffer significant harm. In such a case he may apply to the court for an emergency protection order under s 44, Children Act 1989. Such orders last for a period not exceeding eight days except when the last day is a public holiday and the time can be extended to the next day which is not a Bank Holiday.

The Children Act directs that the police shall not have parental responsibility for the child while he is in police protection but they must do what is reasonable in all the circumstances of the case for the purpose of safeguarding or promoting the child's welfare. The police must allow the child's parents, any person with parental responsibilities and others listed in s 46 (10) to have contact with the child as in the opinion of the designated officer is both reasonable and in the child's best interests.

The powers and duties listed in s 46 can be usefully employed in cases where parents have been arrested and where children are at risk or where they are found in circumstances where they are missing from home and proper care is not being exercised.

COMPUTERS–MISUSE
(Computer Misuse Act 1990)

1. Unauthorised access
(SO only)

Powers of arrest

General powers of arrest under s 25, PACE.

Charge

You did cause a computer namely a . . . (give brief details of computer) *owned by . . .* (give details) *to perform a function with intent to secure access to a programme (or data) held in the said computer and that you knew at that time that the access you intended to secure was unauthorised. Contrary to s 1, Computer Misuse Act 1990.*

2. Unauthorised access with intent
(Triable 'either way', max pen 5 yrs imp)

Powers of arrest

Full powers for 'arrestable offences', see pages 14–15.

Charge

You did commit an offence under s 1, *Computer Misuse Act 1990, with intent to commit an offence of . . .* (name the offence) (or *with intent to facilitate the commission of an offence of . . .* (name the offence)) (or *with intent to facilitate the commission of an offence of . . .* (name the offence) *by . . .* (name the person)) (or *with intent to facilitate the commission of an offence of . . .* (name the offence) *by a person (or persons) unknown). Contrary to s 2, Computer Misuse Act 1990.*

3. Unauthorised modification
(Triable 'either way', max pen 5 yrs imp)

Powers of arrest

Full powers for 'arrestable offences', see pages 14–15.

Charge

You did an act which caused an unauthorised modification of the contents of a computer, namely a . . . (give brief details of computer) *owned by . . .* (give details) *and at the time you did the said act you intended to cause the said modification which you knew was unauthorised and by so doing impair the operation of the computer)* (or *by so doing prevent (or hinder) access to any programme (or data) held in the computer* (or *by so doing impair the operation of a programme (or the reliability of any data) held in the computer). Contrary to s 3, Computer Misuse Act 1990.*

Comments

Computer misuse knows no national boundaries and hence the Act gives power in s 4 for UK courts to exercise jurisdiction in cases where the computer misuse originates from the UK or is directed from abroad against a computer located within the UK. Officers should note that the offence under s 2 will not be complete unless the offence under s 1 ('the unauthorised access offence') has been committed in the first place. The intent must be to commit any criminal offence for which the sentence is fixed by law (eg murder) or a convicted person may be imprisoned for a term of five years or more. Such offences are numerous and will include the majority of offences under the Theft Acts 1968 and 1978, the Offences Against the Person Act 1861, the Criminal Damage Act 1971 and the Misuse of Drugs Act 1971. It is immaterial whether the further offence is to be committed on the same occasion as the unauthorised access or on any future occasion.

The Act provides for amendments to the law on conspiracy so as to make it a substantive offence to conspire to commit offences under the Act. Furthermore, attempts to commit such offences will create an offence under the Criminal Attempts Act 1981. A person may still be guilty of an offence under s 2 of the Computer Misuse Act even though the facts are such that the commission of any further offence is impossible.

CONCEALMENT OF BIRTH
(Triable 'either way', max pen 2 yrs imp)

Powers of arrest

General powers of arrest under s 25 of PACE (see pages 17–18).

Charge

Having been delivered of a certain ... (state sex) *child, by a secret disposition of the dead body of the said child, did endeavour to conceal the birth thereof, contrary to s 60, Offences Against the Person Act 1861.*

Comments

The beat constable will probably meet this crime most often when the dead body of a child is found in some location which indicates an intention to hide it. Under such circumstances, having made certain that life has left the body, make sure nothing is disturbed and send for a senior officer or the CID. If the evidence suggests a more serious offence of homicide then consider using your full powers for arrestable offences.

CONSERVATION OF THE COUNTRYSIDE
(Wildlife and Countryside Act 1981)

Power of search, seizure and arrest

1.   If a constable suspects with reasonable cause that any person is committing or has committed an offence under Part 1 of the Act, the constable may without warrant:

    (a)   Stop and search that person if the constable suspects with reasonable cause that evidence of the commission of the offence is to be found on that person.

    (b)   Search or examine anything which that person may then be using or have in his possession if the constable suspects with reasonable cause that evidence of the commission of the offence is to be found on that thing.

    (c)   Seize and detain for the purpose of proceedings under Part 1 of the Act anything which may be evidence of the commission of the offence or may be liable to be forfeited under s 21.

    In addition to the above a constable may exercise his general power of arrest (see pages 17–18).

2. If a constable suspects with reasonable cause that any person is committing an offence under Part 1 of the Act, he may, for the purpose of exercising the powers in (1) above, enter any land other than a dwelling house.

Specimen charges

1. *Did intentionally kill (or injure or take) a wild bird, namely a . . .* (name the bird species). *Contrary to s 1(1)(a), Wildlife and Countryside Act 1981.*
2. *Did intentionally take (or damage or destroy) the nest of a wild bird, namely a . . .* (name the bird species) *while that nest was in use (or while that nest was being built). Contrary to s 1(1)(b), Wildlife and Countryside Act 1981.*
3. *Did intentionally take (or destroy) an egg of a wild bird namely a . . .* (name the bird species). *Contrary to s 1(1)(c), Wildlife and Countryside Act 1981.*
4. *Did intentionally kill (or injure or take) a wild animal included in Sch 5 of the Wildlife and Countryside Act 1981 namely a . . .* (name the animal species). *Contrary to s 9, Wildlife and Countryside Act 1981.*
5. *Did intentionally pick (or uproot or destroy) a wild plant included in Sch 8 of the Wildlife and Countryside Act 1981, namely a . . .* (name the plant species). *Contrary to s 13, Wildlife and Countryside Act 1981.*

Comments

The Act provides for the protection and conservation of wild creatures and plants. There are numerous offences under the Act which include killing, injuring and taking protected wild creatures. There are restrictions on the sale of live or dead wild birds and their eggs together with measures for the protection of captive birds. There is a prohibition under the Act of certain methods of killing or taking wild birds and animals (see ss 5 and 11). With regard to wild plants, in addition to the offences listed in charge (5) above, there are also offences of selling, offering or exposing for sale live or dead wild plants included in Sch 8.

Licences may be granted for specific purposes under s 16 (eg zoological collections, prevention of disease etc). There are also exceptions listed in ss 4 and 10 to offences contained in the Act.

The Bees Act 1980 makes provisions for the control of pests and diseases affecting bees and provides for powers of entry to premises, vessels etc, by authorised persons where there are reasonable grounds for supposing there are or have been any bees subject to control under an order under s 1 of the Act (see s 2, Bees Act 1980).

CONSPIRACY
(IO, s 1, Criminal Law Act 1977, as amended by s 5, Criminal Attempts Act 1981 and s 7, Computer Misuse Act 1990)

Powers of arrest

The full powers of arrest for 'arrestable offences' will apply where there is a conspiracy to commit any of the following offences:

(a)   Murder or any other offence the sentence for which is fixed by law (eg life imprisonment).

(b)   An offence for which a sentence extending to imprisonment for life is provided.

(c)   An indictable offence punishable with imprisonment for which no maximum term of imprisonment is provided.

(d)   Any offence punishable with imprisonment for five years or more.

(e)   Conspiring to commit any of the offences contained in s 24(2), Police and Criminal Evidence Act 1984 (see comments below).

In cases of conspiracy to commit any offence other than those falling within categories (a) to (e) above, the general power of arrest under s 25, PACE will apply (eg in cases of conspiracy to commit summary offences).

Charges

1.   *You did agree with . . .* (name the person or persons who are party to the agreement) *that a course of conduct shall be pursued which, if the said agreement is carried out in accordance with your intentions, it would necessarily amount to* (or *involve*) *the commission of an offence* (or *the commission of offences*) *namely the offence(s) of . . .* (provide details of the offence concerned) *by . . .* (name the person or persons who is/are party/parties to the agreement and who would commit the offence(s) concerned) *he/they being party to the said agreement*. Contrary to s (1)(a), Criminal Law Act 1977 as amended by s 5(1), Criminal Attempts Act 1981 and s 7, Computer Misuse Act 1990.*

2.   Continue the above charge to the asterisk and then continue with the following:

      . . . albeit the existence of certain facts would render the commission of the said offence(s) impossible. Contrary to s 1(1)(b), Criminal Law Act 1977, as amended by s 5(1) Criminal Attempts Act 1981 and s 7, Computer Misuse Act 1990.

Comments

The detailed provisions relating to the statutory offence of conspiracy are contained in Part 1 of the Criminal Law Act 1977 (as amended by s 5,

Criminal Attempts Act 1981 and the Computer Misuse Act 1990) which implements with some modifications the recommendations of the Law Commission's report published in March 1976. The Act abolished the common law offence of conspiracy apart from that relating to conspiracy to defraud and conspiracy to corrupt public morals or outrage public decency in the circumstances outlined in s 5(3). In addition, the offences of incitement and attempt to commit conspiracies, whether at common law or under the 1977 Act, are also abolished.

The elements of the statutory offence are as follows:

1. An agreement between two or more persons. By virtue of s 2 of the Act a person is exempt from liability for conspiracy if he is an intended victim of the offence to which the conspiracy relates. In addition the same section provides that a person is not guilty of conspiracy in relation to a particular offence if the only other person or persons with whom he conspires are throughout the agreement in any of the following categories: (a) a spouse; (b) a person under the age of criminal responsibility; and (c) an intended victim of that offence.

2. The agreement must be to pursue a course of conduct which will necessarily amount to or involve the commission of an offence by one or more parties if the agreement is carried out in accordance with their intentions. By virtue of s 5(1), Criminal Attempts Act 1981 this element has been extended so as to include agreements to commit an offence which under the circumstances it would be impossible to commit (see charge (2) above). Thus, for example, A and B may agree together to murder C and make all the necessary preparations. If unbeknown to them C dies of natural causes in the meanwhile, they may still be charged with conspiracy.

3. Where there is a conspiracy to commit offences under the Computer Misuse Act 1990 outside England and Wales special provisions apply in relation to the agreement as set out in s 1(1A) of the Criminal Law Act 1977. Officers investigating such conspiracies should refer to this section as well as to ss 4 to 8 of the Computer Misuse Act 1990.

At the practical level evidence relating to the extent of preparation by the parties to the conspiracy and the extent of their involvement will be highly relevant. Personal preparation and the movements and meetings of the conspirators, together with evidence of verbal and written exchanges, or the acquisition of vehicles and equipment, may provide strong evidence tending to show a course of conduct relevant to the agreement to commit an offence. The search for such evidence should be vigorously pursued to provide a strong prosecution case.

In the case of a s 1 conspiracy to commit a **summary offence**, proceedings can only be taken with the consent of the Director of Public Prosecutions. Where a prosecution for a substantive summary offence requires the consent of the Attorney General, a prosecution for conspiracy to commit such an offence will require the same consent. Section 4(3) provides that where the consent of any person is required for a particular offence which is not a summary offence, the same consent is required for the institution of proceedings for conspiracy to commit that offence.

Where there is an agreement to pursue a course of conduct in contemplation or furtherance of a trade dispute which constitutes an offence, the Act provides that such action will not constitute a criminal conspiracy provided that the substantive offence is triable summarily only and is not punishable with imprisonment.

By virtue of s 12, Criminal Justice Act 1987, the common law offence of conspiracy to defraud can now be charged in addition to the statutory offence under s 1 of the Criminal Law Act 1977 where the circumstances dictate. The maximum penalty for conspiracy to defraud is ten years imprisonment, thus making it an arrestable offence.

The offences referred to under (e) in the powers of arrest above are numerous. Those most likely to be met by police officers are:

1. Conspiracy to commit an indecent assault on a woman, causing prostitution of women or procuration of a girl under 21 (all contained in the Sexual Offences Act 1956).
2. Conspiracy to take a motor vehicle or other conveyance without authority etc or going equipped for stealing (all contained in the Theft Act 1968).
3. Conspiracies to commit offences under s 1, Public Bodies Corrupt Practices Act 1889 (corruption in office) or s 1, Prevention of Corruption Act 1906 (corrupt transactions with agents).

COUNTERFEITING AND KINDRED OFFENCES
1. Counterfeiting notes and coins
(Triable 'either way', max pen 10 yrs imp)

Powers of arrest

Full powers for 'arrestable offences', see pages 14–15.

Charge

Did make a counterfeit of a certain currency note (or *a certain protected coin*), *namely* . . . (name the currency note or protected coin) . . .

Then follow with (a) or (b) or (c):

(a) . . . *intending to pass (or tender) the said currency note (or protected coin) as genuine.*

(b) . . . *intending that another person, namely* . . . (name the other person who it is intended should pass the currency note or protected coin) *shall pass the said currency note* (or *protected coin*) *as genuine.*

(c) . . . *intending that another person unknown shall pass (or tender) the said currency note* (or *protected coin*) *as genuine.*

Then continue with the following:

Contrary to s 14(1), Forgery and Counterfeiting Act 1981.

2. Passing counterfeit notes and coins
(Triable 'either way', max pen 10 yrs imp)

Powers of arrest

Full powers for 'arrestable offences', see pages 14–15.

Charge

(a) *You did pass (or tender) as genuine a thing which you knew (or believed) to be a counterfeit of a certain currency note (or a certain protected coin) namely* . . . (name the currency note or protected coin). *Contrary to s 15(1)(a), Forgery and Counterfeiting Act 1981.*

(b) *You delivered to another person, namely* . . . (name the person) (or *you delivered to another person unknown*) *a thing which is, and which you knew (or believed) to be, a counterfeit of a certain currency note (or a certain protected coin)* . . .

Then continue with (a) or (b) or (c):

(a) . . . *intending that the person to whom it was delivered shall pass (or tender) it as genuine.*

(b) . . . *intending that a person other than the person to whom it was delivered, namely* . . . (name the other person concerned) *shall pass (or tender) it as genuine.*

(c) . . . *intending that a person unknown and other than the person to whom it was delivered shall pass (or tender) it as genuine.*

Then continue with:

Contrary to s 15(1)(b), Forgery and Counterfeiting Act 1981.

3. Custody or control of counterfeit notes and coins
(Triable 'either way', max pen 10 yrs imp)

Powers of arrest

Full powers for 'arrestable offences', see pages 14–15.

Charge

You did have in your custody (or under your control) a thing which is, and which you knew (or which you believed to be), a counterfeit of a currency note (or of a protected coin) namely a . . . (name the currency note or protected coin).

Then continue with (a) or (b) or (c) or (d) or (e):

(a)   *. . . intending to pass (or tender) the said counterfeit currency note (or protected coin) as genuine.*
(b)   *. . . intending to deliver the said counterfeit currency note (or counterfeit protected coin) to another person, namely . . .* (name the person) *with the intention that he shall pass (or tender) it as genuine.*
(c)   *. . . intending to deliver the said counterfeit currency note (or counterfeit protected coin) to another person unknown with the intention that he shall pass (or tender) it as genuine.*
(d)   *. . . intending to deliver the said counterfeit currency note (or counterfeit protected coin) to another person, namely . . .* (name the person) *with the intention that another person namely . . .* (name the person it is intended should pass or tender the counterfeit) *shall pass (or tender) it as genuine.*
(e)   *. . . intending to deliver the said counterfeit currency note (or counterfeit protected coin) to another person, namely . . .* (name the person) *with the intention that another person unknown shall pass (or tender) it as genuine.*

Then continue with the following:

Contrary to s 16(1), Forgery and Counterfeiting Act 1981.

4. Making, custody, or control of counterfeiting materials and implements
(Triable 'either way', max pen 10 yrs imp)

Powers of arrest

Full powers for 'arrestable offences', see pages 14–15.

Charge

You did make (or you did have in your custody (or under your control)) a certain thing namely . . . (name the thing) (ie counterfeiting materials or implements) *which you intended to use (or which you permitted another person namely . . .* (name the other person) (or *which you permitted another person unknown) to use), for the purpose of making a counterfeit of a certain currency note (or a certain protected coin) namely . . .* (name the currency note or protected coin), *with the intention that the said counterfeit currency note (or protected coin) shall be passed (or tendered) as genuine. Contrary to s 17(1), Forgery and Counterfeiting Act 1981.*

Comments

The Forgery and Counterfeiting Act 1981 repeals the Coinage Offences Act 1936.

For the purposes of Part 2 of the 1981 Act (which covers all of the above offences) a 'currency note' means: (a) any note which–(i) has been lawfully issued in England and Wales, Scotland, Northern Ireland, any of the Channel Islands, the Isle of Man or the Republic of Ireland; and (ii) is or has been customarily used as money in the country where it was issued; and (iii) is payable on demand *or* (b) any note which–(i) has been lawfully issued in some country other than those mentioned in (a)(i) above and (ii) is customarily used as money in that country.

A 'protected coin' means any coin which–(a) is customarily used as money in any country, *or* (b) is specified in an order made by the Treasury for the purposes of Part 2 of the 1981 Act.

A 'thing' is a counterfeit of a currency note or of a protected coin–(a) if it is not a currency note or a protected coin but resembles these items (whether on one side or both) to such an extent that it is reasonably capable of passing for a currency note or protected coin of that description *or* (b) it is a currency note or protected coin which has been so altered that it is reasonably capable of passing for a currency note or protected coin of some other description.

A thing consisting of one side only of a currency note, with or without the addition of other material is a counterfeit of such a note. A thing consisting of parts of two or more currency notes, or of parts of a currency note, or of parts of two or more currency notes with the addition of other material is capable of being a counterfeit of a currency note.

For the purposes of s 16(1) and (2) (custody or control of counterfeit notes and coins–see above), it is immaterial that a coin or note is not in a fit state to be passed or tendered or that the making or counterfeiting of a coin or note has not been finished or perfected.

Section 24 of the Act provides for the issue of a search warrant by a Justice of the Peace as well as providing powers to seize objects found.

As a practical note, it should be remembered that those who counterfeit and those who pass off the illicit material are generally well organised groups. Whenever any suspicion of these offences arises, the CID and most probably the regional crime squads will need to be involved immediately. If a beat officer does arrest an offender carrying counterfeits, make sure that the material being carried is seized and do not give your prisoner the opportunity of disposing of anything. Make sure that early statements are obtained from any person who may have been offered notes or coins (ie shopkeepers, assistants etc). Consider also your powers under the Theft Acts 1968 and 1978. More often than not counterfeiting offences will be bound up together with offences of deception (see pages 63–67). Where appropriate, offences under the Theft Acts can be charged in addition to the counterfeiting charges. Liaison with the Customs and Excise Authorities, Immigration Offices and Forensic Science Laboratories may also need to be effected at an early stage. Above all seek the guidance of your supervisory officers and the CID.

DAMAGING OR DESTROYING PROPERTY
(Triable 'either way', max pen 10 yrs imp)

(But see under 'Comments', below, where value of property is below £2000 (£5000 when s 46, Criminal Justice and Public Order Act 1994 is in force)).

Powers of arrest

Full powers for 'arrestable offences', see pages 14–15.

Charge

Did without lawful excuse destroy (or *damage)* certain property, namely . . . value . . . belonging to* (name of owner)*, intending to destroy such property* (or *being reckless as to whether such property would be destroyed* or *damaged*)*, contrary to s 1(1), Criminal Damage Act 1971.*

* See 'arson' (page 26) if damage is caused by fire.

Comments

For all purposes of this Act 'property' means property of a tangible nature, whether real or personal, including money and the following:

(a)   Wild creatures which have been tamed or are ordinarily kept in captivity **and** any other wild creatures or their carcasses if, *but only if*, they have been reduced into someone's possession which has not been lost or abandoned, or are in the course of being reduced into possession; but

(b)   **not** including mushrooms (including any fungus) growing wild on any land; or flowers, fruit or foliage of a plant (including any shrub or tree) growing wild on any land.

Property can legally 'belong' to any person who has:

(a)   custody or control of it;
(b)   any proprietary right or interest in it; or
(c)   a charge on it.

A person charged under this heading has an effective legal defence if he maintains that he committed the damage, etc with a 'lawful excuse' in terms as detailed in s 5(2) of the Act. It is essential to such a defence if it is to succeed is that his belief in the 'lawful excuse' *must be honestly held.* For the meaning of 'reckless' see the important decision of the House of Lords in *R v Caldwell* [1981] Crim LR 393. Also on 'recklessness' see *R v Miller* [1983] 2 AC, 161; 1 All ER 978; *Elliot v C (a Minor)* [1983] 2 All ER 1005; *R v R* (1984) 79 Cr App R 334 *R v Rogers* (1984) 149 JP 89. In the case of *R v Whiteley* (1991) Crim LR 436 a computer 'hacker' who made alterations thus impairing the use of the computer was convicted of criminal damage.

The offence covers a very wide field and bears comparison with the similarly wide provisions of theft.

See 'Possessing anything with intent to destroy or damage property', page 103.

By virtue of the Magistrates' Courts Act 1980, this offence is triable 'either way', except where the value of the property destroyed or damage alone does not exceed £2000 (£5000 when new s 46, Criminal Justice and Public Order Act 1994 is in force). In such cases the offence must be tried summarily unless the property is destroyed or damaged by fire. For procedure in cases of damage below £2000 (£5000), see the Magistrates' Courts Act 1980, s 22 and Sch 2 and Criminal Justice Act 1988, s 38.

DAMAGING OR DESTROYING PROPERTY WITH INTENT TO ENDANGER LIFE
(IO, max pen life imp)

Powers of arrest

Full powers for 'arrestable offences', see pages 14–15.

Charge

Did without lawful excuse destroy (or *damage)* certain property (namely)* . . . *intending to destroy* (or *damage*) such property *(or being reckless as to whether such property would be destroyed (or damaged) and intending* *by the destruction* (or *damage*) *to endanger the life of. . .* (name the person) (or *being reckless as to whether the life of . . . would be thereby endangered*). *Contrary to s 1(2), Criminal Damage Act 1971.*

Comments

The definitions and comments under the previous heading are applicable here **excepting** that the special statutory defences relating to 'lawful excuse' in s 5 **do not apply**. Bombing, explosives and similar major incidents are covered by the provision; but lesser matters are equally pertinent. Apply the basic principles and procedures laid down for 'murder' (see page 99) but give priority to the saving and protection of human life. Immediately call the emergency services appropriate if there is any possibility of further risk; also obtain the presence of a senior officer. Threats to commit this offence, with the intention that someone shall fear that the threat will be carried out, is a breach of s 2 of the Act (max pen 10 yrs imp). The special s 5 'lawful excuse' defences apply to the 'threats' offence. See *R v Hardie* [1984] 3 All ER 848 on the question of relevance of self-induced intoxication by alcohol and drugs in relation to this offence. Also see 'possessing anything with intent to destroy or damage property', page 103 and 'Arson', page 26.

*See 'Arson', page 26, if damage is caused by fire.

DANGEROUS DOGS
(Dangerous Dogs Act 1991)
(SO only but aggravated offences triable 'either way')

Powers of arrest

General power of arrest under s 25, PACE (See pages 17–18).

Charges

1. *You were the owner* (or *not being the owner, you were a person for the time being in charge*) *of a dog which was dangerously out of control in a public place called. . .* (name the public place) *contrary to s 3(1), Dangerous Dogs Act 1991.*
2. *You were the owner* (or *not being the owner, you were a person for the time being in charge*) *of a dog which was dangerously out of control in a public place called. . .* (name the public place) *and while the said dog was so out of control it injured . . .* (name and address of person injured) *contrary to s 3(1), Dangerous Dogs Act 1991.*
3. *You were the owner* (or *not being the owner you were a person for*

the time being in charge) of a dog which you allowed to enter a place, which was not a public place, namely . . . (name the place), *where the said dog was not permitted to be and while there the dog injured* . . . (name the injured party) (or *while there, there were reasonable grounds for apprehension that it would injure some person). Contrary to s 3(3), Dangerous Dogs Act 1991.*

Comments

The charges under (2) and (3) above become aggravated offences if a person is in actual fact injured. The maximum penalty on indictment for such an offence is two years imprisonment. Where no injury is caused the offence is summary only.

It is a defence for the owner of the dog concerned, but who was not in charge at the material time, to show that he left the dog in charge of a person whom he reasonably believed to be a fit and proper person.

Under s 4 of the Act, the court may order destruction of the offending animal and they must order destruction where the offence is aggravated.

It is unlawful under s 1 to breed dogs for fighting. The section applies to breeds of a type known as pit bull terrier, Japanese Tosa, Dogo Argentino, and Fila Braziliero. The section makes it clear that it is an offence to breed, sell, exchange, advertise or expose for sale or exchange, make or offer to make a gift of such animals. Dogs of the type described must be kept muzzled and on a lead by a person in charge while in a public place. It is a further offence to abandon such animals or allow them to stray.

DECEPTION
Deception–evasion of liability by
(Triable 'either way', max pen 5 yrs imp)

Powers of arrest

Full powers for 'arrestable offences', see pages 14–15.

Charges

(a)   *You did by a certain deception dishonestly secure the remission of the whole* (or *part) of an existing liability incurred by yourself* (or *incurred by* . . . (name of person by whom a liability was incurred)). *Contrary to s 2(1)(a), Theft Act 1978.*

(b)   (i) *You did by a certain deception with intent to make permanent default in whole* (or *in part) on an existing liability to make a payment, dishonestly induced a creditor, namely* . . . (name the creditor) (or *dishonestly induced a person namely . . . he being a person claiming payment on behalf of . . , a creditor) to wait for payment* (or *to forgo payment). Contrary to s 2(1)(b), Theft Act 1978;* or

(ii) *You did by a certain deception with intent to let another person, namely . . . to make permanent default in whole* (or *in part) on an existing liability to make a payment, dishonestly induce a creditor, namely . . .* (name the creditor) (or *dishonestly induce a person namely . . ., he being a person claiming payment on behalf of . . ., a creditor) to wait for payment* (or *to forgo payment). Contrary to s 2(1)(b), Theft Act 1978.*

(c)   *You did by a certain deception dishonestly obtain an exemption from making* (or *obtain an abatement of liability to make) a certain payment to . . .* (name the person to whom there was a liability to make a payment). *Contrary to s 2(1)(c), Theft Act 1978.*

Comments

Section 2, Theft Act 1978, creates offences of evasion of liability by deception. The offences under charges (a) and (b) above deal with cases where there is an **existing** liability to make a payment and the defendant by deception gets the creditor to remit the whole or part of the debt or induces the creditor to wait for payment or to forgo payment.

The offence under charge (a) applies when the accused gets the creditor to agree that he will never seek payment of an **existing debt**. For example, a man who borrows £50 from his neighbour may give a 'hard luck' story when it comes to the time for repayment. If the neighbour is persuaded by the story and indicates that the loan need never be repaid, the offence may be complete.

The offence under charge (b) is meant to deal with stalling debtors. It will cover those cases where a person induces a creditor to wait for payment and also where a person induces a creditor to forgo payment of an existing debt. It is essential to obtain evidence that the accused *never* intended to pay for there to be a successful prosecution under the charges at (b).

The offence under charge (c) is concerned with the type of fraud where an offender is acting dishonestly from the outset. For example, a person who is not a student may obtain admission to functions which are at a reduced rate for students by stating he is a student. In such a case he has by deception obtained an abatement of liability to make a payment.

For the purpose of s 2 (evasion of liability), the word 'liability' means a legally enforceable liability.

The word 'deception' has the same meaning as in s 15 of the Theft Act 1968 (see 'Deception–obtaining property by', page 66).

Deception–making off without payment
(Triable 'either way', max pen 2 yrs imp)

Powers of arrest

Any person may arrest without warrant anyone who is or whom he, with reasonable cause, suspects to be committing or attempting to commit an offence under this section (ie the offence shown in the charge below).

Charge

You being a person who, knowing that payment on the spot for certain goods supplied, namely ... (name the good(s) supplied) (or *for certain service(s) done, namely* ... (name the service(s) done)) *was required (or expected) from you, you did dishonestly make off without having paid as required (or expected) and with intent to avoid payment of the amount due. Contrary to s 3(1), Theft Act 1978.*

Comments

Conduct of the sort which the above charge is aimed at is commonly called 'bilking'. Everyday examples of such an offence are (1) walking out of a restaurant dishonestly and with intent to avoid paying the bill, and (2) dishonestly driving away from a garage without paying for petrol and with intent to avoid payment. The intention must be to permanently avoid payment altogether and not merely an intent to delay or defer payment (*R v Allen* [1985] 2 All ER 641).

By virtue of s 3(2) 'Payment on the spot' includes payment at the time of collecting goods on which work has been done or in respect of which service has been provided eg collection of clothes from the dry cleaners.

Section 3(3) states that the offence will not apply where the supply of goods or doing of the service is contrary to law, or where the service done is such that payment is not legally enforceable.

Under s 3, dishonesty does not have to be present at the time when goods are supplied or the service done. The time when it does have to be present is when the accused makes off without paying for what he has had. Indeed if dishonesty can be shown at the time the goods were supplied, etc, charges of a more serious nature might be considered (eg theft)–see page 140 or obtaining property by deception–see page 66.

From a practical point of view there is generally a necessity for officers to act quickly in this type of case. Offenders in 'making off' do so as quickly and inconspicuously as possible, often by motor vehicle. As soon as a report is received of a person bilking, a description of the offender and any vehicle he was using should be circulated at the earliest possible time after the commission of the offence.

Deception–obtaining pecuniary advantage by
(Triable 'either way', max pen 5 yrs imp)

Powers of arrest

Full powers for 'arrestable offences', see pages 14–15.

Charge

By a certain deception, namely . . . (give particulars) *dishonestly obtained for himself (or for . . .) a certain pecuniary advantage, namely* (give particulars of pecuniary advantage falling within s 16(2) of the Act), *contrary to s 16(1), Theft Act 1968.*

Comments

'Pecuniary advantage' covers:

(i)   the obtaining of overdraft, insurance policies and annuity contracts–including the obtaining of more favourable terms; or

(ii)   the obtaining of an opportunity to earn remuneration (or more remuneration) in an office or employment or to win money on betting (s 16(2)). In all cases the **advantage must be obtained by the 'deception'** as defined under 'comments', page 67.

This provision covers a wide field–from obtaining by deception a free seat in the cinema, to a better job, a credit balance with a bookmaker, or the removal of an overdraft with a bank manager.

Deception–obtaining property by
(Triable 'either way', max pen 10 yrs imp)

Powers of arrest

Full powers for 'arrestable offences', see pages 14–15.

Charge

By a certain deception (See 'comments' below for definition), *namely . . .* (give particulars) *dishonestly obtained . . .* (specify property) *belonging to . . . with the intention of permanently depriving the said . . . of it, contrary to s 15, Theft Act 1968.*

(See 'Comments' under 'theft', page 141 for definitions of 'property' and 'owner'.)

Comments

This offence is alternatively known as 'cheat'.

'Deception' means any deception (whether deliberate or reckless) by words or conduct as to fact or as to law. This includes any deception as to the present intentions of the person using the deceit–or of any other person (s 15(4)). While deceptions in writing are not included in this definition, it would seem that words which deceive can properly take either written or spoken form.

A person 'obtains property' for the purposes of the offence if he acquires (i) ownership; or (ii) possession; or (iii) control over it. 'Obtains' **includes** (i) obtaining for another; or (ii) enabling another to obtain, or to retain, the property. 'Intent' is discussed under 'Wounding, etc (with intent)', page 149. For the general interpretation of the word 'dishonesty' see *R v Ghosh* [1982] 2 All ER 689.

In using the powers of arrest much will depend upon the gravity and circumstances applying. While unnecessary apprehensions must be avoided, be certain that when an accused retains his liberty he does not have the opportunity thereby improperly to interfere with evidence.

Deception–obtaining services by
(Triable 'either way', max pen 5 yrs imp)

Powers of arrest

Full powers for 'arrestable offences', see pages 14–15.

Charge

Did by a certain deception dishonestly obtain a service (or obtained services) from . . . (name the person from whom the service was obtained). Contrary to s 1(1), Theft Act 1978.

Comments

This section makes it an offence to obtain any service from another by means of deception. A typical example would be where a person hires a car and is required to pay in advance and he pays by means of a worthless cheque. Another common occurrence involving this type of offence is where a person hires a taxi knowing full well that he has not got the money to pay for the fare at the end of the journey. Subsection 1(2) of the Act does in fact spell out that it is an obtaining of services where the other is induced to confer a benefit by doing some act, or causing or permitting some act to be done, on the understanding that the benefit has been or will be paid for.

For the meaning of the word 'deception' see under 'Obtaining property by deception', page 66.

From a practical viewpoint it is important for the person deceived to provide full details of the offender or his description. If he is not known, details of the deception employed by the offender, any documents, particularly signed documents passed by the offender (eg cheques) and the service which was supplied by the aggrieved person. The latter should also make clear in his statement that he acted on what the accused said or the conduct he used. Any witnesses who saw the transaction take place should also provide corroborative evidence to create a firm prosecution case.

DOMESTIC VIOLENCE
1. Domestic Violence and Matrimonial Proceedings Act 1976.
2. Domestic Proceedings and Magistrates' Courts Act 1978.

The above two Acts of Parliament relate to domestic proceedings before a judge and magistrates' courts respectively. A power of arrest is contained in both sets of legislation which, although worded differently, provide the same broad powers. The following is a composite of the powers contained in both Acts.

Powers of arrest

Where a power of arrest is:

(a)   attached to an injunction granted by a judge under the Domestic Violence and Matrimonial Proceedings Act 1976; or

(b)   attached to an order made by a magistrates' court under s 16 of the Domestic Proceedings and Magistrates' Courts Act 1978; and

such an injunction or order respectively makes the following provisions:

That the other party to the marriage (in the case of an injunction granted by a judge) or by the respondent (in the case of an order made by a magistrates' court):

(i)   shall not use violence against the person of the applicant; or
(ii)   shall not use violence against a child of the family; or
(iii)   shall not enter the matrimonial home,

then a constable may arrest, without warrant, a person whom he has reasonable cause for suspecting of being in breach of any of the provisions mentioned in (i) to (iii) above by reason of that person's violence or, as the case may be, entry into the matrimonial home.

Comments

A judge or magistrates' court may only attach a power of arrest if satisfied that physical injury (magistrates' court) or actual bodily harm (judge) has befallen the applicant or child of the family and that it is likely to do so again.

Both Acts provide that where a power of arrest is attached, and a person is arrested, then he shall be brought before a judge or Justice of the Peace, as the case may be, within a period of 24 hours beginning with the time of his arrest. In the case of an arrest made by virtue of a judge's direction, the prisoner shall not be released during the 24 hour period except on the direction of the judge concerned. The Domestic Violence and Matrimonial Proceedings Act 1976 also puts the onus upon the police to seek forthwith directions from the High Court or county court concerned as to the time and place the offender is to be brought before a judge.

Where an offender is brought before a Justice of the Peace, the Justice may remand him and the provisions of ss 128 and 129, Magistrates' Courts Act 1980, will apply. The Bail Act 1976, does not apply to civil proceedings and a recognizance must be taken if bail is allowed.

The above power in no way precludes the police from exercising other powers of arrest under the criminal law where circumstances warrant it (eg in cases of assault occasioning actual bodily harm, grievous bodily harm etc) and prosecutions should be taken in appropriate cases. Battered wives, however, are usually the main witnesses in such prosecutions and experience has shown that prosecutions have failed or could not be pursued because of a withdrawal by the wife of her complaint or her nervous reaction against giving evidence against a bullying husband. In cases where an injunction has been granted, the above Acts will make the constable's job easier when dealing with domestic disputes of this sort. Your force will have directions on the use of the Acts and these should always be adhered to.

DRUGS–UNLAWFUL POSSESSION OF
(Including attempting and inciting) (Triable 'either way', Class 'A' drug max pen 7 yrs imp; Class 'B' drug max pen 5 yrs imp; Class'C' drug max pen 2 yrs imp)

Powers of search and arrest

To search

If a constable has reasonable grounds to suspect that any person is in possession of a controlled drug (see 'Comments' for definition) in contravention of the Misuse of Drugs Act 1971, or any Regulations made under it, he may–

(a)   search that person and detain him for the purpose;
(b)   search any vehicle or vessel in which he suspects that the drug may be found. For the purpose of searching he can require the person in control of the vehicle or vessel to stop it (see s 23(2) of the Act);
(c)   seize and detain anything found in the course of the search which appears to be evidence.

To arrest

(a)   *Class 'A' or 'B' drug involved* (see 'comments' for definitions)–Full powers for 'arrestable offences' (see pages 14–15).
(b)   *Class 'C' drug involved*–General power of arrest under s 25, PACE (see pages 17–18).

Charge–for possession of a controlled drug

Did have in his possession (or did incite . . . (name of person) *to possess) a certain drug called* . . . (describe the drug eg an ampoule containing a preparation designed for injection called morphine) *being a Class 'A' (or Class 'B') (or Class 'C') controlled drug* (see 'comments' below for definitions). *Contrary to s 5(1) and (2) (and s 19* if the charge is 'inciting') *of the Misuse of Drugs Act 1971.*

Comments

Types of drugs

A 'controlled drug' means any substance or product listed as a Class 'A', 'B', or 'C' drug in Sch 2 of the Act. Many drugs are listed, with Class 'C' being generally the least potent. Among those most often illegally used are:

(a)   morphine (Class 'A'–usually injected);
(b)   lysergide and other N-alkyl derivatives of lysergamide (Class 'A'– better known as LSD, 'acid', etc);
(c)   cannabis and cannabis resin (Class 'B'–better known as 'pot', 'dope', 'grass' (ie any plant of the genus cannabis or any part of such plant (see also–'Cannabis cultivation of plant' page 40, etc. 'Cannabis resin' is the separated resin obtained from the cannabis plant); and
(d)   amphetamines (Class 'B'–which include 'double blues', 'French blues', pep-pills, etc–all currently referred to as 'speed' by pushers and drug-takers).

Class 'C' drugs include products such as benzedrine and methedrine.

Practical

Offences will usually come to your notice through:

(a) information received; or
(b) you having to deal with someone who seems to be 'on a trip' (ie under the influence of a drug); or
(c) you seeing a known or suspected 'pusher' being approached by a possible customer, or vice versa.

Watch out for the companion (male or female) who might be carrying drugs for your suspect; also for vehicles and hiding places in the vicinity where drugs might be concealed. Pushers are often well organised and their unfortunate dupes will often resort to subterfuge. If the provable facts known to you amount to no more than to an attempt to possess the drug or show only the pusher (or middleman) incited or attempted to incite possession of the drug, this remains an offence. When this applies, the powers to search, arrest and punishment are the same as for the appropriate substantive offence, depending on the classification of the drug involved– 'A', 'B' or 'C' (see 'powers' and 'comments', on page 73 and above).

Searching

Officers should make full use of their wide powers of stop and search and their powers of search, seizure and arrest as provided by the Police and Criminal Evidence Act 1984. In particular officers should comply with the Codes of Practice under the Act in order to negate any allegations of malpractice. In particular it may be necessary to make intimate and strip searches under s 55, PACE (see page 6) as this is often the only totally satisfactory way to deal with drug offenders. Never leave the suspect in control of anything which might contain evidence eg handbag, jewellery etc. Unless there are exceptional circumstances never put your prisoner in the cells before searching. Realise that everything taken into possession which is believed or suspected to be a drug must go to the forensic science laboratory for identification.

Amphetamine-takers

If you believe a suspect has taken this drug during the preceding 24 hours or thereabouts, invite him voluntarily to provide a urine sample. Should he agree:

(1) take it in a clean, dry container *without* a preservative;
(2) divide the contents and offer one sample to the suspect in a similar container;

(3)   send your sample for HO Lab analysis.

If the analysis shows the presence of the drug and a 'possession' prosecution is consequently to be undertaken *on this finding alone*, the charge should cite the date on which the drug was known or believed to have been taken (*Hambleton v Callinan* [1968] 2QB 427).

This urine sample procedure should be applied in particular if the suspect was driving or in charge of a motor vehicle, etc when arrested (see 'Driving, etc, when unfit through drug', page 163).

Special defence for 'possession'

There is a special defence for the individual who takes possession of a drug maintainedly:

(1)   with the knowledge or suspicion of what it is and with the intention of delivering it into the possession of a person lawfully entitled to take custody of it; *or*

(2)   to prevent someone else committing an offence under the Act. His purpose when taking possession must have genuinely been to hand it over as described at (1) above (eg to a doctor, a pharmacist, a responsible hospital practitioner–or possibly to a police officer eg if he contends that he found the drug, etc). For the defence to be effective, he must do this as soon as possible and have taken all reasonable steps to hand the drug over. Alternatively, if his maintained purpose was to prevent someone committing an offence, the defence remains effective if he has taken all reasonable steps to try to destroy the drug (see s 5(4)).

Further defences relating to lack of knowledge that the substance or product was a controlled drug are available under s 28 of the Act.

For case law on 'Possession' see *Warner v Metropolitan Police Com* [1968] 2 All ER 356; *R v Searle* [1971] Crim LR 592; *R v Colyer* [1974] Crim LR 243; *R v Ashton -Rickardt* [1978] 1 All ER 173; *Chief Constable of Cheshire v Hunt* (1983) 147 JP 567; *R v Maginnis* [1987] AC 303.

General

Contact a senior officer and your Force Drug Squad *as soon as ever possible* in the enquiry.

Investigation of drug offences often brings other crimes to light–thefts, blackmail and even worse.

See 'Drugs–unlawful supply of', below and 'Cannabis–cultivation of plant', page 40.

The Misuse of Drugs Act 1971, additionally deals comprehensively with drugs matters relating to importing (s 3), exporting (s 3), production (s 4), use of premises, etc. A working knowledge of the 'possession' and 'supply' offences covers basic matters likely to require **immediate** action by the non-specialist police officer.

*DRUGS–UNLAWFUL SUPPLY OF
(including attempting and inciting) (Triable 'either way', max pen Class 'A' Drug–life imp; Class 'B' Drug–14 yrs imp; Class 'C' Drug–5 yrs imp)
(*Note all definitions under previous heading apply here).

Powers of search and arrest

To search

As for 'Drugs–unlawful possession of', page 69.

To arrest

Full powers for 'arrestable offences', see pages 14–15.

Charge

. . . That you supplied (or offered to supply, or incited . . . (name of person) *to supply) a class 'A' (or 'B' or 'C') controlled drug, namely . . .* (describe drug) to . . . (name of person), *contrary to s 4* of the Misuse of Drugs Act 1971 (* and s 19 if charge is 'inciting').*

Comments

This 'pusher' offence is significantly more serious than the related 'possession' offence. Deal with it accordingly. All 'Comments' under 'Drugs–unlawful possession of', page 69 apply–**excepting the special defence provisions** (see 'Special defence' subheading, page 72). Classes of persons authorised legally to possess or supply controlled drugs are detailed in s 7 of the Act (doctors, dentists, veterinary practitioners and surgeons, etc–together with those obtaining drugs on proper prescription). Be alert, however, to the registered addict who 'pushes' his prescribed drug to other people.

Immediate involvement of the Force Drug Squad is even more important here than when dealing with 'possession' of a controlled drug.

See also 'Cannabis–cultivation of plant', page 40.

DRUG TRAFFICKING OFFENCES
Assisting another to retain the benefit of drug trafficking
(Triable 'either way', max pen 14 yrs imp)

Powers of arrest

Full powers for 'arrestable offences', see pages 14–15.

Charge

1.   *Knowing (or suspecting) that another person named A is a person who carries on (or has carried on or has benefited from) drug trafficking, you entered into an arrangement (or you were concerned in an arrangement) whereby the retention (or the control by another or the control on behalf of another) of A's proceeds of drug trafficking was facilitated. Contrary to s 24(1)(a), Drug Trafficking Offences Act 1986.*

2.   *Knowing (or suspecting) that another person named A is a person who carries on (or has carried on or has benefited from) drug trafficking you entered into an arrangement (or you were concerned in an arrangement) whereby A's proceeds of drug trafficking are used to secure that funds are placed at A's disposal (or whereby A's proceeds of drug trafficking are used for A's benefit to acquire property by way of investment. Contrary to s 24(1)(b), Drug Trafficking Offences Act 1986.*

Comments

The Drug Trafficking Offences Act 1986 creates powers for the Crown Court to make confiscation orders against persons convicted of drug trafficking offences. Thus the illicit gain made by those who deal in drugs can now no longer benefit them provided the courts vigorously apply the procedures laid down in ss 1–5 of the Act. Sections 7–10 create machinery to prevent a person suspected of drug trafficking to dispose of property before it can be dealt with by the Crown Court. Officers should be prepared to present to the court details of all property owned by the drug trafficker or under his control. There are special provisions in ss 27–33 of the Act to enable officers to investigate drug trafficking and which facilitate the gathering of evidence in relation to the property of the accused.

The offences of production, supply, and possession for the supply of controlled drugs under the Misuse of Drugs Act 1971 are all deemed to be 'drug trafficking offences' and will thus attract confiscation orders under the Act. The same applies to offences of conspiracy or attempts or incitement to commit or aiding, abetting, counselling or procuring any of these offences.

The offences under charges (1) and (2) above are newly created under the Act and they are in themselves deemed to be 'drug trafficking offences' which will attract confiscation orders by the court.

DRUNK AND DISORDERLY

DRUNKENNESS (DRUNK AND INCAPABLE)

DRUNK IN CHARGE OF CARRIAGE, ETC

DRUNK IN CHARGE OF LOADED FIREARMS

(Note: Offences of drunkenness and the control of alcohol at sporting events is dealt with under the heading 'Sporting Events' (see page 132).)

Powers of arrest

Any person may arrest any offender who:

(a) in any public place is guilty, while drunk, of disorderly behaviour; or

(b) in any highway or other public place (whether a building or not) or on any licensed premises is found drunk and incapable of taking care of himself; or

(c) in any highway or other public place is drunk while in charge of any carriage, horse, cattle or steam engine; or

(d) anywhere is drunk when in possession of any loaded firearm.

Charges

1. Drunk and disorderly (SO only)

In a certain public place called . . . (name the public place) *you were guilty, while drunk, of disorderly behaviour. Contrary to s 91(1), Criminal Justice Act 1967.*

2. Drunkenness (drunk and incapable) (SO only)

In a certain highway (or *public place*) *called . . .* (name the highway or public place) (or *in certain licensed premises called . . .* (name the premises)) *you were found drunk. Contrary to s 12, Licensing Act 1872.*

3. Drunk in charge of a carriage etc (SO only)

In a certain highway (or *public place*) *called . . .* (name the highway or public place) *you were drunk while in charge of a certain carriage, namely*

... (name the type of carriage (eg cycle, cart etc)) (or *you were drunk while in charge of a horse* (or *cattle)*) (or *you were drunk while in charge of a steam engine). Contrary to s 12, Licensing Act 1872.*

4. Drunk in charge of loaded firearms (SO only)

You were drunk when in possession of a loaded firearm. Contrary to s 12, Licensing Act 1872.

Comments

For the purpose of s 91, Criminal Justice Act 1967 (drunk and disorderly) a 'public place' means any highway and any other premises or place to which, at the material time, the public has or is permitted to have access, whether on payment or otherwise. There is a similar definition prescribed for the offences under the Licensing Act 1872 by virtue of the Licensing Act 1902.

A bicycle, whether ridden or pushed, is a carriage within the meaning of s 12, Licensing Act 1872 (*Corkery v Carpenter* [1951] 1 KB 102). For the offence of 'riding a pedal cycle while under the influence of drink', see page 165. A person cannot be charged with an offence under s 12, Licensing Act 1872 in addition to a charge under s 19, Road Traffic Act 1988.

A licensee and the persons he employs are obliged to take all reasonable steps to prevent drunkenness on licensed premises. If the licensee permits (i) drunkenness, or (ii) violent, or (iii) quarrelsome, or (iv) riotous conduct he commits an offence (summons procedure only: s 172, Licensing Act 1964). Magistrates now have the power to make an 'exclusion order' against persons who are convicted of offences in licensed premises and violence is involved. (See 'Licensed premises–excluded persons', page 95.) The Licensing (Amendment) Act 1977 provides powers for the entry of police into licensed premises.

It is extremely important to remember that illness or certain injuries can sometimes be mistaken for drunkenness. If there is any doubt it is best to seek medical aid straight away. The primary duty of the police is to protect life.

Drunken persons placed in police cells should be visited frequently in accordance with your force orders and code of practice. It is essential that these orders are carried out and a careful physical check made of the prisoner. If there is any concern about his condition then medical aid must be sought immediately. A careful record of all visits to such prisoners should be made on the detention sheet or record.

DRUNK IN CHARGE OF A CHILD UNDER 7 YEARS
(SO only)

Powers of arrest

Any person may arrest any offender found drunk while having the charge of a child apparently under the age of seven years, *in any highway or public place or licensed premises* (including any place to which the public have access whether on payment or otherwise) (s 2(1), Licensing Act 1902).

Charge

Was found drunk in a certain highway (or *public place,* or *on licensed premises) while having the charge of a child apparently under the age of seven years, contrary to s 2(1), Licensing Act 1902, as amended.*

Comments

Remember that, for the purposes of this and the other offences of drunkenness mentioned, a public place includes any place to which the public has a right of access, whether on payment or otherwise. This would include a football ground during a match to which the public were admitted, a theatre during a public performance, etc.

See 'comments' under previous heading concerning illness and drunken prisoners placed in police cells.

ENCLOSED PREMISES, BEING FOUND IN OR UPON, ETC
(SO, max pen 3 mths imp)

Powers of arrest

Any person may arrest anyone found committing this offence.

Charge

Was found in (or *upon) a dwelling house* (or *warehouse,* or *coach house,* or *stable,* or *out-house,* or *garden,* or *area) in the occupation of . . . for a certain unlawful purpose, namely to . . . contrary to s 4, Vagrancy Act 1824.*

Comments

The various places described in the charge should be studied and strictly interpreted. Lord Caldecote CJ considered that an 'area' denotes the basement area, namely, the open space below the level of the ground which has been excavated for the purpose of building a house on the site (*Knott v Blackburn* [1944] KB 77). Railway sidings are not 'areas'. The 'unlawful purpose' intended must be the commission of some criminal offence (eg stealing) and *not* some immoral act which is not so punishable (*Haynes v Stevenson* (1860)).

In view of the provision relating to burglary (see page 38) in the Theft Act 1968 and the law relating to adverse occupation of premises (see page 000) in the Criminal Law Act 1977, the **practical value** of this provision relates to 'being found in a garden or area or **upon** a dwelling house, warehouse, etc' and it is included mainly to cover this.

'Intent' is discussed under 'Wounding, etc (with intent)' page 149.

FIREARM–CARRYING WITH CRIMINAL INTENT, ETC
(IO, max pen life imp)

Powers of arrest

Full powers for 'arrestable offences', see pages 14–15 (SAO).

Charge

Did have with him a firearm (or imitation firearm) namely . . . (see 'comments' below for definitions) with intent to commit a certain indictable offence, namely . . . (or to resist or to prevent the arrest of . . .) while he had the said firearm (or imitation firearm) with him). Contrary to s 18, Firearms Act 1968.

Comments

The charge contains the necessary ingredients to the crime. The following definitions are essential to a working understanding of this and related firearms offences in the handbook.

'Firearms' means a lethal barrelled weapon (which includes such a weapon not designed to kill or inflict injury, but capable of doing so if misused (*Read v Donovan* [1947] K 326) of any description from which any shot, bullet or other missile can be discharged, and includes:

(i)   any prohibited weapon (*see* s 5(1) *and* (2) *of the Act–a gas gun, machine guns etc*) whether it is a lethal weapon as aforesaid, or not; (note that by virtue of s 1, Firearms Act 1988 the Secretary of State can by order add to the types and classes of prohibited weapons and ammunition); and

(ii)   any component part of such a lethal or prohibited weapon; and

(iii) any accessory to any such weapon designed or adapted to diminish the noise or flash caused by firing the weapon (*silencers, etc*).

'Ammunition' means ammunition for any firearm (as defined) and includes grenades, bombs and other like missiles, whether capable of use with a firearm or not; together with prohibited ammunition (including ammunition containing noxious or liquid gas, etc).

'Imitation firearm' means anything which has the appearance of being a firearm whether or not it is capable of discharging any shot, bullet or other missile–but **excluding** weapons designed, etc for the discharge of noxious liquid, gas, etc (s 5(1)(b)).

'Intent' is discussed under 'Wounding, etc (with intent)', page 149.

Stop and search, etc, powers

On reasonable suspicion that a person has a firearm with him, (i) in a public place; or (ii) anywhere else while committing or being about to commit this or the offence of trespassing with a firearm (page 83), a constable may detain and search that person and stop and search any vehicle then and there being used. It is an offence to fail to hand over a firearm and ammunition in such circumstances and the constable may arrest under his powers for 'arrestable offences' (see pages 14–15).

When using these powers, a constable may enter any place–but only for the purpose of this and the 'trespassing with a firearm' offence, page 83 (s 47, Firearms Act 1968).

FIREARM–OR IMITATION–USING WITH INTENT TO RESIST OR PREVENT ARREST
(IO, max pen life imp)

Powers of arrest

Full powers for 'arrestable offences', see pages 14–15 (SAO).

Charge

Did make (or attempt to make) use of a certain firearm (see 'Firearm– carry with criminal intent' page 78, for definition and 'comments', below) (or *imitation firearm* (similarly, see above for definition) *with intent to resist* (or *prevent) the lawful arrest* (or *detention) of himself* (or *of . . .), contrary to s 17(1), Firearms Act 1968.*

Comments

Where officers suspect that firearms are being carried, senior officers must be informed immediately. Force firearms policy will then be adhered to in order to safeguard the public and the police officers involved. (See general comments under the heading 'Firearm, trespassing with' (page 83).)

A component part of a firearm or an accessory to diminish noise or flash is not a 'firearm' for the purpose of this and the following offence (see ss 17(4) and 57(1)(b) and (c) of the Act).

FIREARM–OR IMITATION–HAVING POSSESSION WHEN COMMITTING, OR BEING ARRESTED FOR, CERTAIN OFFENCES
(IO, max pen life imp)

Powers of arrest

Full powers for 'arrestable offences', see pages 14–15.

Charge

At the time of committing (or *at the time of being arrested for*) *the offence of* . . . (describe shortly one of the offences specified in Sch 1 of the Firearms Act 1968, as amended by Sch 2 of the Theft Act 1968), *had in his possession a certain firearm** (or *an imitation* firearm*), *namely* . . . *contrary to s 17(2), Firearms Act 1968.*

*See pages 78–79 for definitions

Comments

The Sch 1 offences referred to in this charge are offences under the Criminal Damage Act 1971; offences under the following provisions of the Offences Against the Person Act 1861–ss 20–22, 30, 32, 38, and 47 (Criminal assaults); offences under Part I of the Child Abduction Act 1984 (abduction of children); theft; burglary; blackmail; taking a motor vehicle without consent; assaulting a constable in the execution of his duty; rape; offences under ss 17, 18 and 20, Sexual Offences Act 1956 (abduction of women); aiding and abetting the commission of the above offences and attempting to commit them. The Sch 1 offence must be proved before the offence is complete (*R v Baker* [1961] 3 All ER 703).

FIREARM (including shotgun and air weapon)–CARRYING LOADED, ETC, IN PUBLIC
(Triable 'either way' except if an air weapon (SO only), max pen 5 yrs imp. Air weapon–6 mths imp)

Powers of arrest

If a firearm other than an air weapon–full powers for 'arrestable offences', see pages 14–15.

If an air weapon, the general power of arrest under s 25, PACE will apply (see pages 17–18).

Charge

Without lawful authority or reasonable excuse did have with him in a certain place called . . . (name the place) *a loaded shotgun (*or *loaded air weapon) (*or *a firearm with ammunition suitable for use in the firearm).* (See 'Firearm carrying with criminal intent', pages 78-79 for 'firearm' definition). *Contrary to s 19, Firearms Act 1968.*

Comments

The proof of 'lawful authority or reasonable excuse' lies on the person having the weapon. In many cases an acceptable reason for possession will be immediately forthcoming. Be alert, however, for potential troublemakers and others who may have well-prepared pretexts to offer. Relate your facts to the powers of arrest given when deciding what action to take.

Important

Recognise that–(i) if it is an 'air weapon' or 'shot gun' **this must be loaded**; (ii) if it is any other sort of firearm it need **not be loaded** provided the person concerned has suitable ammunition with him (not necessarily **on** him).

A 'shotgun' is a smoothbore gun (not being an air gun) which has a barrel not less than 24 inches in length and does not have any barrel with a bore exceeding 2 inches in diameter; either has no magazine or has a non-detachable magazine incapable of holding more than two cartridges and is not a revolver gun.

An 'air weapon' is an air rifle, air gun or air pistol, not declared by the Secretary of State to be specially dangerous. Those so declared are air weapons (air rifles, air guns and air pistols) capable of discharging a missile so that on discharge the missile has kinetic energy above 12 ft lb–or 6 ft lb if an air pistol (see Firearms Dangerous Air Weapons Rules 1969). As such weapons become 'firearms' for the purposes of this offence, your immediate problem relates to (i) whether any air weapon is loaded; or (ii) whether the possessor has ammunition with him. Pass a detailed description to your police firearms department for guidance.

A 'public place' includes any highway and any premises or place to which at the material time the public have, or are permitted to have, access whether on payment or otherwise (eg a football ground or stadium during a public match, a railway carriage which is in use, etc).

Common sense use of this provision can nip potentially serious hooligan and gang troubles in the bud.

In suspect cases the possessor of a **firearm** or a **shotgun** will generally be legally required to hold a certificate. A constable may demand the production of certificates and if these are not produced or the suspect fails to allow the officer to read them or show he is exempt from holding a certificate, the constable may seize and detain the firearm, shotgun or ammunition and require the person to declare his name and address. It is an offence for such a person to refuse or fail to give his true name and address. If the offence is committed the general power of arrest under s 25, PACE will apply (see pages 17–18).

FIREARM POSSESSION WITH INTENT TO ENDANGER LIFE OR CAUSE INJURY TO PROPERTY
(IO, max pen life imp)

Powers of arrest

Full powers for 'arrestable offences', see pages 14–15 (SAO).

Charge

Did have in his possession a certain firearm, namely ... (describe) *[or certain ammunition namely ...* (describe; see 'comments' under 'Firearm–carrying with criminal intent', pages 78–79 for definitions of 'firearm' and 'ammunition') *with intent by means thereof to endanger life (or to enable another person, namely ... by means thereof to endanger life). Contrary to s 16, Firearms Act 1968.*

Comments

It does not matter whether injury to the person is caused, so long as the **intent to carry this out by means of the firearm or ammunition is proved**. 'Intent' is discussed under 'Wounding, etc (with intent)', page 82.

Very often officers will be forewarned of situations where a person is committing this offence. Quarrels between individuals, matrimonial disputes, jealous lovers and rival gangs are a few of the main reasons why people in the heat of the moment or after harbouring a grudge take up arms and go out to settle the score. If information is received that a person is committing this offence, be particularly careful. Obtain as much information as you can if time permits and inform senior officers immediately. The danger will then be assessed and instructions given under your force's firearms policy. Above all there should be no heroics when time is on your side enabling the implementation of force policy. If there is no time and you are faced with a dangerous situation whilst you are on patrol duty, radio for assistance straightaway and try to defuse the situation. If it is practicable, take the weapon from the offender and make the arrest. Above all remember your first duty as a police officer is to preserve life and that includes the life of the offender no matter how deranged he may be.

FIREARM, TRESPASSING WITH
(Triable 'either way' (except if an air weapon–SO only or any firearm where trespass is on land–SO only), max pen (i) on indictment–5 yrs imp; (ii) summary trial–6 months imp; (iii) summary trial–on land with any firearm 3 mths imp)

Powers of arrest

(i) Having firearm (not an air weapon) with him *in a building*, etc–full powers for 'arrestable offences', see pages 14–15.

(ii) Having an air weapon with him in a building etc, or having any type of firearm with him on land use the general power of arrest under s 25, PACE (see pages 17–18).

Charge

Having a firearm (see 'Firearm, carrying with criminal intent', page 78 for definition) (or *an air weapon* (see 'Firearm, carrying loaded etc in public', page 81 for definition) *with him, he did enter* (or *was in) a building* (or *part of a building) namely . . . (or did enter)* (or *was on) land at . . .) as a trespasser without reasonable excuse, contrary to s 20, Firearms Act 1968.*

Comments

The 'stop and search, etc' powers under the Act, which related both to **persons and vehicles** (see 'Firearm–carrying with criminal intent', page 78) apply to this offence. Where a trespass with a firearm is into a building 'entry as a trespasser' marries closely to 'Burglary', page 38, but under the Firearms Act the only two extra essentials are (i) possession of a firearm; and (ii) absence of reasonable excuse. This applies equally to trespass on land–which, incidentally, includes 'land covered in water' (s 20(3)).

Important

Proof of 'reasonable excuse' lies on the trespasser.

Note that a **firearm without ammunition** is adequate to the charge. Possession of an **imitation firearm is not, however, an offence here**. Use of the right to arrest will depend on the gravity and circumstances of each particular case–but always seize the firearm if practicable and legally permissible–it may be your most important evidence.

FORGERY AND KINDRED OFFENCES

1. Forgery
(Triable 'either way', max pen 10 yrs imp)

Powers of arrest

Full powers for 'arrestable offences', see pages 14–15.

Charge

You did make a false instrument namely a . . .(name the false instrument). Then follow with (a) or (b) or (c) or (d) or (e):

(a)   . . . *with the intention that it shall be used to induce* . . . (name the person it is intended should accept the false instrument); or

(b)   . . . *with the intention that it shall be used to induce some person unknown;* or

(c)   . . . *with the intention that it shall be used by another person, namely* . . . (name the person it is intended should use the false instrument) *to induce* . . . (name the person it is intended should accept the false instrument); or

(d)   . . . *with the intention that it shall be used by another person namely* . . . (name the person it is intended should use the false instrument) *to induce some person unknown;* or

(e)   . . . *with the intention that it shall be used by another person unknown to induce* . . . (name the person it is intended should accept the false instrument)

Then continue with the following:

. . . *to accept the said false instrument as genuine, and by reason of so accepting it to do* (or *not to do*) *some act to his prejudice* (or *some act to the prejudice of another person namely* . . . (name the person)). *Contrary to s 1, Forgery and Counterfeiting Act 1981.*

2. Copying a false instrument
(Triable 'either way', max pen 10 yrs imp)

Powers of arrest

Full powers for 'arrestable offences', see pages 14–15.

Charge

You did make a copy of a certain instrument, namely ... (name the instrument) *which is, and which you knew* (or *believed*) *to be, a false instrument*

Then follow with (a) or (b) or (c) or (d) or (e):

(a)   ... *with the intention that it shall be used to induce* ... (name the person it is intended should accept the copy of the false instrument); or

(b)   ... *with the intention that it shall be used to induce some person unknown;* or

(c)   ... *with the intention that it shall be used by another person, namely* ... (name the person it is intended should use the copy of the false instrument) *to induce* ... (name the person it is intended should accept the copy of the false instrument); or

(d)   ... *with the intention that it shall be used by another person namely* ... (name the person it is intended should use the copy of the false instrument) *to induce some person unknown*; or

(e)   ... *with the intention that it shall be used by another person unknown to induce* ... (name the person it is intended should accept the copy of the false instrument)

Then continue with the following:

... *to accept the said copy of the false instrument as a copy of a genuine instrument and by reason of so accepting it to do* (or *not to do*) *some act to his prejudice* (or *some act to the prejudice of another person namely* ... (name the person)). *Contrary to s 2, Forgery and Counterfeiting Act 1981.*

3. Using a false instrument
(Triable 'either way', max pen 10 yrs imp)

Powers of arrest

Full powers for 'arrestable offences', see pages 14–15.

Charge

You did use a certain instrument, namely . . . (name the instrument) *which was, and which you knew* (or *believed*) *to be, false, with the intention of inducing. . .* (name the person it was intended to induce) (or *with the intention of inducing some person unknown) to accept the said instrument as genuine, and by reason of so accepting it to do* (or *not to do) some act to his prejudice (*or *some act to the prejudice of . . .* (name the person)). *Contrary to s 3, Forgery and Counterfeiting Act 1981.*

4. Using a copy of a false instrument
(Triable 'either way', max pen 10 yrs imp)

Powers of arrest

Full powers for 'arrestable offences', see pages 14–15.

Charge

You did use a copy of a certain instrument, namely . . . (name the instrument) *which is, and which you knew to be, a false instrument, with the intention of inducing . . .* (name the person it is intended to induce) (or with the intention of inducing some person unknown) *to accept the said copy of the said false instrument as a copy of a genuine instrument and by reason of so accepting it to do* (or *not to do*) some act to his prejudice (or some act to the prejudice of . . . (name the person)). *Contrary to s 4, Forgery and Counterfeiting Act 1981.*

5. Custody or control of false instruments
(Triable 'either way', max pen–s 5(1), 10 yrs imp; s 5(2), 2 yrs imp)

Powers of arrest

Section 5(1)–Full powers for 'arrestable offences', see pages 14–15.
Section 5(2)–General power of arrest under s 25, PACE (see pages 17–18).

Charges

(a) Section 5(1)
You did have in your custody (or *control) a certain instrument namely . . .* (name the instrument), *to which s 5 of the Forgery and Counterfeiting Act 1981 applies, which is, and which you knew to be, false, with the intention that it shall be used* (or *with the intention that it shall be used by . . .* (name the person it is intended should use the false instrument), (or *with the intention that it shall be used by some person unknown) to induce. . .* (name the person it is intended to induce) (or *to induce some person unknown)*

to accept the said false instrument as genuine and by reason of so accepting it to do (or not to do) some act to his prejudice (or some act to the prejudice of. . . (name the person)). Contrary to s 5(1), Forgery and Counterfeiting Act 1981.

(b) Section 5(2)

You did have in your custody (or under your control), without lawful authority or excuse, an instrument, namely . . . (name the instrument), to which s 5 of the Forgery and Counterfeiting Act 1981 applies which is and which you knew (or believed) to be false. Contrary to s 5(2), Forgery and Counterfeiting Act 1981.

Comments

The Forgery and Counterfeiting Act 1981 repeals the Forgery Act 1913. By virtue of s 8 of the 1981 Act, the word 'instrument' means: (a) any document whether of a formal or informal character; (b) any stamp issued or sold by the Post Office; (c) any Inland Revenue Stamp; (d) any disc, tape, sound track or other device on or in which information is recorded or stored by mechanical, electronic or other means. It should be noted that a currency note within the meaning of Part 2 of the Act (counterfeiting) is **not** an instrument for the purposes of Part 1 (forgery).

Investigating officers should bear in mind the meaning of the words 'false'; 'making'; 'prejudice'; and 'induce'. Their definitions will be found in ss 9 and 10 of the Act where they are set down in considerable detail. Home Office circulars and your force orders relevant to the Act will also explain these terms and should be referred to.

Section 5(3) and (4) relate to the offences of making or having custody or control of machines, implements, paper or other materials for the purpose of making false instruments.

With regard to all of the offences under s 5, the instruments to which the section applies are money orders, postal orders, United Kingdom postage stamps, Inland Revenue stamps, share certificates, passports and documents which can be used instead of passports, cheques, traveller's cheques, cheque cards, and credit cards. Also included are entries in a register of births, adoptions, marriages or deaths and certificates relating to entries in such registers.

A magistrate may issue a search warrant under s 7 of the Act. A constable holding such a warrant may enter any premises specified and search for and seize things used for the making of false, or copies of false, instruments in contravention of ss 1 or 2; or any false instrument or copy of a false instrument which has been used or it is intended should be used in contravention of ss 3 or 4; or any thing the custody or control of which without lawful authority or excuse is an offence under s 5. A magistrates' court may order forfeiture of such objects and their subsequent destruction or disposal.

From a practical viewpoint it is best in every case to use the powers of arrest as outlined above where the circumstances warrant such powers being exercised. Be careful to preserve all the evidence and remember that it is very easy for offenders to dispose of documents which have been forged. Make sure you give your prisoner no opportunity to do this. Very often offences of forgery and the like arise simultaneously with the commission of other criminal offences especially theft, burglary or deception. For example by burglary a criminal may steal a wallet containing a cheque book and cheque card. If he signs one of the cheques with a forged signature and presents it for payment for goods, he not only commits an offence under ss 1 and 3 of the Act, he also clearly commits a number of offences under the Theft Acts 1968 and 1978 (burglary, theft and deception). It may be that the evidence obtained in relation to the Theft Act offences make it more convenient to arrest for those offences. The forgery matters could then be included as additional charges when the relevant evidence was established. Note that the offence under s 5(2) carries only the general powers of arrest. In cases under this section, officers should try to establish how the offender came to have custody or control of the false instrument. He may well have stolen it or received it. If that is so, use the 'arrestable offences' power given on pages 14–15.

As far as the evidence is concerned, remember that in all of the offences under ss 1–4 and 5(1) and (3) the necessary 'intent' must be proved. 'Intent' in these cases is best proved where a person accepts a false instrument as genuine and actually does some act to his prejudice. For example, the shopkeeper handing over goods as a result of being given a forged cheque. If it is a case of keeping observation on a person using a false instrument, do not jump in too quickly, obtain as much evidence as possible to show his intention.

GROSS INDECENCY
1. Indecency between men
(Triable 'either way', max pen–by man over 21 with man under 18–5 yrs imp: in other cases 2 yrs imp)

Powers of arrest

Full powers for 'arrestable offences', see pages 14–15, **in case of man over 21 years with man under 18.** In all other cases used the general powers of arrest under s 25, PACE (see pages 17–18).
Important–See also comments under the heading 'Buggery', page 37, re homosexual acts committed in private.

Charge

Being a man did commit (or *was party to the commission by . . . a man of*)
(or procured the commission by . . . a man of) an act of gross indecency
with another man, namely . . . (or *himself*). *Contrary to s 13, Sexual*
Offences Act 1956.

2. Indecent conduct towards a child
(Triable 'either way', max pen 2 yrs imp)

Powers of arrest

General power of arrest under s 25, PACE, see pages 17–18.

Charge

Did commit an act of gross indecency with (or *towards) . . .* (name the
child), *a child under the age of 14 years, namely of the age of . . . years,*
(or *Did incite . . .* (name the child), *a child under the age of 14 years,*
namely of the age of . . . years to an act of gross indecency with him (or
. . . (name of another person)). *Contrary to s 1, Indecency with Children*
Act 1960.

Comments

The powers of arrest and the compass of these offences are restricted and
worthy of study. Carefully consult the gross indecency 'comments' under
'Buggery' at page 37, in particular.

If confronted with offenders in the act of committing the crime of gross
indecency, take whatever action is possible to obtain corroboration of what
you see, preserve all evidence and, if you arrest, make sure your prisoners
do not have the opportunity to dispose of possible evidence. Do not lose
sight of the fact that one male person can be charged alone with the crime
(eg if the other party to the crime acted innocently or through ignorance–
possibly a juvenile).

The two accused must be acting in concert, but actual physical contact
is not necessary (*R v Hornby and Peaple*[1946] 2 All ER 487. There must
be an element of participation and cooperation of two men (*R v Preece*
and Howells [1976] Crim LR 392).

The second charge shown, remedies a defect in the law revealed in the
case of *Fairclough v Whipp* [1951] 2 All ER 834. In this case it was held
that if a child merely accepted a man's invitation to touch him in an
indecent manner, this did not amount to an indecent assault (see 'Indecent
assault on a female' (page 91) and 'Indecent assault upon a male' (page
90)). The Indecency with Children Act 1960 provides that any person,
whether a male or female, who commits an act of gross indecency with a

child of either sex under the age of 14 years, or who incites such a child to the act with himself, herself or someone else, is guilty under this provision.

No proceedings shall be instituted for the offence under s 13, Sexual Offences Act 1956 (charge (1)) except by or with the consent of the DPP where either of the men was at the time of its commission under 18 years of age (s 8, Sexual Offences Act 1967). This provision does not apply to proceedings under the Indecency with Children Act 1960 (charge (2)) (s 48, Criminal Justice Act 1972).

Proceedings for the s 13 offence (charge (1)) must be taken within 12 months of its commission.

HANDLING STOLEN GOODS, ETC
(Triable 'either way', max pen 14 yrs imp)

Powers of arrest

Full powers for 'arrestable offences', see pages 14–15.

Charge

Was guilty of handling stolen goods in that, knowing (or *believing*) *certain goods, namely* . . . (specify) *to be stolen goods within the meaning of the Theft Act 1968 he dishonestly:*

(a)   *received the said goods (from . . .);* or

(b)   *arranged to receive the said goods (from . . .);* or

(c)   *undertook* (or *assisted (. . .) in) the retention* (or *removal* or *disposal* or *realisation) of the said goods by* (or *for the benefit of) . . . contrary to s 22 of the Theft Act 1968.*

Comments

This crime covers the handling of goods which have either been (i) stolen (see 'Theft', page 140); or (ii) obtained by deception (see page 66); or (iii) obtained by blackmail (see page 34). The essential requirements are contained in the charge–with the alternatives.

'Goods' means money and every other description of property except land, and includes goods severed from the land by stealing (s 34(2)(b)).

'Stolen goods' are goods obtained by theft, blackmail, or deception (see headings already referred to) (s 34(2)(b), etc). They additionally include any other goods which directly or indirectly represent or have represented the 'stolen goods' in the hands of the 'thief' or handler as being the whole or part of the proceeds of any disposal or realisation of the goods stolen, etc (eg money or other property, etc, received from the sale of it (s 24(2)).

Defences to charges of this sort are frequently directed to prove that the accused did not know, or **believe**, that the goods were stolen, etc. Bear in mind the rebuttable presumption in law that 'recent possession' of stolen property indicates that the possessor stole it, or came into possession of it, with guilty knowledge. Additional to this, s 27(3) of the Act contains 'special evidence of guilty knowledge' provisions. ·

Arrest is generally advisable in most cases in which the facts reasonably justify such action–and, in any case, **preserve all likely evidence.**

INDECENT ASSAULT ON A FEMALE
(Triable 'either way', max pen 10 yrs imp)

Powers of arrest

Full powers for 'arrestable offences', see pages 14–15 (SAO if assault constitutes gross indecency).

Charge

Did make an indecent assault on . . . a woman (or *a girl*), *contrary to s 14, Sexual Offences Act 1956.*

Comments

An indecent assault can be briefly defined as 'an assault accompanied by circumstances or gestures of an indecent nature'. A girl under 16 cannot in law give any consent which would prevent an act being an assault upon her. In cases where children are indecently assaulted and the circumstances dictate, consideration should be given to taking the child into police protection under the Children Act 1989 (see page 48).

See 'Comments' under 'Gross indecency and indecent conduct towards a child' (page 89).

INDECENT ASSAULT UPON A MALE
(Triable 'either way', max pen 10 yrs imp)

Powers of arrest

Full powers for 'arrestable offences', see pages 14–15 (SAO if assault constitutes gross indecency).

Charge

Did make an indecent assault on . . . a man (or *a boy*), *contrary to s 15, Sexual Offences Act 1956.*

Comments

This crime is usually committed upon young boys who, in some instances, are persuaded to be willing subjects to the intimacy, either because of ignorance or the inducement of money. If the assault is committed upon a youth under 16 years of age, consent is not material. A woman can commit this offence (*R v Hare* (1934)).

See 'comments' under 'Gross indecency and indecent conduct towards a child' (page 89).

INDECENT DISPLAYS
Indecent Displays (Control) Act 1981, s 1
(Triable 'either way', max pen 2 yrs imp)

Powers of arrest

General power of arrest under s 25, PACE (see pages 17–18).

Charge

Did publicly display (or *did cause*) (or *did permit the public display of*) *certain indecent matter namely* . . . (name the indecent matter displayed). *Contrary to s 1(1), Indecent Displays (Control) Act 1981.*

Comments

Section 1(2) of the Act states that any matter which is displayed in or so as to be visible from any public place shall be deemed to be publicly displayed.

'Public place' in relation to the display of any matter, means any place to which the public have or are permitted to have access (whether on payment or otherwise) while that matter is displayed except:

(a)   a place to which the public are permitted to have access only on payment which is or includes payment for that display; or

(b)   a shop or any part of a shop to which the public can only gain access by passing beyond an adequate warning notice.

The Act makes it clear, however, that the exclusions in (a) and (b) shall only apply where persons under 18 are not permitted to enter while the display is continuing.

The warning notice referred to in (b) must comply with the requirements of s 1(6) as follows–'WARNING: Persons passing beyond this notice will find material on display which they may consider indecent. No admittance to persons under 18 years of age'. The word 'WARNING' must appear as a heading to the notice and no pictures or other matter shall appear on the notice. The notice must be so situated that no one could reasonably gain access to the shop or part of the shop in question without being aware of the notice and it must be easily legible by any person gaining such access.

A constable may seize any article which he has reasonable grounds for believing to be or to contain indecent matter and to have been used in the commission of an offence under the Act. Section 2(3) authorises the issue of a search warrant.

'Matter' includes anything capable of being displayed except that it does not include a human body or any part thereof.

Television broadcasts, displays in art galleries, museums, Crown buildings, theatre plays, and cinemas are exempt from the offence under s 1 in the circumstances outlined in s 1(4).

INDECENT EXPOSURE IN STREET, CAUSING ANNOYANCE (SO only)

Powers of arrest

General power of arrest under s 25, PACE (see pages 17–18).

Charge

In a certain street called . . . to the annoyance (or *obstruction*, or *danger*) *of residents* or *passengers did wilfully and indecently expose his person, contrary to s 28, Town Police Clauses Act 1847.*

Comments

This charge is rarely used. Remember that the exposure must be related to circumstances of indecency and it must be to the annoyance etc of residents or passengers. Merely urinating in the street will rarely justify this charge unless there were some additional circumstances to indicate indecency. The expression 'street' for the purpose of this offence, includes any place of public resort or recreation belonging to or controlled by the local authority and includes any open and unfenced ground adjoining or abutting upon any street.

INDECENT EXPOSURE, WITH INTENT TO INSULT FEMALE (SO only)

Powers of arrest

Any person may arrest anyone found committing. However, a constable should use the general power of arrest under s 25, PACE (see pages 17–18).

Charge

Did wilfully, openly, lewdly and obscenely expose his person, with intent to insult a certain female named . . ., contrary to s 4, Vagrancy Act 1824.

Comments

This offence can be committed anywhere and any person can arrest provided the offender is caught in the act. The indecent condition of the offender's mind is all-important.

'Intent' is discussed under 'Wounding, etc (with intent)', page 149.

LICENSED PREMISES, REFUSING OR FAILING TO QUIT (SO, only)

Powers of arrest

Should the offender be drunk and incapable, see 'Drunkenness' or, if drunk and disorderly, see 'Drunk and disorderly', etc, pages 75–76. Any constable shall, on the demand of the licensee, his agent, or servant, help to expel from the licensed premises any person who is drunken, violent, quarrelsome or disorderly, or whose presence would render the licensee liable to penalty under the Licensing Act, 1964, and may use such force as may be necessary for the purpose. (See s 174(3), Licensing Act 1964.) The general power of arrest under s 25, PACE will apply (see pages 17–18).

Charge

On certain premises at . . . in respect of which a licence for the sale of intoxicating liquor by retail had been granted to . . . was drunken (or *violent,* or *quarrelsome,* or *disorderly,* or *a person whose presence on the said premises of the said . . . would subject him the said . . . to a penalty under the Licensing Act 1964) and being then requested by the said . . . (or by . . . the servant* or *agent of the said . . . or by . . . a constable) to quit the said premises, he failed to do so, contrary to s 174, Licensing Act 1964.*

LICENSED PREMISES–EXCLUDED PERSONS
(Licensed Premises (Exclusion of Certain Persons) Act 1980)
(SO only)

Power to expel

A constable shall on the demand of the licensee or his servant or agent help to expel from licensed premises any person whom the constable reasonably suspects of having entered in breach of an exclusion order.

Charge

Being a person subject to an exclusion order made by . . . (name the court making the order) *on . . .* (name the date the order was made) *under the Licensed Premises (Exclusion of Certain Persons) Act 1980, entered certain premises namely . . .* (name the premises entered) *in breach of the said exclusion order. Contrary to s 2(1), Licensed Premises (Exclusion of Certain Persons) Act 1980.*

Comments

The Licensed Premises (Exclusion of Certain Persons) Act 1980 provides that where a person is convicted of an offence committed on licensed premises and the court is satisfied that in committing the offence he resorted to violence or he offered or threatened to resort to violence, the court may make an 'exclusion order' prohibiting the offender from entering those premises or any other specified premises without the express consent of the licensee or his servant or agent. An exclusion order may be made in addition to any sentence which is imposed in respect of the offence for which the person is convicted.

An 'exclusion order' shall have effect for such period which the court may specify and shall not be less than three months or more than two years unless terminated.

Under s 3 of the Act, power is given to the licensee, his servant, or agent to expel those persons whom they reasonably suspect to have entered their premises in breach of an exclusion order. Any constable shall help the licensee to expel on demand of the licensee where the constable himself reasonably suspects the offender of having entered in breach of an order.

The powers under this Act are in addition to the general power to expel under s 174, Licensing Act 1964 (see previous heading). When being called upon to assist under either Act, remember that it is highly likely that the power of arrest for being drunk and disorderly (see page 75), or causing a breach of the peace (see page 36) can be used, depending on the circumstances. People subject to exclusion orders may well, in addition, be violent or cause damage, in which case the wider powers of arrest in relation to those offences (generally arrestable offences) can be used.

In the unlikely event that persons subject to exclusion orders are not involved in other offences which warrant arrest, he should be told politely to leave the premises and then reported for summons procedure for being in breach of the relevant order. Powers of arrest under s 25, PACE (see pages 17–18) can be used in appropriate cases.

MALICIOUS COMMUNICATIONS
(SO only)

Powers of arrest

General power of arrest under s 25, PACE (see pages 17–18).

Charges

1.   *Did send to another person, namely* . . . (name of recepient), *a letter* (or *an article*), *namely* . . . (specify) *which conveyed a message which was indecent* (or *grossly offensive*) [or *which conveyed a threat*] [or *which conveyed information which was false and which you knew or believed to be false*] *your purpose being* (or *one of your purposes being*) *in sending the said letter* (or *article that it should cause distress (or anxiety) to the said* . . . (name recipient) [or *your purpose being* (or *one of your purposes being*) *in sending the said letter* (or *article*) *that it should cause distress* (or *anxiety*) *to* . . . (name of third person to whom it was intended the message etc should be communicated) *to whom you intended that it should be communicated*]. *Contrary to s 1(1)(a), Malicious Communications Act 1988.*

2.   *Did send to another person, namely* . . . (name of recipient) *an article which was* (or *part of which was) of an indecent* (or *grossly offensive*) *nature, your purpose being* (or *one of your purposes being*) *in sending the said article that it should cause distress* (or *anxiety*) *to the said* . . . (name of recipient) [or *your purpose being* (or *one of your purposes being*) *in sending the said article that it should cause distress* (or *anxiety*) *to* . . . (name of third person to whom it was intended article etc should be communicated) *to whom you intended that the said article (or the contents of the said article) (or the nature of the said article) should be communicated*]. *Contrary to s 1(1)(b), Malicious Communications Act 1988.*

Comments

The Malicious Communications Act 1988 was brought into force to stem the growing practice (often with racial overtones) of sending malicious and offensive materials to others. The above charges can be applied to all communications whether sent through the post or otherwise.

The first charge and its variations deals with letters and articles which convey messages of an indecent or grossly offensive nature or where the letter or article conveys a threat or information which is false and known to be false by the sender. The second charge deals with indecent or offensive articles of whatever nature. In both cases it must be shown that the purpose of the sender was to cause distress or anxiety to the recipient or to any third person whom it was intended the material should be communicated.

There is a defence open to a person charged with sending a letter etc conveying a threat. If the defendant can show that he had reasonable grounds for making a demand and that he believed the threat was a proper means of reinforcing that demand he will not be guilty of the offence under s 1(1)(a)(ii). Officers should note that this defence is not open to those who send letters etc which are indecent, grossly offensive or which contain false information.

In all cases it must be shown that the purpose of the sender was to cause distress or anxiety to the recipient or to any third person to whom it was intended the material should be communicated.

The Act makes it clear that sending will include delivery and a person who causes the sending or delivery will come within the scope of its provisions.

MANSLAUGHTER
(IO, max pen life imp)

Powers of arrest

Full powers for 'arrestable offences'(see pages 14–15 (SAO)).

Charge

Unlawfully did kill . . . (or a certain man whose name is unknown) against the peace of Our Sovereign Lady, the Queen, Her Crown and Dignity, contrary to Common Law.

Comments

This type of case should be treated in the same manner as murder. It often happens that it is not possible to establish whether a crime is murder or manslaughter until some considerable time after the commencement of the investigation.

See also 'Dangerous driving, causing death by' (see page 155).

MENTAL DISORDER
Police Powers–Mental Health Act 1983

1. If a constable finds in a place to which the public have access a person who appears to him to be suffering from mental disorder and to be in immediate need of care or control, the constable may, if he thinks it is necessary to do so in the interests of that person or for the protection of other persons, remove that person to a place of safety within the meaning of s 135, Mental Health Act 1983.
2. A person who is detained by virtue of (1) above in a place of safety is deemed to be in legal custody. If such a person escapes, he may be retaken:

   (a) In any case, by the person who had custody immediately before the escape; or by any constable; or by an approved social worker.

   (b) If at the time of his escape he was liable to be detained in a hospital or mental nursing home or subject to guardianship under the Mental Health Act 1983 – by any approved social worker or by any officer of the staff of the hospital; or by any person authorised in writing by the managers of the hospital; or by any constable.

Comments

It is important to note that a person who escapes while being taken to or detained in a place of safety shall not be retaken after the expiration of the period of 72 hours beginning with the time he escapes or the period during which he is liable to be so detained, whichever expires first. There are also time limits on the retaking of escapees under (b) above and appropriate reference should be made by officers to the hospital concerned.

A person who is detained by an officer in a place of safety may be kept for up to 72 hours so that he can be examined by a doctor and interviewed by an approved social worker in order to make suitable arrangements for his care. Police officers should become involved in matters relating to mentally ill persons only if it is absolutely necessary; for example if the person concerned has committed crime or the officer on patrol finds a person in a public place and from his observations it is clear he is suffering from some mental disorder. Expert assistance should be summoned straight away. Home Office circulars direct that a person who is removed to a place of safety should normally be taken to a hospital or if this is not practicable the assistance of a social worker should be sought.

A 'place of safety' is defined in the Act as accommodation provided by the social services, a hospital as defined by the Mental Health Act 1983, a mental nursing home, a residential home for the mentally disordered, a police station or any other suitable place the occupier of which is willing temporarily to receive the patient. Once removed to a place of safety, the person can be detained for up to 72 hours.

Under s 128 of the Act it is an offence for any person to induce or knowingly assist another person who is in legal custody by virtue of the above provisions to escape from such custody. It is also an offence knowingly to harbour a patient absent without leave or otherwise at large and liable to be retaken under the Act.

MURDER
(IO–pen life imp)

Powers of arrest

Full powers for 'arrestable offences', see pages 14–15 (SAO).

Charge

Did murder . . . (or *a certain man whose name is unknown) against the peace of our Sovereign Lady the Queen, Her Crown and Dignity, contrary to Common Law.*

Comments

Detail all suspects and request persons who are able to assist the enquiry to remain. Arrest the suspected murderer if possible. Make a careful note of his demeanour, etc, and everything he says. Ensure that he has no opportunity to interfere with his clothing or body before the arrival of senior or CID officers. See that nothing is disturbed at the scene, most particularly the body, until the arrival of senior officers. Do not permit the doctor who confirms death to move the position of the body more than is necessary, unless senior officers are present and authorise such procedure. Should the crime be committed out of doors, keep sightseers well away and do everything possible to avoid the surroundings of the body being trampled on, etc. Keep calm and be deliberate in your actions. Make a mental note of everything you see and hear and supplement this with a written note, if possible.

Obtain the immediate assistance of senior officers.

OFFENSIVE WEAPON, CARRYING WITHOUT AUTHORITY OR EXCUSE
(Triable 'either way', max pen 2 yrs imp)

Powers of arrest

General power of arrest under s 25, PACE (see pages 17–18).

Charge

Without lawful authority or reasonable excuse had with him in a certain public place called . . . (name the public place) *an offensive weapon, namely . . .* (name the weapon). *Contrary to s 1, Prevention of Crime Act 1953.*

Comments

Proper and wise use of this provision can often prevent serious crimes of violence and gang troubles–including hooligan conduct at football matches and other games which attract partisan crowds. The Act is widely drawn; a 'public place' includes any premises or place to which at the material time the public have or are permitted to have access, on payment or otherwise; an 'offensive weapon' means any article which can be used for causing personal injury or is intended by the possessor for such use by him or some other person. This could be, for example, a flick-knife (used for causing personal injury) or a half-brick (if the possessor intends to use it to cause such injury).

Important

The offence is committed only if the possessor of the 'weapon' *does not have lawful authority* for possessing it *or cannot give a reasonable excuse*. He is not required to establish this, however, until the prosecution has proved that the accused had an 'offensive weapon' with him. Any explanation so given must relate to the carrying of the weapon and not the manner of its use (*R v Jura* [1954] 1 QB 503). If the weapon has been used to cause injury or frighten or intimidate anyone, this is good evidence to offset an explanation that it was being carried with lawful authority or reasonable excuse (*Woodward v Koessler* [1958] 3 All ER 557). It is the responsibility of the prosecution to prove that the accused **knowingly** had the weapon with him (*R v Cugullere* [1961] 2 All ER 343) and, if two or more are jointly charged, that each knew of the weapon that the other had with him and that there was a common purpose (*R v Edmonds* [1963] 2 QB 142).

Persons who sell or have flick knives or gravity knives in their possession for sale (or hire) commit an offence contrary to the Restriction of Offensive

Weapons Acts 1959 and 1961. The importation of such weapons is also prohibited. Moreover, s 141, Criminal Justice Act 1988, makes it a summary offence to manufacture, sell, hire, offer for sale or have or have in possession or expose any weapon listed in the Criminal Justice Act 1988 (Offensive Weapons) Order 1988. Officers should refer to these Regulations where some 14 different types of weapon are listed.

OFFENSIVE WEAPON–HAVING ARTICLE WITH BLADE OR POINT IN PUBLIC PLACE
(SO only)

Powers of arrest

General power of arrest under s 25, PACE, see pages 17–18.

Charge

Did have with you in a public place, an article to which s 139, Criminal Justice Act 1988 applies, namely a . . . (specify the article), *contrary to s 139(1) Criminal Justice Act 1988.*

Comments

The articles to which s 139 refers are those with a blade or a sharply pointed article. It does not include a folding pocket knife unless it has a blade with a cutting edge exceeding three inches.

This section extends considerably the liability for carrying knives and sharp articles. An officer will not have to show that such articles were offensive weapons under the provisions of the Prevention of Crime Act 1953 (see above). Merely having the above types of weapon in a public place is sufficient.

It is a defence for a person charged with the offence if he can show that he had good reason or lawful authority for having the article with him in a public place.

A further defence is provided in the Act if the accused can show that he had the article with him for use at work, for religious reasons or as part of any national costume.

A public place is defined in the Act so as to include any place to which at the material time the public have or are permitted to have access whether on payment or otherwise.

OFFENSIVE WEAPONS–POSSESSION OF CROSSBOWS
(**SO only**)

Powers of arrest, search and seizure

1.   General power of arrest under s 25, PACE (see pages 17–18).
2.   If a constable suspects with reasonable cause that a person is committing or has committed an offence under s 3, Crossbows Act 1987 (see below), the constable may:

   (a)   search that person for a crossbow or part of a crossbow;
   (b)   search any vehicle, or anything in or on a vehicle, or in which the constable suspects with reasonable cause there is a crossbow, or part of a crossbow, connected with the offence.

3.   A constable may detain a person or vehicle for the purpose of a search under (2) above.
4.   A constable may seize and retain for the purpose of proceedings for an offence under the Crossbows Act 1987 anything discovered by him in the course of a search under (2) above which appears to him to be a crossbow or part of a crossbow.

Charges

1.   *Being a person under the age of 17 years, namely . . . years* (state age) *and not being under the supervision of a person over the age of 21 years, you had with you a crossbow capable of discharging a missile. Contrary to s 3(a), Crossbows Act 1987.*
2.   *Being a person under the age of 17 years, namely . . . years* (state age) *and not being under the supervision of a person over the age of 21 years, you had with you parts of a crossbow which together can be assembled to form a crossbow capable of discharging a missile. Contrary to s 3(b), Crossbows Act 1987.*

Comments

For the purpose of exercising the above powers, a constable may enter any land but he cannot enter a dwelling house.

Under ss 1 and 2 of the Crossbows Act 1987, it is an offence for a person under seventeen to purchase or hire a crossbow. It is also an offence to sell, or let, or hire such weapons to persons under seventeen.

Possession by persons over seventeen is not an offence as such in normal circumstances. However, officers should always bear in mind that such weapons could be 'offensive weapons' if they fall within that definition in the Prevention of Crime Act 1953. Possession of crossbows in these circumstances in a public place by a person of any age would be an offence (see above).

POLICE, CAUSING WASTEFUL EMPLOYMENT OF
(SO, max pen 6 mths imp)

Powers of arrest

General power of arrest under s 25, PACE (see pages 17–18). (See, however, power of arrest for bomb hoaxes (page 35)).

Charge

Did cause certain wasteful employment of the police by knowingly making to . . . a false report.

(a) *tending to show that an offence . . . (specify) had been committed;* or,
(b) *tending to give rise to apprehension for the safety of certain persons, namely . . . (specify) (or certain property situate at . . .);*or
(c) *tending to show that he had information material to a certain police enquiry relating to* (specify), *in that he . . .* (give particulars of false report).

Contrary to s 5(2) of the Criminal Law Act 1967.

Comments

Proceedings may not be instituted for this offence except by, or with the consent of, the Director of Public Prosecutions (Criminal Law Act, s 5(3)). The offence is included because of its topicality and value when the police waste time, etc, on false reports deliberately made. Whenever you seriously question the genuineness of what is being reported by anyone, try to get his signed statement in writing. He may even be prepared to write it himself, which is all the better.

Note that a **'false report'** can be made to **any person**–not necessarily direct to the police. Your senior officers will decide on policy and procedure in all cases of this sort. The Criminal Law Act 1977 provides for the offence of making bomb hoaxes and a charge under this Act might usefully be employed together with a charge under this particular section should the circumstances fit.

POSSESSING ANYTHING WITH INTENT TO DESTROY OR DAMAGE PROPERTY
(Triable 'either way', max pen 10 yrs imp)

Powers of arrest

Full powers for 'arrestable offences', see pages 14–15.

Charge

Did have in his custody (or *under his control) a* . . . (describe article or substance, etc) *intending without lawful excuse to use it* (or *to cause or permit)*. . . (name of individual) *to use it* (a) *to destroy* (or *damage) certain property namely* . . . belonging to . . . (or (b) *to destroy (or damage) his own* (or . . .'s (name of owner)) *property, namely* . . . *in a way which he knew was likely to endanger the life of* . . .).*Contrary to s 3, Criminal Damage Act 1971.*

Comments

All 'comments' in paras 1, 2 and 3 under 'Damaging or destroying property' (page 60) are pertinent here (ie 'property,' 'belonging' and 'lawful excuse'). A possessor can commit this offence in his own house as well as elsewhere.

The section has important practical preventative values and properly used can be the means of averting major tragedies. Search warrants on 'reasonable cause' grounds can be issued by a JP (s 6(1) and (2)–information on oath). The offence is widely drawn and among other things, for example, covers the case of a person possessing materials for constructing home-made bombs. The isolated possession of a milk bottle, some petrol, cotton wool, or a wad, may be innocent–but in combination can be conclusive *if proof of intention to endanger life can be clinched.* Obtain instructions and guidance in all cases if there is no imminent hazard.

PROPERTY–OFFENCES RELATING TO ENTERING AND REMAINING ON PROPERTY

1. Violence for securing entry (SO, max pen 6 mths imp)

Powers of arrest

A constable in uniform may arrest without warrant anyone who is, or whom he, with reasonable cause suspects to be, guilty of an offence under s 6(1) of the Criminal Law Act 1977 (for offences see 'charges' and 'comments' (below)).

Charge

Did without lawful authority use (or threaten) violence for the purpose of securing entry for himself (or for . . . (name the person for whom violence was used or threatened for the purpose of securing entry)) *into certain premises situate at . . . (give the address of the premises concerned) at a time when he knew that . . . (name the person present who was opposed to entry) was present on the said premises and who was opposed to the entry which the violence was intended to secure. Contrary to s 6(1), Criminal Law Act 1977.*

Comments

For this offence to be complete it should be borne in mind that some person must be present on the premises in question who is opposed to the entry and this fact must be known by the offender. The defence of lawful authority will cover those persons who need to obtain entry to carry out their duties, eg bailiffs executing court orders. It is immaterial whether the violence in question is directed against the person or against property (s 6(4)). Under the same provision the offence will still be complete even if the violence was used for the purpose of gaining entry for something other than acquisition of the premises. Section 6(2) declares that the fact that a person has an interest in, or right to possession of, premises does not constitute lawful authority for the use of violence to secure entry into the premises. Section 6(3) provides two defences to a prosecution for this offence. First, if the accused proves that at the time of the offence he or a person on whose behalf he was acting was a 'displaced residential occupier' (for definition see under heading, 'Adverse occupation of premises' (page 106)). Secondly, if the accused can prove that part of the premises into which entry was sought constituted premises of which he or the person on whose behalf he acted was a displaced residential occupier and that part of the premises into which entry was sought constituted an access of which he or the other person was also a displaced residential occupier. Thus, under the first defence, a person who goes away on holiday and finds on his return that he is excluded by a trespasser might plead that he committed the act constituting the offence in order to regain possession of his property. Under the second defence, for example, a person occupying a flat in a building from which he has been excluded by trespassers might plead that the only means of getting to his residence was by gaining access to the hall and to effect this he necessarily committed the act constituting the offence.

It is important for officers to note that when s 72, Criminal Justice and Public Order Act 1994 comes into force, s 6(2) will operate subject to a new s 6(1A) which will be inserted into the Criminal Law Act 1977. In effect this means that the offence under s 6(1) (see charge above) can no longer be committed by a person who is a displaced residential occupier or a protected intending occupier or a person acting on their behalf. By reason of this change in the law, the above defences under s 6(3) will no longer be necessary and will be ommitted from the Criminal Law Act.

2. Adverse occupation of residential premises (SO, max pen 6 mths imp)

Powers of arrest

A constable in uniform may arrest without warrant any person who is, or whom he, with reasonable cause, suspects to be guilty of an offence of being on premises as a trespasser after having entered as such and failing to leave those premises on being required to do so by or on behalf of:

(a)   a displaced residential occupier of the premises; or
(b)   an individual who is a protected intending occupier of the premises.

(See 'comments' below).

Charge

Being a person who was on premises situate at . . . (give the address or location of the premises concerned) *as a trespasser after having entered as such did fail to leave the said premises on being required to do so by* [(a) . . . (name the person making the request) *a displaced residential occupier (or a protected intending occupier)*][or (b) by . . . (name the person making the request) *acting on behalf of* . . . (name the displaced residential occupier or protected intending occupier) *a displaced residential occupier (or a protected intending occupier]* *of the said premises. Contrary to s 7, Criminal Law Act 1977.*

Comments

Section 7, Criminal Law Act 1977 provides powers for dealing with squatters. The extensive definitions of 'displaced residential occupier' and 'protected intending occupier' are contained in s 12. However, when s 74, Criminal Justice and Public Order Act 1994 comes into force, the definition of protected intending occupier will change and will be set out in a new s 12 (A) which will be inserted into the Criminal Law Act. At that time the protection against squatters will be provided to the following:

1.   Displaced residential occupiers under s 12, ie those persons who occupied premises as a residence immediately before being excluded from occupation by squatters.
2.   Protected intending occupiers under s 12A where the following applies in the case of an individual.

   (a)   he has in the premises concerned a freehold or leasehold interest with not less than two years still to run;
   (b)   he requires the premises for his own occupation as a residence;
   (c)   he is excluded from occupation of the premises by a person

who entered them, or any access to them, as a trespasser; and
(d) he holds a written statement specifying his interest and that
he requires the premises for occupation as a residence for
himself. This statement must be signed by the individual
concerned in the presence of a JP or Commissioner for Oaths
(usually a solicitor) and is then signed by them as witnesses.

Similar provisions to the above provide protection for tenants and licensees
of premises. In such cases it is the landlord and the tenant or licensee who
sign the statement in the presence of the JP etc.

Officers should refer to the full text of s 12 and s 12A for the extent of
those classified as displaced residential occupiers and protected intending
occupiers.

Generally arrests under s 7 will be made under the supervision of a senior
officer acting on force directions. It should be noted that the requirements
that the trespasser should have entered as such excludes from the offence
tenants remaining on property after the expiry of their tenancy.

There are a number of defences open to persons charged under s 7
contained in s 7(2) and (3) and in the new s 12A(9), Criminal Law Act
1977.

3. Trespassing with a weapon of offence
(SO, max pen 3 mths imp)

Powers of arrest

A constable in uniform may arrest without warrant any person who is, or
whom he, with reasonable cause, suspects to be in the act of committing
an offence of being on premises as a trespasser, having entered as such,
and having with him on those premises without lawful authority or
reasonable excuse a weapon of offence.

Charge

Being on premises situate at . . . (give the address or location of the
premises) *as a trespasser, after having entered as such, did without lawful
authority or reasonable excuse have with him on the said premises a
weapon of offence namely* . . . (name the weapon of offence). *Contrary to
s 8, Criminal Law Act 1977.*

Comments

This offence is very similar to the offence of being in possession of an
offensive weapon in a public place without lawful authority or reasonable
excuse. To secure a conviction it will be necessary to prove that: (a) there

was an absence of lawful authority or there was no reasonable excuse for possession of the weapon concerned (the type of weapon and the circumstances in which it was found or was being used will be very relevant); and (b) that the offender had entered the premises as a trespasser in the first instance (tenants who remain after the expiration of their tenancy will therefore be excluded from the offence); and (c) that he had remained on those premises as a trespasser. Evidence from the occupier that this state exists should be obtained before any arrest is made. The expression 'Weapon of Offence' means any article made or adapted for use for causing injury to or incapacitating a person or intended by the person having it with him for such use.

4. Trespassing on premises of foreign missions etc (SO, max pen 6 mths imp)

Powers of arrest

A constable in uniform may arrest without warrant anyone who is, or whom he, with reasonable cause, suspects to be in the act of committing an offence under s 9(1), Criminal Law Act 1977 (see 'Charge' below).

Charge

Did enter (or *was on) certain premises to which s 9(2) of the Criminal Law Act 1977 applies, namely* . . . (name the diplomatic mission, consular premises, premises entitled to inviolability, or private residence of the diplomatic agent concerned) *situate at* . . . (give the address or location of the premises) *as a trespasser. Contrary to s 9(1), Criminal Law Act 1977.*

Comments

Section 9(1) of the Criminal Law Act 1977 makes it an offence to enter, or be on, premises defined in s 9(2) as follows: (a) the premises of a diplomatic mission within the terms of the Vienna Convention on Diplomatic Relations (set out in Sch 1 of the Diplomatic Privilege Act 1964); (b) consular premises as defined in the Vienna Convention on Consular Relations (set out in Sch 1, Consular Relations Act 1968); (c) any premises entitled to inviolability under any enactment; (d) any premises which are the private residence of a diplomatic agent or any person entitled to inviolability of residence under any enactment.

A certificate issued by or under the authority of the Secretary of State that at the time of the alleged offence the premises concerned fell within s 9(2) shall be conclusive evidence of that fact. It is a defence for the accused to prove that he believed that the premises were not premises to which the section applies. Proceedings under s 9 shall not be taken without the consent of the Attorney General.

5. Obstruction of court officers executing process against unauthorised occupiers
(SO, max pen 6 mths imp)

Powers of arrest

A constable in uniform or any officer of a court may arrest without warrant anyone who is, or whom he, with reasonable cause, suspects to be guilty of resisting or intentionally obstructing an officer of a court engaged in executing any process issued by the High Court or any county court for the purpose of enforcing any judgment or order for the recovery of any premises or for the delivery of possession of any premises.

(Note: See 'Comments' below relating to the scope of this power and related 'Charge'.)

Charge

Did resist (or intentionally obstruct) . . . (name the court officer concerned) *who was in fact an officer of a court, namely* . . . (name the court concerned) *engaged in executing process issued by the High Court (or county court) for the purpose of enforcing a judgment (or order) for the recovery of premises situate at* . . . (give the address of the premises concerned) *(or for the delivery of possession of premises situate at* . . . (give the address of premises concerned)), *contrary to s 10, Criminal Law Act 1977.*

Comments

This offence is restricted solely by virtue of s 10(2) to those judgments or orders which have been made following proceedings in which a person claiming possession alleges that the premises concerned are occupied solely by a person or persons (not being a tenant or tenant remaining after the termination of tenancy) who entered into or remained in occupation of those premises without the consent of the person claiming possession. This effectively limits the offence to cases where court officers are seeking to enforce orders for possession under the above circumstances (ie, possession under summary procedure in RSC Ord 113 or CCR Ord 26). Officers should seek the guidance of a senior officer before the power of arrest is exercised or any charge is made.

It is a defence for the accused to show that he believed that the person he was resisting or obstructing was not a court officer.

An 'officer of a court' is defined as a sheriff, under sheriff, deputy sheriff, bailiff or officer of a sheriff, and any bailiff or other person who is an officer of a county court within the meaning of the County Courts Act 1959.

PROPERTY–POWERS OF ENTRY FOR THE PURPOSE OF ENFORCING PART 2, CRIMINAL LAW ACT 1977

For the purpose of arresting a person under any power conferred by any provision under Part 2, Criminal Law Act 1977 other than s 9(7) (ie arrest of persons trespassing on premises of foreign missions etc), a constable may enter and search any premises (s 17, PACE).

Comment

This power of entry will apply to the four foregoing powers of arrest and charges under ss 6, 7, 8 and 10 (listed under the heading 'Property–offences relating to and remaining on property', pages 104–110).

PROSTITUTE, COMMON, LOITERING OR SOLICITING (SO, only)

Powers of arrest

A constable may arrest any common prostitute whom he finds in a street or public place and suspects, with reasonable cause, to be committing this offence (s 1(3), Street Offences Act 1959).

Charge

Being a common prostitute, did loiter (or *solicit) in . . . a street (or public place) for the purpose of prostitution, contrary to s 1, Street Offences Act 1959.*

Comments

In practice a woman who has not been previously convicted of this offence will not be charged with it unless she has been cautioned by the police on previous occasions and had such cautions officially recorded. There are variations in the procedure adopted by police forces and your own force instructions should be consulted.

'Street' includes roads, lanes, passages and other similar places for the time being open to the public together with doorways and entrances to premises abutting upon, or any ground adjoining and open to a street.

'Public place' is not defined in the Act and should be construed in its general and literal meaning: a field to which the public were admitted for one day and an enclosure where cars were parked at the rear of an inn (entered through an open gateway) are examples of public places. If the prostitute is on a balcony or at a window of a house adjoining a street or public place and she solicits a person in the street or public place she is guilty of this offence (*Smith v Hughes* (1960)).

See 'Prostitution by a woman, man living on earnings of' page 112, in relation to males who 'aid and abet'.)

PROSTITUTION BY A MAN–LIVING ON HIS EARNINGS
(Triable 'either way', max pen 7 yrs imp)

Powers of arrest

Anyone may arrest any person **found committing** this offence (s 5(3), Sexual Offences Act 1967).

Charge

Being a man (or *woman*) *knowingly did live wholly or in part on the earnings of the prostitution of a* (or *another*) *man, called . . . contrary to s 5, Sexual Offences Act 1967.*

Comments

It is well to remember that special evidence relating to a man who lives with, or is habitually in the company of, a **female prostitute** (s 30(2), Sexual Offences Act 1956–see 'Prostitution by woman–man living on earnings of', below) is **not specifically recognised** in similar terms for the male prostitute. Admissible evidence of this sort could, however, have significance in support of the allegation–especially if the individual charged is another man. The case-law (*Calvert v Mayes* [1954] 1 QB 342–see page 112) seems pertinent to this offence in respect of indirect earnings accruing to a man, or woman, who, in some measure, *knowingly* lives on financial advantages from an association with a male prostitute.

It is advisable to seek guidance and instruction from a senior officer before confronting any suspect with the allegation–especially if he, or she, is likely to be traceable afterwards.

PROSTITUTION BY A WOMAN, MAN LIVING ON EARNINGS OF
(Triable 'either way', max pen 7 yrs imp)

Powers of arrest

Full powers for 'arrestable offences', see pages 14–15.

Charge

Being a man, knowingly did live wholly or in part on the earnings of prostitution, contrary to s 30, Sexual Offences Act 1956.

Comments

A man who lives with or is habitually in the company of a prostitute, or who exercises control, direction or influence over her movements in a way which shows he is aiding, abetting or compelling her prostitution with others, is presumed to be committing this offence unless he proves otherwise (see s 30(2), Sexual Offences Act 1956).

He may receive the earnings indirectly, as for example, when he receives payment from other men who resort to his house or use his motor vehicle to have intercourse with women with whom he associates and knows to be prostitutes (*Calvert v Mayes* [1954] 1 QB 342).

'Prostitution' means the offering for reward by a female of her body commonly for purposes of lewdness–not necessarily sexual intercourse (*R v De Munck* [1918] 1 KB 635).

It is generally advisable to seek advice and instructions from senior officers before confronting a suspect with this allegation–especially if his identity is known or he can easily be traced.

PROSTITUTION–SOLICITING OF WOMEN BY MEN
(SO only)

Powers of arrest

General power of arrest under s 25, PACE (see pages 17–18).

Charges

1. Kerb-crawling
Being a man you solicited a woman, namely . . . (name the woman solicited) (or *a number of different women) for the purpose of prostitution from a motor vehicle while it was in a street called* . . . (name the street) or *public place called* . . . (name the public place)[(or *being a man you*

solicited a woman named . . . (name the woman) (*or a number of women)
for the purpose of prostitution in a street named* . . . (name the street) *or
public place called* . . . (name the public place) *while you were in the
immediate vicinity of a motor vehicle that you had just got out of* (or *off*)]
persistently [*or in such a manner* (or *in such circumstances) as to be likely
to cause annoyance to the said woman solicited* (or *the said women
solicited) or in such a manner* (or *in such circumstances) as to be likely to
cause a nuisance to other persons in the neighbourhood. Contrary to s 1,
Sexual Offences Act 1985.*

2. Persistently soliciting women for prostitution

Being a man you did in a certain street called . . . (name the street) *or public
place called* . . . (name the public place) *persistently solicit a woman
named,* . . . (name the woman) (*or a number of different women) for the
purpose of prostitution. Contrary to s 2, Sexual Offences Act 1985.*

Comments

Information about kerb-crawling and similar acts of soliciting for
prostitution will often come from long suffering people living in
neighbourhoods where such activities take place. Where such complaints
are received, observation should be laid on straight away in order to gather
the necessary evidence. Officers should make careful notes of the type
and number of any vehicle used, the position of the vehicle or whether it
was being driven, the demeanour and activities of the man in the vehicle
and the number of women he approaches. If plain-clothes women officers
are used on such operations, they should make full notes immediately after
the offender is apprehended of what he said at the time he approached them
in the street and also his reaction at the time of being arrested or reported
for the offence. It may be that the only available evidence will come from
police observations and therefore it is essential that what is seen of the
offender's activities is carefully recorded. Women who are approached
for prostitution may quite naturally be reluctant to provide statements but
nevertheless officers should always endeavour to obtain such testimony
in order to back up evidence obtained by observation. This will mean that
officers will have to act quickly to obtain details of the woman's identity
shortly after she has been approached by the offender. She should be
interviewed as quickly after the event as possible in order to obtain exact
details of what the offender did and said to her.

For the purposes of the Act, a street includes any bridge, road, lane,
footway, subway, square, court, alley or passage, whether a thoroughfare
or not, which is for the time being open to the public, and the doorways
and entrances of premises abutting on to a street, and any ground adjoining
and open to a street shall be treated as forming part of the street.

PUBLIC EXHIBITIONS, ETC OPEN TO THE PUBLIC–
REMOVING ARTICLES, ETC
(Triable 'either way', max pen 5 yrs imp)

Powers of arrest

Full powers for 'arrestable offences', see pages 14–15.

Charge

From (the ground of) a certain building, namely . . . (specify) *situate at
. . . to which* (or *to part of which, namely . . .* (specify part)) *the public
had access in order to view it* (or *to view a collection* (or *part of a
collection) of . . .* (specify) *housed therein), did without lawful authority
remove . . .* (give particulars of article or part of article removed) *displayed*
(or *kept for display) to the public in the said (part of the) building (or the
said grounds), contrary to s 11, Theft Act 1968.*

Comments

This offence applies to exhibitions etc, in places which are open to the
public, but not when the collection, premises, etc, is on show for the
purpose of effecting sales or other commercial dealings. Commercial art
galleries and the like are thereby generally excluded. It differs from theft
(see page 140) and burglary (see page 38) in that, among other things
'intent permanently to deprive' and 'entering as a trespasser' do not apply.
The offence is complete when the article in the exhibited collection (or as
the case may be) is removed from the building, grounds, etc, while the
public have access. The place need not be in permanent use for such public
exhibitions; it is sufficient if such use is limited to a particular period or
occasion. This makes the offence applicable to the country's stately homes
and other similar places when used for public exhibitions, provided sales
and commercial dealings do not apply.

   The offence is **not** committed when the remover of the thing believes
himself to have lawful authority to remove it–or that such authority would
be forthcoming if the person entitled to give this knew of the circumstances
(s 11(3)).

PUBLIC ORDER–ANTICIPATION OF VIOLENCE
(S 60, Criminal Justice and Public Order Act 1994–when in force)

Power to stop and search

1.   Where a police officer of or above the rank of superintendent*
     believes that–

(a)   incidents involving serious violence may take place in any locality in his area, and

(b)   it is expedient to do so to prevent their occurrence he may give an authorisation that the powers to stop and search persons and vehicles conferred by s 60 shall be exercisable at any place within that locality for a period not exceeding 24 hours.

* A chief inspector or inspector may exercise this power if he reasonably believes incidents involving serious violence are imminent and no superintendent is available.

2.   Where an authorisation has been given under (1) above, s 60 of the Act confers on any constable in uniform power–

(a)   to stop any pedestrian and search him or anything carried by him for offensive weapons or dangerous instruments

(b)   to stop any vehicle (including a caravan) and search the vehicle, its driver and any passenger for offensive weapons or dangerous instruments.

3.   If in the course of a search under s 60 of the Act, a constable discovers a dangerous instrument or an article which he has reasonable grounds for suspecting to be an offensive weapon, he may seize it.

Power of arrest

The general power of arrest under s 25, PACE (see pages 17–18) will apply in relation to the offence mentioned under 'Charge' below.

Charge

You did fail to stop (or *you did fail to stop a certain vehicle, namely a . . .* (specify, make and type of vehicle and registration number) *when required to do so by . . .* (name the officer with his rank and number), *a constable of the . . . constabulary* (name the force) *under powers conferred upon him by s 60, Criminal Justice and Public Order Act 1994. Contrary to s 60(8), Criminal Justice and Public Order Act 1994.*

Comments

There is a general power to stop and search under PACE (see pages 17–18). The above power can only be used where a superintendent or above gives the appropriate authorisation in writing which must specify the locality and the period during which it is operative. Where a vehicle is stopped, the driver is entitled to obtain a written statement that his vehicle was stopped by reason of these powers. Such a statement can be obtained from the police at any time for up to a year after the vehicle was stopped.

Section 60 declares that a 'dangerous instrument' is an instrument which has a blade or is sharply pointed. An 'offensive weapon' has the same meaning as given by s 1(9), PACE.

PUBLIC ORDER OFFENCES

1. Riot
(IO, max pen 10 yrs imp)

Powers of arrest

Full powers for 'arrestable offences', see pages 14–15.

Charge

You did use unlawful violence for the common purpose of twelve or more persons present together who used (or threatened) unlawful violence for the said common purpose and where the conduct of the said twelve or more persons taken together was such as would cause a person of reasonable firmness present at the scene to fear for his personal safety. Contrary to s 1, Public Order Act 1986

2. Violent disorder
(Triable 'either way', max pen 5 yrs imp)

Powers of arrest

Full powers for 'arrestable offences', see pages 14–15.

Charge

You did use (or threaten) unlawful violence where three or more persons who were present together used (or threatened) unlawful violence and the conduct of the said three or more persons taken together was such as would cause a person of reasonable firmness present at the scene to fear for his personal safety. Contrary to s 2, Public Order Act 1986.

3. Affray
(Triable 'either way', max pen 3 yrs imp)

Powers of arrest

A constable may arrest without warrant anyone he reasonably suspects is committing affray (see 'charge' below).

Charge

You did use (or threaten) unlawful violence towards another and your conduct was such as would cause a person of reasonable firmness present at the scene to fear for his personal safety. Contrary to s 3, Public Order Act 1986.

4. Fear or provocation of violence
(SO only, max pen 6 mths imp)

Powers of arrest

A constable may arrest without warrant anyone he reasonably suspects is committing the following offences:

(a) using towards another person threatening, abusive or insulting words or behaviour; or

(b) distributing or displaying to another person any writing, sign or other visible representation which is threatening, abusive or insulting.

Either:

(i)   with intent to cause the other person to believe that immediate unlawful violence will be used against him or another person by any person, or

(ii) to provoke the immediate use of unlawful violence by the other person or another person, or

(iii) whereby the other person is likely to believe that unlawful violence will be used or it is likely that such violence will be provoked.

Charges

1. *Did use towards another person* (or *persons*), *namely* . . . (name the person(s) threatened etc), *certain threatening words* (or *behaviour*) (or *certain abusive words* (or *behaviour*)* or *certain insulting words* (or *behaviour*))* or *did distribute* (or *display*) *to another person* (or *persons*) *namely* . . . (name the person(s) to whom distributed etc), *a certain writing* (or *sign* or *certain visible representation, namely* . . . (name the sign etc) *which was threatening* (or *abusive* or *insulting*)]** *with intent to cause the said* . . . (name person(s) threatened etc) *to believe that immediate unlawful violence would be used against him* (or *a certain person named* . . . (name the other person). *Contrary to s 4, Public Order Act 1986*; or

2. Read to whichever asterisk above is appropriate and then add: *to provoke the immediate use of unlawful violence by the said* . . . (name

the person provoked) [or *to provoke the immediate use of unlawful violence by a certain person named* . . . (name the other person provoked into using unlawful violence). *Contrary to s 4, Public Order Act 1986.*

3.   Read to whichever asterisk is appropriate in (1) above and then add: *whereby the said* . . . (name the person threatened etc) *was likely to believe that such violence would be used or [whereby the said* . . . (name the person threatened etc) *was likely to be provoked into using such violence. Contrary to s 4, Public Order Act 1986.*

5. Harassment, alarm or distress
(SO only)

Powers of arrest

1.   A constable may arrest without warrant anyone he reasonably suspects of intending to cause a person harassment, alarm or distress by

    (a)   using threatening, abusive or insulting words or behaviour or disorderly behaviour or

    (b)   displays any writing, sign or other visible representation which is threatening, abusive or insulting

thereby causing that or another person harassment, alarm or distress.

(Note: The above powers will not come into force until the appropriate commencement order under the Criminal Justice and Public Order Act 1994 has been made.)

2.   A constable may arrest a person without a warrant if:

    (a)   he engages in the use of threatening, abusive or insulting words or behaviour or distributes or displays to another person any writing, sign or other visible representation which is threatening, abusive or insulting within the hearing or sight of a person likely to be caused harassment, alarm or distress thereby which the constable warns him to stop; and

    (b)   he engages in further offensive conduct immediately or shortly after the warning.

Charges

1(a)   *You did with intent to cause* . . . (name the person) *harrassment, alarm or distress use threatening (or abusive) (or insulting) words (or behaviour) (or disorderly behaviou) thereby causing the said* . . . (name) *or thereby causing* . . . (name of other person) *harrassment, alarm or distress. Contrary to s 4A (1)(a), Public Order Act 1986.*

(b)   *You did with intent to cause . . .* (name the person) *harrassment, alarm or distress display a certain writing (or sign) or a certain visible representation) which was threatening (or abusive) (or insulting) thereby causing the said . . .* (name) *or thereby causing . . .* (name of other person) *harrassment, alarm or distress. Contrary to s 4A (1) (b), Public Order Act 1986.*

(Note: The above charges will not come into force until the relevant commencement order relating to s 154, Criminal Justice and Public Order Act 1994 has been made.)

2.   *Did use threatening (or abusive or insulting) words (or behaviour or disorderly behaviour) within the hearing (or sight) of a person likely to be caused harassment (or alarm or distress) thereby. Contrary to s 5(1)(a), Public Order Act 1986.*

3.   *Did display a certain writing, namely . . .* (name the writing) *(or sign, namely . . .* (name the sign) *or visible representation, namely . . .* (name the representation)) *which was threatening (or abusive or insulting) within the hearing (or sight) of a person likely to be caused harassment (or alarm or distress) thereby. Contrary to s 5(1)(b), Public Order Act 1986.*

Comments

Section 9 of the Public Order Act 1986 abolishes the common law offences of riot, rout, unlawful assembly and affray.

With regard to the statutory offences of riot, violent disorder and affray, these can all be committed in both public and private places. Thus disturbances at football matches, places of public entertainment and disorderly picketing in industrial disputes are all situations where arrest and subsequent charging should be considered. Invariably your senior officers will provide guidelines which should be followed.

In the case of riot, it is immaterial whether or not the twelve or more persons, or three or more in the case of violent disorder, use or threaten violence simultaneously. In both offences the common purpose may be express or may be inferred from the conduct of those present. Moreover, in both offences there need not be any person of reasonable firmness actually present or likely to be present at the scene of the disturbance. It appears that if on an objective view a person of reasonable firmness would fear for his personal safety, that is sufficient.

The offence of fear or provocation of violence under s 4 may be committed in a public or private place, except that no offence is committed where the words or behaviour etc are used by a person inside a dwelling and the person receiving the threats etc is also inside the dwelling.

In all of the above offences, the word 'violence' means violent conduct and includes (except in the context of affray), violent conduct towards persons and property. In addition, the violent conduct is not restricted to conduct causing or intended to cause injury or damage but includes any violent conduct, for example throwing towards a person a missile capable of causing injury but which falls short.

All of the above public order offences can be combined with charges of assault, carrying offensive weapons, and criminal damage in appropriate cases.The Public Order Act 1936 is not entirely repealed by the 1986 Act; ss 1 and 2 of the former legislation remain (ie the prohibition of uniforms and quasi military organisations with political objects). The Public Meetings Act 1908 which makes it an offence to act in a disorderly manner for the purpose of breaking up public meetings also remains on the statute book.

The Contempt of Court Act 1981, s 12, makes it an offence for any person who:

(a)   wilfully insults the justice or justices, or any witness or an officer of the court or any solicitor or counsel having business in the court, during his or their sitting or attendance in court or in going to or returning from the court; or

(b)   wilfully interrupts the proceedings of the court or otherwise misbehaves in court.

Where such offences are committed, the court may order an officer of the court or any constable, to take the offender into custody and detain him until the rising of the court. The court may commit the offender to custody for a specified period, not exceeding one month or impose a fine not exceeding £1000 or both.

PUBLIC PROCESSIONS AND ASSEMBLIES
1. Public processions–failing to comply with conditions

Powers of arrest

A constable in uniform may arrest without warrant anyone he reasonably suspects of:

(a)   organising, or
(b)   taking part in, or
(c)   inciting another to take part in–

a public procession, who knowingly fails to comply with any condition imposed by a senior police officer under s 12, Public Order Act 1986.

Charge

You did organise (or *take part in or incite another person, namely* ... (name the person incited) *to take part in) a public procession and you did knowingly fail to comply with a condition made in relation to the said procession, namely* ... (name the condition) *imposed by* ... (insert the rank and name of the senior police officer), *a senior police officer of the* ... (name the police force), *by virtue of his powers under s 12(1), Public Order Act 1986. Contrary to s 12, Public Order Act 1986.*

2. Public processions–prohibition offences

Powers of arrest

A constable in uniform may arrest without warrant anyone he reasonably suspects of:

(a)   organising, or
(b)   taking part in, or
(c)   inciting another to take part in—

a public procession, the holding of which he knows is prohibited by virtue of an order made under s 13, Public Order Act 1986.

Charge

You did organise (or *take part in or incite another person, namely* ... (name the person incited) *to take part in) a public procession knowing that the said public procession was prohibited by virtue of an order made on* ... (insert date of order) *by* ... (name the chief officer of police), *the chief officer of police of the* ... (name the police force), *by virtue of the powers vested in him under s 13(1), Public Order Act 1986. Contrary to s 13, Public Order Act 1986.*

3. Public assemblies–failure to comply with conditions

Powers of arrest

A constable in uniform may arrest without warrant anyone he reasonably suspects of:

(a)   organising, or
(b)   taking part in, or
(c)   inciting another to take part in—

a public assembly who knowingly fails to comply with a condition imposed by a senior police officer under s 14, Public Order Act 1986.

Charge

You did organise (or *take part in or incite another person, namely* . . . (name the person incited) *to take part in*) *a public assembly and you did knowingly fail to comply with a condition made in relation to the said public assembly, namely* . . .(name the condition) *imposed by* . . . (insert the rank and name of the senior police officer), *a senior police officer of police of the* . . . (name the police force), *by virtue of his powers under s 14(1), Public Order Act 1986. Contrary to s 14, Public Order Act 1986.*

Comments

Under s 12 (public processions) and s 14 (public assemblies), Public Order Act 1986, senior police officers are given wide powers to prevent public disorder. Where senior officers reasonably believe that on the occasion of a public procession or an assembly that such gatherings may result in serious public disorder or serious damage to property or serious disruption of the life of the community they may give directions and impose conditions on the organisers and those taking part. Such directions and conditions may also be given where the purpose of the organisers is to intimidate others with a view to compelling them not to do an act they have a right to do or to do an act they have a right not to do. Before imposing conditions senior police officers must have regard to the time or place at which and the circumstances in which any public procession or assembly is being or is intended to be held. In addition, in the case of processions, the route or proposed route to be taken must also be considered. In the case of processions or assemblies which spring up spontaneously, the senior officer making the conditions can be the most senior officer present at the scene. The directions and conditions which may be imposed must be with a view to prevent disorder, damage, disruption or intimidation. The conditions may also specify the route of a procession or a prohibition on entering specified public places. Organisers and those who take part in public processions or assemblies who knowingly breach the conditions imposed commit the offences listed above.

Under s 13 of the Act, if the chief officer of police of the district where a public procession is to be held considers that his powers under s 12 (above) are not sufficient to prevent serious public disorder at public processions he must apply to the District Council for an order prohibiting the holding of public processions or processions of a specified class for such period (not exceeding three months) as may be specified in the order. On receiving the application the Council may, with the consent of the

Secretary of State, make an order in the exact terms applied for or with modifications. In the Metropolitan Police District and the City of London the application is made to and the subsequent approval is made by the Secretary of State. Organisers and those taking part in prohibited processions commit the offences under (2) above.

Section 16 of the Act states that a 'public assembly' means an assembly of 20 or more persons in a public place which is wholly or partly in the open air. A 'public place' means any highway and any place to which at the material time the public or any section of the public has access on payment or otherwise as of right or by virtue of express or implied permission. A 'public procession' means a procession in a public place.

RACIAL HATRED–ACTS INTENDED OR LIKELY TO STIR UP RACIAL HATRED
(Triable 'either way', max pen 2 yrs imp)

Powers of arrest

A constable may arrest without warrant anyone he reasonably suspects of using threatening, abusive or insulting words or behaviour, or displays any written material which is threatening, abusive or insulting if:

(a) he intends thereby to stir up racial hatred; or
(b) having regard to all the circumstances racial hatred is likely to be stirred up thereby.

Charge

Did use threatening (or *abusive* or *insulting*) *words* (or *behaviour*) (or *did display certain written material, namely* . . . (name the written material) *which was threatening* (or *abusive* or *insulting*)) *whereby you intended to stir up racial hatred* (or *having regard to all the circumstances, racial hatred was likely to be stirred up thereby*). *Contrary to s 18(1), Public Order Act 1986.*

Comments

The offence under s 18 can be committed in a public or a private place except no offence is committed where the words used or the material displayed is by a person inside a dwelling and such words etc are not heard or seen except by persons in that or another dwelling. It is a defence for the accused to prove that he was inside a dwelling and had no reason to believe that the words or behaviour used etc would be heard or seen by a person outside that or any other dwelling.

The consent of the Attorney General must be obtained before proceedings are commenced under s 18.

RAPE OF WOMEN AND MEN
(IO, max pen life imp; attempted rape, life imp)

Powers of arrest

Full powers for 'arrestable offences', see pages 14–15 (SAO).

Charge

Had sexual intercourse with . . . (name the person against whom the offence was committed) *without her (or his) consent. Contrary to s 1, Sexual Offences Act 1956.*

Comments

Section 142, Criminal Justice and Public Order Act 1994 redefines the offence of rape. Section 1, Sexual Offences Act 1956 now reads as follows:

1.   It is an offence for a man to rape a woman or another man
2.   A man commits rape if:

   (a)   he has sexual intercourse with a person (whether vaginal or anal) who at the time of the intercourse does not consent to it; and

   (b)   at the time he knows that the person does not consent to the intercourse or is reckless as to whether that person consents to it.

3.   A man also commits rape if he induces a married woman to have sexual intercourse with him by impersonating her husband.

Section 1(2), Sexual Offences (Amendment) Act 1976 states that if at a trial for a rape offence the jury has to consider whether a man believed that a woman was consenting to sexual intercourse, the presence or absence of reasonable grounds for such a belief is a matter to which the jury is to have regard in conjunction with any other relevant matters in considering whether he so believed.

Officers engaged in investigating cases of rape should ensure that appropriate evidence is obtained in order to fully support the above section. This will include the absence of consent of the assaulted person **at the time intercourse took place** or evidence relating to the recklessness of the accused as to whether the person consented to it. Such proof may be established by much of the circumstantial evidence available. The victim's demeanour, the condition of the person's clothing, the nature and severity of any injuries the person received will be highly relevant as to whether there was consent. The question of early complaint is important because a victim, as a first reaction, may complain to the first person contacted, perhaps to an individual or by telephone. Such early complaint is always excellent evidence to show the demeanour of the victim and demonstrates the authenticity of the story. However, officers should never lose sight of the fact that some rape victims are terrified of telling anybody about what has happened and indeed of being questioned and examined subsequently. If there is a late complaint, officers should always keep an open mind and investigate thoroughly. Above all, a rape victim should be treated with sympathy and understanding bearing in mind the severe physical and psychological trauma experienced. Victim Support Agencies will be of great assistance in this respect. Great care should be exercised where children are concerned. Often through fear they may not readily relate circumstances of any sexual assault upon them until well after the event. The full co-operation of parents, etc, should be sought and tact, patience and understanding exercised by the investigating officer, in such circumstances. If a person makes a complaint of rape to you, make a careful note of the time, the words used, the person's demeanour, state of clothing and injuries. There should be no delay in reporting the matter to the senior officer on duty, who will make the necessary arrangements for attendance by the CID, scenes of crime staff and the doctor who will perform the necessary medical examinations.

It is absolutely essential that all evidence, whether at the scene, on the clothing of any person arrested or on the person of the assaulted person, are preserved as far as ever possible. The scene of the crime should be guarded immediately the complaint has been made and officers first there should ensure that they do not trample over the area.

The arrest may be made if you are reasonably satisfied that the crime has been committed and that you have got the right man. Evidence of identification, the movements of the accused, his explanations, the colour, type and index number of the vehicle he used (if any), articles and material found on his clothing, at the scene, in his dwelling or in his car will all be highly relevant to the investigation.

Section 4, Sexual Offences (Amendment) Act 1976, restricts the written publication or broadcast of any matter likely to lead members of the public to identify a woman or man as the complainant in a criminal rape case in England and Wales.

See 'Burglary', page 38, for offence of entering a building, or inhabited vehicle or vessel as a trespasser with intent to commit rape.

RAVES
(Criminal Justice and Public Order Act 1994)

(Note: At the time of writing the powers under s 63 and s 65 (see (a), (b) and (e) below) are in force but the powers under s 64 are not (see (c) and (d) below). Before using (c) and (d) officers should check whether the relevant commencement order has been made).

Police powers

(a) Powers to remove persons attending or preparing for a rave–s 63(1) and (2)

(1)   The following powers apply to a gathering on land in the open air of 100 or more persons (whether or not trespassers) at which amplified music is played during the night (with or without intermissions) and is such as, by reason of its loudness and duration and the time at which it is played, is likely to cause serious distress to the inhabitants of the locality; and for this purpose–

    (i)   such a gathering continues during intermissions in the music and, where the gathering extends over several days, throughout the period during which amplified music is played at night (with or without intermissions); and

    (ii)   'music' includes sounds wholly or predominantly characterised by the emission of a succession of repetitive beats.

(2)   If, as respects any land in the open air, a police officer of at least the rank of superintendent reasonably believes that–

    (i)   two or more persons are making preparations for the holding there of a gathering to which (1) above applies,

    (ii)   ten or more persons are waiting for such a gathering to begin there, or

    (iii)   ten or more persons are attending such a gathering which is in progress,

he may give a direction that those persons and any other persons who come to prepare or wait for, or to attend the gathering are to leave the land and remove any vehicles or other property which they have with them on the land.

(b) Power of arrest (s 63(8))

Where a constable in uniform reasonably suspects that a person knows that a direction under s 63(2), Criminal Justice and Public Order Act 1994 has been given and that the said direction applies to him and that person either–

(i)   fails to leave the land to which the direction applies as soon as reasonably practicable or

(ii)   having left the said land, be enters the land within the period of 7 days beginning with the day on which the direction was given,

the constable may arrest that person without a warrant.

(c) Power of entry (s 64)

If a police officer of at least the rank of superintendent reasonably believes that circumstances exist in relation to any land which would justify the giving of a direction under s 63 (see (a) above) in relation to a gathering to which that section applies, he may authorise any constable to enter the land for any of the following purposes–

(i)   to ascertain whether such circumstances exist; and

(ii)   to exercise any power conferred on a constable by s 63 or to exercise any power of seizure (see (b) above and (d) below).

A constable who is so authorised to enter land for any purpose may enter the land without a warrant.

(d) Power of seizure (s 64)

If a direction has been given under s 63 (see (a)(2) above) and a constable reasonably suspects that any person to whom the direction applies has without reasonable excuse–

(i)   failed to remove any vehicle or sound equipment on the land which appears to the constable to belong to him or to be in his possession or under his control; or

(ii)   entered the land as a trespasser with a vehicle or sound equipment within the period of 7 days beginning with the day on which the direction was given,

the constable may seize and remove that vehicle or sound equipment.

(e) Power to stop persons from proceeding to raves (s 65)

If a constable in uniform reasonably believes that a person is on his way to a gathering to which s 63 applies (see (a)(1) above) in relation to which a direction under s 63(2) is in force (see (a)(2) above), he may–

(i)   stop that person, and

(ii)   direct him not to proceed in the direction of the gathering.

(Note: (1) The above power may only be exercised at a place within 5 miles of the boundary of the site of the gathering; (2) The above power will not apply to an exempt person (see 'Comments' below)).

(f) Additional power of arrest (s 65 (5)

Where a constable in uniform reasonably suspects a person knows that a direction under s 65(1)(b) (see (ii) above) has been given to him and he has failed to comply with that direction, the constable may arrest him without warrant.

Charges

1. *You, knowing that a direction under s 63(2), Criminal Justice and Public Order Act 1994 had been given by* . . . (name the officer), *a superintendent (or higher rank) of the* . . . *police force on the* . . . (give date) *and which applied to you,* * *you did fail to leave land specified in the said direction situate at* . . . (give location) *as soon* as reasonably practicable (or continue from asterisk . . . you having *left land specified in the said direction situate at* . . . (give location) *on* . . . (give date of leaving) *again entered it on* . . . (give date of return), *such date being within the period of seven days beginning with the day in which the said direction was given. Contrary to s 63(6), Criminal Justice and Public Order Act 1994.*

2. *You, knowing that a direction under s 65(1)(b), Criminal Justice and Public Order Act 1994 had been given to you by* . . . (name the officer), *a constable of the* . . . *police force on the* . . . (give date), *you did fail to comply with the said direction. Contrary to s 65(4), Criminal Justice and Public Order Act 1994.*

Comments

The direction given by the superintendent (or above) may be communicated to the people concerned either by him or by any constable irrespective of rank. All that needs to be done is for reasonable steps to be taken by the police to bring the direction to the notice of the gathering.

A direction under s 63 cannot be made in respect of an 'exempt person' who is defined as the occupier of the land concerned, any member of his family, any employee or agent of the occupier and any person whose home is situated on the land.

ROBBERY
(IO, max pen life imp)

Powers of arrest

Full powers for 'arrestable offences', see pages 14–15.

Charge

Did steal . . . (specify property) belonging to . . . and immediately before (or at the time of) doing so, and in order to do so,

(a) *used force on the said . . . (or . . .); or*
(b) *put (or sought to put) the said . . . (or . . .) in fear of being then and there subjected to force.*
Contrary to s 8, Theft Act 1968.

Comments

The charge provided is framed to contain all essential ingredients–including the alternatives. *It is not required that the property shall be taken from the person, or in the presence of, the victim, or that it must be in his immediate and personal care and protection.* In effect the crime amounts to a theft (see page 140) accompanied by the use of some **immediate** physical force, or threat of force, towards someone **in order to commit the theft**. The use of such violence to facilitate an escape after a theft would not amount to robbery. Force used solely to enable appropriation of the property stolen **could** justify the charge (eg a street wages snatch in which a cash bag was forcibly pulled from the determined grasp of a resisting cashier, etc). For practical purposes much will depend upon the degree of force involved when deciding whether a 'theft' or 'robbery' charge is appropriate. Notice that an unaccompanied individual can commit this crime; a gang with a 'show of force' is not essential.

ROBBERY, ASSAULT WITH INTENT TO COMMIT
(IO, max pen life imp)

Powers of arrest

Full powers for 'arrestable offences', see pages 14–15.

Charge

Did assault . . . with intent to rob, contrary to s 8, Theft Act 1968.

Comments

See 'Robbery', page 129, and 'Theft', page 140, for amplifying comments.

An **assault is necessary** to this crime. That is an aggressive use of force or violence, or the attempted use of such force, etc, directed to cause bodily injury to someone. This force must necessarily relate to the intention to rob. If the motive of theft can be proved, then, for example, an unsuccessful slash with a razor which misses the intended victim might well justify the charge. 'Intent' is discussed under 'Wounding, etc (with intent)' page 149.

SEXUAL INTERCOURSE WITH A GIRL UNDER 13 YEARS (IO, max pen life imp)

Powers of arrest

Full powers for 'arrestable offences', see pages 14–15 (SAO).

Charge

Had unlawful sexual intercourse with . . . a girl under the age of 13 namely the age of . . . years, contrary to s 5, Sexual Offences Act 1956.

Comments

It is advisable to arrest in every case in which this charge is alleged *and the evidence justifies such action.* The remarks under the heading 'Rape' (page 124) apply here.

SEXUAL INTERCOURSE WITH A GIRL UNDER 16 YEARS (Triable 'either way', max pen 2 yrs imp. Time limit on proceedings, 12 mths)

Powers of arrest

General power of arrest under s 25, PACE see pages 17–18.

Charge

Had unlawful sexual intercourse with . . . a girl under the age of 16, namely the age of . . . years, contrary to s 6, Sexual Offences Act 1956.

Comments

This crime has, in recent years, become increasingly prevalent. Bear in mind that the consent of the female does not affect the issue. If there is an absence of consent the crime will be rape. The original complaint of the female can be given in evidence even though it is 'hearsay' (if the accused was not present at the time). It must be remembered that such evidence of complaint is not in itself evidence of the facts which it alleges but evidence of the consistency of the conduct of the complainant. The exercise of the power to arrest will vary according to the circumstances of each case. The remarks under 'Rape', page 124, are equally applicable to this crime. Should the circumstances indicate, it may be necessary to take the girl into police protection under the Children Act 1989 (see page 48).

Section 6(3), Sexual Offences Act 1956, provides that a man under 24 years of age who has not previously been tried on such a charge is not guilty of this crime if he believes the girl with whom he is intimate to be over 16 years **and** has reasonable cause for this belief. Section 47, however, recognises that proof in this respect lies on the man–although the standard of proof required is less than that demanded of the prosecution.

Officers should obtain corroborative evidence, and evidence of the female's dress, demeanour and use of cosmetics in order to assist the court should the accused invoke the above defence.

SOLICITATION BY MEN
(Triable 'either way', max pen 2 yrs imp)

Powers of arrest

Anyone may arrest a person found committing this offence but a constable may only do so in accordance with s 25, PACE (see pages 17–18) (s 41, Sexual Offences Act 1956 as amended by the Police and Criminal Evidence Act 1984, Sch 6).

Charge

Being a man, did persistently solicit (or *importune*) *in a certain public place called . . . for immoral purposes, contrary to s 32, Sexual Offences Act 1956.*

Comments

Solicitation may be by actions without words being spoken and evidence that some person complained or was annoyed is not essential (*Horton v Mead* [1913] 1 KB 154). It must involve the physical presence of the alleged offender–displaying an advertisement in a shop window is not sufficient (*Burge v DPP* [1962 1 All ER 666n etc). Remember that persistence in the soliciting or importuning is necessary to the charge. The offender is guilty whether soliciting, etc, men or women for homosexuality, prostitution or any immoral purpose. A 'public place' is any place to which the public have a lawful right of access. If the male is 'poncing' for a prostitute, reference to the heading 'Prostitution by a woman, man living on earnings of', may reveal a second offence (page 112).

If the immoral purpose is a homosexual act, proceedings must start within 12 months of the offence being committed (s 7, Sexual Offences Act 1967).

SPORTING EVENTS–CONTROL OF ALCOHOL ETC AND EXCLUSION ORDERS
1. Offences in connection with alcohol on coaches and trains and at sporting events

Police powers of enforcement

(a)   A constable may, at any time during the period of a designated sporting event at any designated sports ground, enter any part of the ground for the purpose of enforcing the provisions of the Sporting Events (Control of Alcohol etc) Act 1985.

(b)   A constable may search a person he has reasonable grounds to suspect is committing or has committed an offence under the Sporting Events (Control of Alcohol etc) Act 1985 and he may arrest such a person.

(c)   A constable may stop a public service vehicle which is being used for the principal purpose of carrying passengers for the whole or part of a journey to or from a designated sporting event and may search such a vehicle or a railway passenger vehicle if he has reasonable grounds to suspect that an offence under s 1, Sporting Events (Control of Alcohol etc) Act 1985 is being or has been committed in respect of the vehicle. (For offences–see charges below.)

(d)   A constable may stop a motor vehicle which is not a public service vehicle but is adapted to carry eight or more passengers and is being used for the principal purpose of carrying two or more passengers for the whole or part of a journey to or from a designated sporting event and may search such a vehicle if he has reasonable grounds to suspect that an offence under s 1A, Sporting Events (Control of Alcohol etc) Act 1985 is being or has been committed in respect of the vehicle.

Charges

(a)   *You being the operator* (or *servant of* or *agent of the operator*) (or *you being the hirer* or *servant of* or *agent of the hirer*) *of a public service vehicle* (or *railway passenger vehicle*) *and the said public* *service vehicle (*or *railway passenger vehicle) was being used for the principal purpose of carrying passengers for the whole (*or *part) of a journey to (*or *from) a designated sporting event namely . . .* (name the designated event), *knowingly caused (*or *permitted) intoxicating liquor to be carried on the said public service vehicle (*or *railway passenger vehicle). Contrary to s 1(2), Sporting Events (Control of Alcohol etc) Act 1985.*

(b) *You being the person who was the driver (*or *you being a person who was not the driver but the keeper (*or *servant of or agent of the keeper) (or you being a person who was not the driver but a person to whom a motor vehicle as defined in s 1A(1) of the Sporting Events (Control of Alcohol etc) Act 1985 was made available by hire (*or *loan or by means of . . .* (name the means the vehicle was made available)) *by the keeper (*or *by the keeper's servant or by the keeper's agent or by your servant or by your agent)) of a motor vehicle which was not a public service vehicle but was adapted to carry more than eight passengers and the said vehicle was being used for the principal purpose of carrying two or more passengers for the whole (*or *part) of a journey to (*or *from) a designated sporting event, namely . . .* (name the event), *did knowingly cause (*or *permit) intoxicating liquor to be carried on the said motor vehicle. Contrary to s 1A, Sporting Events (Control of Alcohol etc) Act 1985 as added by the Public Order Act 1986.*

(c) *Did have in your possession certain intoxicating liquor namely . . .* (name the quantity and type of intoxicant) *while on a public service vehicle (*or *railway passenger vehicle or motor vehicle to which s 1A, Sporting Events (Control of Alcohol etc) Act 1985 applies) and which was being used for the principal purpose of carrying passengers (*note: for the words 'carrying passengers' substitute the words 'carrying two or more passengers' if the motor vehicle is not a public service vehicle and section 1A applies) *for the whole (*or *part) of a journey to (*or *from) a designated sporting event, namely . . .* (name the event). *Contrary to s 1(3) (*or, *in the case of non PSV's, contrary to s 1A(3)), Sporting Events (Control of Alcohol etc) Act 1985.*

(d) *You were drunk on a public service vehicle (*or *railway passenger vehicle or motor vehicle to which s 1A, Sporting Events (Control of Alcohol etc) Act 1985 applies) and which was being used for the principal purpose of carrying passengers (*note: for the words 'carrying passengers' substitute the words, 'carrying two or more passengers' if the motor vehicle is not a public service vehicle and s 1A applies) *for the whole (*or *part) of a journey to (*or *from) a designated sporting event namely . . .* (name the event). *Contrary to s 1(4) (*or, *in the case of non PSV's, contrary to s 1A(4)), Sporting*

Events (Control of Alcohol etc) Act 1985.

(e)   *Did have in your possession intoxicating liquor namely . . .* (name the quantity and type of intoxicant) (or *did have in your possession an article to which s 2, Sporting Events (Control of Alcohol etc) Act 1985 applies, namely . . .* (name the article)) *at a time during the period of a designated sporting event namely . . .* (name the event) *when you were in an area of a designated sports ground, namely . . .* (name the ground) *from which the said event may be directly viewed.*

(f)   *Did have in your possession an article* (or *substance to which s 2A, Sporting Events (Control of Alcohol etc) Act 1985 applies, namely . . .* (name the article) *(eg a flare, or fog signal or firework etc)* at a time during the period of a designated sporting event, namely . . .* (name the event) *when you were in an area of a designated sports ground, namely . . .* (name the ground) *from which the said event may be directly viewed* (or carry on to * and then add) *. . . while entering* (or *trying to enter) a designated sports ground, namely . . .* (name the ground) *at a time during the period of a designated sporting event, namely . . .* (name the event) *at the said ground. Contrary to s 2A(1), Sporting Events (Control of Alcohol etc) Act 1985 as added by para 3, Sch 1 Public Order Act 1986).*

(g)   *You were drunk in a designated sports ground, namely . . .* (name the ground) *at a time during the period of a designated sporting event, namely , . . .*(name the event) *at the said ground. Contrary to s 2(2), Sporting Events (Control of Alcohol etc) Act 1985.*

Comments

The Sporting Events (Control of Alcohol etc) Act 1985 as amended by the Public Order Act 1986 provides wide powers for the police to control unruly elements not only at specified sporting events, notably football, but also while spectators are travelling to and from such events. Officers will invariably find that charges additional to those above can also be brought against individual offenders eg assaults, carrying offensive weapons, criminal damage etc. Once convicted the courts have power to make exclusion orders against offenders (see page 135). The term, 'designated sports ground', means any place used wholly or partly for sporting events where accommodation is provided for spectators and for the time being designated, or of a class designated by order made by the Secretary of State. The Sports Grounds and Sporting Events (Designation) Order 1985 has been made. Schedule 1 of that order lists the sports grounds concerned. A 'designated sporting event' means an event or proposed events outside Great Britain. The classes of sporting events are listed in Sch 2 to the above order.

The period of a designated sporting event is the period beginning two hours before the start of the event or (if earlier) two hours before the time at which it is advertised to start and ending one hour after the end of the event. There are modifications to this general rule as shown in s 9(4).

2. Exclusion orders–football matches and other sporting events (SO, max pen for breach–1 month imp)

Powers of arrest

1. A constable who reasonably suspects that a person has entered premises in breach of an exclusion order may arrest him without warrant.
2. If a person to whom an exclusion order relates, fails to comply with an order made under s 35, Public Order Act 1986 (ie where the court orders photographs to be taken), a constable may arrest him without a warrant in order that his photograph may be taken (see 'Comments' below).

Charge

Being a person to whom an exclusion order made by the . . . (name the court making the order) *on . . .* (name the date of the order) *under s 30, Public Order Act 1986, applies, you did enter certain premises namely . . .* (name the premises) *in breach of the said exclusion order. Contrary to s 32(3), Public Order Act 1986.*

Comments

Under s 30, Public Order Act 1986, courts can make exclusion orders prohibiting convicted persons from entering premises for the purpose of attending association football matches prescribed by order made by the Secretary of State. The Secretary of State also has power to extend the provisions relating to exclusion orders to sporting events other than football matches. Before making any arrest officers should ensure that the offender was entering or had entered one of the prescribed matches in breach of the order.

The courts can make exclusion orders in relation to any offence which fulfils one or more of three conditions as follows:

1. The offence must be committed during a relevant period as determined under s 31(6) to (8) of the Act, while the accused was at or was entering or leaving or trying to enter or leave the football ground concerned.

2.   The offence must be one which involved the use or threat of violence towards another person or towards property or under the provisions of the Act relating to racial hatred (see page 123) and committed on journeys to or from the football match concerned.

3.   The offence was committed under s 1(3) or (4) or 1A(3) or (4) of the Sporting Events (Control of Alcohol etc) Act 1985 and the designated sporting event concerned was an association football match.

Once an exclusion order is made it has effect for such time mentioned in the order which must be for not less than three months. The exclusion order can only be made in addition to a sentence imposed in respect of the offence for which the accused was convicted or in addition to a probation order or order of absolute or conditional discharge. The court which makes the order must give copies of the order to the offender, to the chief officer of police and to any prescribed person.

The court which makes the exclusion order may make an order which requires the police to take a photograph of the excluded offender and requiring that person to go to a specified police station for this purpose. The requirement to go to a police station for the purpose of photography must be not later than seven clear days after the date on which the order was made. If the offender fails to comply with the order he may be arrested under the powers shown above.

In relation to football matches played outside England and Wales, Part 2 of the Football Spectators Act 1989 provides the court with power to make a 'restriction order' where a person is convicted of offences listed in Sch 1 of the Act. The court must consider that such an order would help prevent violence or disorder. The effect of such an order is to place an obligation on the convicted person to report to a police station within five days of making the order and to further report on the occasion of a designated football match when the offender is required to do so. Failure to comply with these provisions is an offence. Moreover, under the Act the court has power to make a restriction order on those who are convicted of offences abroad and which correspond with the UK offences in Sch 1. The proper use of the restriction order should help control those unruly elements who travel to international football events and cause mayhem abroad.

3. Football Offences (Football (Offences) Act 1991–All SO only)

Powers of arrest

Full powers for 'arrestable offences', see pages 14–15.

Charges

(a)   Throwing missiles. *On* . . . (Give day and date of match) at . . . (location of football ground) *on the occasion of a designated football match between* . . . (name the teams) *you threw something at or towards the playing area of the said ground* (or *you threw something at or towards an area adjacent to the playing area of the said ground to which spectators are not generally admitted*) (or *you threw something at or towards an area in which spectators or other persons were present* (or *might be present*) *without lawful authority or lawful excuse. Contrary to s 2, Football (Offences) Act 1991.*

(b)   Indecent or racialist chanting. *On* . . . (give day and date of match) *at* . . . (location of football ground) *on the occasion of a designated football match between* . . . (name the teams) *you took part in chanting of an indecent* (or *racialist) nature. Contrary to s 3, Football (Offences) Act 1991.*

(c)   Going on to the playing area. *On* . . . (give day and date of match) *at* . . . (location of football ground) *on the occasion of a designated football match between* . . . (name the teams) *you did without lawful authority* (or *lawful excuse) go on to the playing area of the said ground* (or *you did without lawful authority* (or *lawful excuse) go on to an area adjacent to the playing area of the said ground to which spectators are not generally admitted. Contrary to s 4, Football (Offences) Act 1991.*

Comments

The provisions of the Act only apply to 'designated football matches'. The Football (Offences) (Designation of Football Matches) Order 1991 has designated the relevant matches and officers should refer to this particular instrument.

References in the Act to things done at a designated football match includes anything done at the ground:

(a)   Within the period beginning two hours before the time at which it is advertised to start and ending one hour after the match; or

(b)   Where the match is advertised to start at a particular time on a particular day, but does not take place on that day, within the period beginning two hours before and ending one hour after the advertised starting time.

In s 3, 'chanting' means the repeated uttering of words or sounds in concert with one or more others. The words 'of a racialist nature' mean chanting of or including matter which is threatening, abusive or insulting to a person by reason of his colour, race, nationality (including citizenship) or ethnic or national origins.

The Football (Offences) Act 1991 provides further useful powers for the police to deal with the hooligan elements. However, officers should always remember that where circumstances dictate, more serious charges under the Public Order Act 1986 should always be considered (see pages 116 to 120).

STEALING, GOING EQUIPPED FOR
(Triable 'either way', max pen 3 yrs imp)

Powers of arrest

Full powers for 'arrestable offences', see pages 14–15. In addition any person may arrest anyone who is, or whom he, with reasonable cause, suspects to be committing this offence.

Charge

At . . . (specify place), *not being his place of abode, had with him a certain article, namely* . . . (specify) *for use in the course of (or in connection with)*:

(a)   *a burglary* (at . . . (specify building)); or
(b)   *a theft* (of . . .(give particulars)); or
(c)   *an offence under s 12(1), Theft Act 1968, of taking a conveyance, namely, a* . . . (specify) *without the consent of the owner or other lawful authority;* or
(d)   *an offence under s 15, Theft Act 1968, of obtaining property (namely* . . . (specify)) *by deception.*

Contrary to s 25, Theft Act 1968

Comments

All essentials to the crime, including alternatives, are contained in the charge provided. It is essential that the possessor of the article/s or implement/s shall be **away from his place of abode** at the material time. A person who is living rough in a car is at his place of abode when on a site with the intention of abiding there, but not when the vehicle is in transit from one site to another (*R v Bundy* [1977] 2 All ER 382). The power to arrest **covers reasonable suspicion that he has such articles, etc, with him** and that his intended use is for one or other of the purposes–'burglary' (page 38), 'theft' (page 140), or 'cheat' (page 60). The 'taking of a conveyance' (s 12) **is a theft** for the purposes of this offence (s 15(5)). 'Intent' is discussed under 'Wounding, etc (with intent)', page 149.

The fact that an accused has an article with him which was made, or has been adapted, for use to commit the crime alleged (burglary, theft, cheat) is evidence that he had it with him for such use (s 25(3)).

A 'cheat' is 'obtaining property by deception' (s 15, Theft Act, page 66).

TELECOMMUNICATIONS–FRAUDULENT AND IMPROPER USE OF SYSTEM
(Fraudulent use –triable 'either way', max pen 2 yrs imp. Improper use–SO only)

Powers of arrest

General power of arrest under s 25, PACE, see pages 17–18.

Charges

1. *Did dishonestly obtain a service provided by means of a licensed telecommunications system with intent to avoid payment of a charge applicable to the provision of the said service. Contrary to s 42(1), Telecommunications Act 1984.*
2. *Did send by means of a public telecommunications system, a message (or a certain matter) which was grossly offensive (or of an indecent or obscene or menacing character). Contrary to s 43(1)(a), Telecommunications Act 1984.*
3. *Did send by means of a public telecommunications system for the purpose of causing annoyance (or inconvenience or needless anxiety) to another, a message that you knew to be false. Contrary to s 43(1)(b), Telecommunications Act 1984.*
4. *Did persistently make use of a public telecommunications system for the purpose of causing annoyance (or inconvenience or needless anxiety) to another by sending messages that you knew to be false. Contrary to s 43(1)(b), Telecommunications Act 1984.*

Comments

All of the above charges cater for the misuse of the telephone and other modern telecommunications systems. Where the misuse consists of indecent telephone calls, the co-operation of the appropriate telecommunications manager will need to be sought.

Persistent offenders can be tracked down by means of specialist equipment and liaison with telephone operators. The person on the receiving end may also have to assist in detecting the offender. By keeping him talking there is always a better chance of detection. Officers will have to be guided by the physical and mental state of the victim before any decision is taken in relation to his or her involvement in tracking the offender. If the call is traced, officers must act quickly. If caught, the offender should be asked to stay at the telephone source while an officer checks with the Telecom service that he has the source of the offending call. Careful notes should be taken of all conversations and the actions taken to trace the offenders.

THEFT
(Triable 'either way', max pen 10 yrs imp)

Powers of arrest

Full powers for 'arrestable offences', see pages 14–15. Exceptions are (i) taking or destroying fish in private, etc waters; and (ii) attempting this offence. Any person may arrest anyone reasonably suspected to be committing (i) or (ii). (See Sch 1, Theft Act 1968 for full particulars.)

Charges

(1) Theft

Did steal . . .(specify property) (*of the value of* (specify)) *belonging to . . .* (name of owner), *contrary to ss 1 and 7, Theft Act 1968.*

(2) Theft of things forming part of land by person not in possession of the land

Not being in possession of certain land, namely . . . , situate at . . . did steal (specify thing forming part of the land) *belonging to . . .* (name of person), *and forming part of the said land by severing it* (or *causing it to be severed*) *from the land* (or *after it had been severed, from the land*), *contrary to ss 1 to 7, Theft Act 1968.*

(3) Theft of fixture or structure by person in possession of land under a tenancy

Being in possession of certain land, namely, . . .situate at . . . under a tenancy granted by . . . did steal (part of) a certain fixture (or *structure*) *namely* (specify) *belonging to the said . . .* (or *to . . .*) *let to be used with the said land, contrary to ss 1 to 7, Theft Act 1968.*

(4) Theft by picking mushrooms, flowers, fruit, etc, growing wild on land

Not being in possession of certain land, namely . . . situate at . . . did steal certain mushrooms belonging to . . . and growing wild on the said land (or certain flowers or fruit or foliage from a plant (or tree), namely (specify), belonging to . . . and growing wild on the said land) by picking them (or it) for reward (or for sale) (or for a commercial purpose, namely (state purpose)), contrary to ss 1 to 7, Theft Act 1968.

Comments

Every ingredient of the charge must be proved. The following amplifies and defines, in summarised form, the main points requiring clarification:

'Dishonesty'–it is not dishonest if a person appropriates in the genuine belief that he has a lawful right to deprive the owner (see 'Belonging to another' (below) (either for himself or for someone else) or if he similarly believes that the owner would have consented to the appropriation had he known of the circumstances, or, if he appropriates in the belief that the owner cannot be discovered by taking reasonable steps. (Note: trustees and the owner's personal representatives are excluded from this.) **It can be dishonest** even if the appropriator is willing to pay for the property (s 2).

'Appropriating' need not be for gain or benefit to the thief. It can be appropriation even when a person comes by property (innocently or not) without stealing it and afterwards assumes the rights of the owner (s 3), (eg the dishonest appropriation by a parent of things taken and brought home by a child under the age of criminal responsibility (under 10 yrs)).

'Property' can mean almost anything tangible or intangible (eg stocks and shares). The following cannot be stolen, however:

(i)   land and certain things forming part of it–but only in particular circumstances not likely to be met with on the beat (except in circumstances provided in s 4(2) of the Act);

(ii)   mushrooms, flowers, fruit and foliage growing wild and not **picked** for reward, sale or some other commercial purpose; and

(iii)   untamed wild creatures, and their carcasses, not ordinarily kept in captivity and not reduced into the possession of someone at the time of 'appropriation' (s 4).

(Note: See 'Comments' under 'Damaging or destroying property', page 60).

'Belonging to another' (owner)–covers any person having genuine rights of possession or control or proprietary claim or interest in, or to, the property (s 5), (eg the treasurer of a holiday fund).

'With the intention of permanently depriving'–means what it says, subject to certain exceptions–and borrowing or lending can only amount to this if the property is borrowed, etc, for a period, and in circumstances, which make it equivalent to an outright taking or disposal (s 6): but *'where a person having possession or control (lawful or not) of property belonging to another,* **parts** *with the property under a condition as to its return which he may not be able to perform, this (if done for purposes of his own and without the other's authority) amounts to treating the property as his own to dispose of regardless of the other's rights'* (*s* 6(2)). The overall effect is that if a person **'appropriates'** under conditions mentioned in the italics, with the intention of parting with the 'property' he may be guilty of theft. If consent to the appropriation was obtained dishonestly this is still theft (see *R v Lawrence* (1970)).

'Intent' is discussed under 'Wounding, etc (with intent)', page 149.

For the full definition of 'theft', consult ss 1 to 6 of the Theft Act 1968. The offence embraces almost every conceivable type of dishonest appropriation.

The following headings in this book deal with Theft Act provisions **not** amounting to 'theft': *blackmail* (page 34), *obtaining property by deception* (page 66), *obtaining services by deception* (page 67), *evasion of liability by deception* (page 63), *making off without payment* (page 65), *obtaining pecuniary advantage by deception* (page 66), *handling stolen goods* (pages 90–91), *taking any conveyance without authority* (pages 169–170), and *removing articles from places open to the public* (page 114).

Compare the offence of 'theft' with that of 'damage' (page 60) if the circumstances of an enquiry include damage to, or destruction of, property. A damage, etc charge may be more appropriate–*and* easier to prove. Powers to arrest are the same.

TRESPASS OR NUISANCE ON LAND
(Criminal Justice and Public Order Act 1994)
(SO only: max pen 3 mths imp)

(Note: At the time of writing the following powers under (1) and (2) below are in force but the powers under (3) are not. They may be used from the date of the relevant commencement order made under the Criminal Justice and Public Order Act 1994).

Police powers (s 61)

1. Power to remove trespassers (s 61)

If the senior police officer present at the scene reasonably believes that two or more persons are trespassing on land and are present there with the common purpose of residing there for any period, that reasonable steps have been taken by or on behalf of the occupier to ask them to leave and–

(a)   that any of those persons has caused damage to the land or to any property on the land or used threatening, abusive or insulting words or behaviour towards the occupier, a member of his family or an employee or agent of his, or

(b)   that those persons have between them six or more vehicles on the land,

he may direct those persons, or any of them, to leave the land and to remove any vehicles or other property they have with them on the land.

2. Power of arrest (s 61(5))

Where a constable in uniform reasonably suspects that a person knows that a direction under s 61(1), Criminal Justice and Public Order Act 1994 has been given and that the said direction applies to him and that person either–

(a)   fails to leave the land to which the direction applies as soon as reasonably practicable, or

(b)   having left the said land, he enters the land as a trespasser within the period of three months beginning with the day on which the direction was given,

the constable may arrest that person without a warrant.

3. Power of seizure (s 62)

Where a direction under s 61(1), Criminal Justice and Public Order Act 1994 has been given and a constable reasonably suspects that any person to whom the direction applies has, without reasonable excuse–

(a)   failed to remove any vehicle on the land which appears to the constable to belong to him or to be in his possession or under his control; or

(b)   entered the land as a trespasser with a vehicle within the period of three months beginning with the day on which the direction was given,

the constable may seize and remove that vehicle.

(Note: A 'vehicle' will include any vehicle whether or not it is in a fit state for use on roads, any chassis or body with or without wheels, appearing to have formed part of such a vehicle and any load carried by and anything attached to such a vehicle. It will also include a caravan as defined in s 29(1), Caravan Sites and Control of Development Act 1960.)

Charges

You knowing that a direction under the authority of s 61(1), Criminal Justice and Public Order Act 1994 and made on . . . (give date of direction) *had been given in respect of certain land situate at . . .* (give location) *and occupied by . . .* (give name of occupier) *and which direction applied to you,* you did fail to leave the said land in accordance with the direction as soon as reasonably practicable* (or continue from asterix . . . *you having left the said land again entered it as a trespasser on . . .* (give date of entry) *such date being within three months beginning with the day on which the said direction was given). Contrary to s 61(4), Criminal Justice and Public Order Act 1994.*

Comments

It sometimes happens that people enter land with the permission of the occupier which means they are not trespassers. However, they may outstay their welcome. Once the occupier makes it known that they should leave and they do not do so then they become trespassers. Section 61(2) makes it clear that the senior officer must reasonably believe that the other conditions specified are satisfied *after* the trespass occurred before he can make a direction under s 61(1). A direction made can be communicated to the persons to whom it is to apply by any constable, not necessarily by the officer making the order.

It is a defence for a person charged with an offence to show either–(a) he was not trespassing on the land or (b) that he had a reasonable excuse for failing to leave the land as soon as reasonably practicable or, as the case may be, for again entering the land as a trespasser.

TRESPASS–AGGRAVATED
(Criminal Justice and Public Order Act 1994)

Police powers

1. Power to remove persons from land (s 69)

If the senior police officer present at the scene reasonably believes—

(a)   that a person is committing, has committed or intends to commit the offence of aggravated trespass on land in the open air; or

(b)   that two or more persons are trespassing on land in the open air and are present there with the common purpose of intimidating persons so as to deter them from engaging in a lawful activity or of obstructing or disrupting a lawful activity, he may direct that person or (as the case may be) those persons (or any of them) to leave the land.

2. Powers of arrest (s 68(4) and s 69(5))

(a) A constable in uniform who reasonably suspects that a person is committing an offence of aggravated trespass under s 68 Criminal Justice and Public Order Act 1994 may arrest him without a warrant (see 'Charges' below).

(b) Where a constable in uniform reasonably suspects that a person knows that a direction under s 69(1) Criminal Justice and Public Order Act 1994 has been given and that the said direction applies to him and that person either–

(i) fails to leave the land to which the direction applies as soon as practicable, or

(ii) having left the said land, he again enters it as a trespasser within the period of three months beginning with the day on which the direction was given,

the constable may arrest that person without a warrant.

Charges

1. *You did trespass on land in the open air situate at* . . . (give location) *and occupied by* . . . (name occupier) *and upon which persons were engaging in* (or . . . *and upon which persons were about to engage in*) *a lawful activity upon the said land* [or . . . *and upon which persons were engaging in* (or . . . *and upon which persons were about to engage in*) *a lawful activity on land in the open air adjoining the land aforesaid and in relation to that lawful activity you did something which was intended by you to have the effect* of intimidating those persons* (or *intimidating (one of* or *some of) those persons) so as to deter (him or them) from engaging in the said lawful activity* [or continue from asterisk . . . *of obstructing the said lawful activity*] [or continue from asterisk . . . *of disrupting the said lawful activity*]. *Contrary to s 68(3), Criminal Justice and Public Order Act 1994.*

2. *You knowing that a direction under the authority of s 69(1) Criminal Justice and Public Order Act 1994 made on* . . . (give date) *had been given in respect of your aggravated trespass upon land situate at* . . . (give location) *and occupied by* . . . (give name of occupier) *and which direction applied to you, you did fail to leave the said land in accordance with the direction as soon as practicable* (or continue from asterisk . . . *you having left the said land on* . . . (give date of leaving), *again entered it as a trespasser on* . . . (give date

of return), *such date being within three months beginning with the day on which the direction was given. Contrary to s 69(3), Criminal Justice and Public Order Act 1994.*

Comments

Section 68(1) defines aggravated trespass as follows:

'A person commits the offence of aggravated trespass if he trespasses on land in the open air and, in relation to any lawful activity which persons are engaging in or are about to engage in on that or adjoining land in the open air, does there anything which is intended by him to have the effect–

(a)   of intimidating those persons or any of them so as to deter them from engaging in that activity,

(b)   of obstructing that activity, or

(c)   of disrupting that activity.'

Section 68(2) states that activity on any occasion in the part of a person or persons on land is 'lawful' for the purpose of s 68 if he or they may engage in the activity on the land on that occasion without committing an offence of trespassing on land. For the definition of 'land' see s 68(5).

The comments applicable to raves in relation to communicating the direction to the offenders applies also to aggravated trespass (see page 128).

In proceedings for an offence under (2) above there is a defence open to the accused on identical terms to that in relation to the offence under s 61 (see page 144).

TRESPASSORY ASSEMBLIES

1. Powers of arrest– organising etc trespassory assembly

A constable in uniform may arrest without warrant anyone he reasonably suspects of–

(a)   organising, or

(b)   taking part in, or

(c)   inciting another to take part in

a trespassory assembly, the holding of which he knows is prohibited by an Order made under s 14A, Public Order Act 1986.

Charge
(SO only–max pen 3 mths imp)

You did organise (or *take part in* or *make another person, namely* . . . (name the person incited) *to take part in*) *a trespassory assembly knowing that the said trespassory assembly was prohibited by virtue of an order made on . . . (name date of order) by the . . . District Council under powers vested in them by s 14A, Public Order Act 1986. Contrary to s 14B, Public Order Act 1986.*

2. Powers to stop persons proceeding to trespassory assemblies– s 14C, Public Order Act 1986

If a constable in uniform reasonably believes that a person is on his way to an assembly within the area to which an Order under s 14A, Public Order Act 1986 applies, which the constable reasonably believes is likely to be an assembly which is prohibited by that Order, he may:

(a)   stop that person and
(b)   direct him not to proceed in the direction of the assembly.

The above power may only be exercised within the area to which the order applies.

3. Power of arrest–failing to comply with direction

A constable in uniform may arrest without warrant anyone he reasonably suspects to be committing an offence under s 14C, Public Order Act 1986 (see 'charge' below).

Charge
(SO only–max pen 3 mths imp)

You knowing that a direction under s 14C(1), Public Order Act 1986 had been given to you by . . . (name the officer), a constable of the . . . (name the force) police force on the . . . (give date) you did fail to comply with the said direction. Contrary to s 14(C), Public Order Act 1986.

Comments

The Criminal Justice and Public Order Act 1994 provides new powers to chief police officers and District Councils to control large trespassory gatherings on land. Section 70 inserts a new s 14A into the Public Order Act 1986. This allows a chief officer of police to apply to the District Council for an order to prohibit trespassory assemblies. The Chief Officer must reasonably believe firstly that the assembly is intended to be held on land to which the public has no right of access (or only a limited right) and that the assembly is likely to be held without the permission of the occupier. As an alternative the reasonable belief must be that the assembly is likely to conduct itself in such a way as to exceed the limits of any permission of the occupier or the limits of the public's right of access.

Secondly the chief officer must reasonably believe that the assembly may result in either serious disruption to the life of the community or where the land itself or buildings or monuments upon the land is of historical, architectural, archaeological or scientific importance, significant damage may be caused to these sites. Similar powers are provided for the Commissioner of the Metropolitan Police and the Secretary of State as far as London is concerned.

An Order may be revoked or varied by subsequent Orders and no Order shall prohibit the holding of assemblies for a period exceeding 4 days or in an area exceeding an area represented by a circle with a radius of 5 miles from a specified centre. An assembly means an assembly of 20 or more persons. An 'occupier' is defined in England as the person entitled to possession of the land by virtue of an estate or interest held by him.

VAGRANTS, SLEEPING OUT, ETC
(SO, max pen 3 mths imp)

Powers of arrest

Any person may arrest any offender found committing. However, a constable should use his general power of arrest under s 25, PACE, see pages 17–18.

Charge

Unlawfully did wander abroad and lodge in a certain barn (or *outhouse, or deserted,* or *unoccupied building situate at . . .;* or *in the open air in . . . street;* or *under a tent,* or *in a certain cart,* or *wagon, in . . . street), and not giving a good account of himself, and:*

(a) *having been directed to a reasonably accessible place of shelter, he failed to apply for* (or *refused) accommodation there;* or

(b) *he is a person who persistently wanders abroad and notwithstanding that a place of shelter was reasonably accessible he lodged* (or *attempted to lodge), as aforesaid,* or

(c) *that by* (or *in the course of) lodging as aforesaid, he caused damage to property* (or *infection with vermin,* or *other offensive consequence); (or that he lodged as aforesaid in such circumstances as to appear to be likely to cause damage to property etc) to . . . the property of . . .; contrary to s 4, Vagrancy Act 1824, as amended.*

Comments

It is important to note the provisos (a), (b) and (c) stated in the charge. Should a person be discovered wandering abroad and lodging out and he is a stranger, he must be referred to a reasonably accessible place of shelter (*that is, 'a place where provision is regularly made for giving (free of charge) accommodation for the night to such persons as apply therefor'*) and he must refuse or neglect to go there before he can be arrested. The only exception to this is when the vagrant has caused or is likely to cause damage or offensive consequences to property. Homelessness is becoming an increasing social problem and officers should be guided by local force policy. There are a number of social agencies (such as the Salvation Army, 'Shelter', etc) who may be able to assist in cases of this sort. Arrest should really be the last resort.

WOUNDING OR CAUSING GRIEVOUS BODILY HARM (NO INTENT)
(Triable 'either way', max pen 5 yrs imp)

Powers of arrest

Full powers for 'arrestable offences', see pages 14–15.

Charge

Unlawfully and maliciously did wound ... (or *unlawfully and maliciously did inflict upon* ... *certain grievous bodily harm*) *contrary to s 20, Offences Against the Person Act 1861*.

Comments

See remarks under 'Wounding, causing grievous bodily harm, etc with intent', below and 'Assault occasioning bodily harm', page 27.

WOUNDING, CAUSING GRIEVOUS BODILY HARM, ETC (WITH INTENT)
(IO, max pen life imp)

Powers of arrest

Full powers for 'arrestable offences', see pages 14–15.

Charges

1. General charge–wounding with intent to do grievous bodily harm

Unlawfully and maliciously did wound (or *unlawfully and maliciously did cause grievous bodily harm*) *to* ... (name the person wounded, etc) *with intent to do grievous bodily harm to the said* . . .(name the person wounded, etc) (or *to* . . . (name the person to whom grievous bodily harm was intended if other than the person wounded, etc)). *Contrary to s 18, Offences Against the Person Act 1861.*

2. Wounding with intent to resist arrest

Unlawfully and maliciously did wound (or *unlawfully and maliciously did cause grievous bodily harm) to*. . . (name the person wounded, etc) *with intent to resist* (or *prevent) the lawful apprehension* (or *detainer) of yourself* (or *of* . . . (name the person whose arrest it was intended to resist if other than the accused)). *Contrary to s 18, Offences Against the Person Act 1861.*

Comments

Always arrest in respect of this crime if the injury appears serious. Remember your first duty is to the injured person, particularly if his life is endangered. The essential feature which distinguishes the offence is intent to cause the injury or resist arrest. There is no obligation here for the alleged offender to prove that his act of wounding, etc, was accidental. The definition of the word 'maliciously' laid down in *R v Cunningham* [1957] 2 QB 396 is not appropriate for a charge under this section or s 20 (see previous heading) and the word is best ignored *R v Mowatt* [1968] 1 QB 421. See, however, other important case law on this point in *R v Pembliton* (1874) R2 CCR 119 *R v Latimer* (1886) 17 QB 359; *R v Martin* (1881) 8 QBD 54; *R v Wilson* [1984] Crim LR 173; *R v Savage and Parmenter* [1991] 4 All ER 698.

'Intent'–A court is not bound to draw an inference by reason *only* of the result of an action being the natural and probable consequences of it. It will decide the 'intent' by considering all the evidence and drawing from this the conclusion which seems the proper one (see s 8, Criminal Justice Act 1967).

To constitute a wound, the skin must be broken and to constitute grievous bodily harm, really serious bodily harm must be caused (*R v Methavam* (1961)).

If a trespasser enters any building, or inhabited vehicle or vessel, and there inflicts, or attempts to inflict, grievous bodily harm upon someone, he is guilty of burglary (see 'Burglary', page 38)–an offence that equally applies, if, when entering as a trespasser, it can be proved he intended grievous bodily harm.

Officers should note that in connection with offences of causing bodily harm to others, a new offence of 'torture' has been created by s 134, Criminal Justice Act 1988. This offence is committed by public officials or any person acting in an official capacity or any person acting with the consent or acquiescence of public officials etc, no matter what their nationality may be. The offence is committed when any person is subjected to the intentional infliction of severe pain or suffering at the hands of the above people. The offence can be committed in the UK or elsewhere and the maximum penalty for the offence is life imprisonment.

PART THREE

Road Traffic Law
Specific Powers of Arrest and Charges

DANGEROUS DRIVING AND CYCLING
(a) **Dangerous driving–causing death by (IO max pen 10 yrs imp)**

Powers of arrest

Full powers for 'arrestable offences'; see pages 14–15 (SAO).

Charge

Did cause the death of . . . (name the victim) *by driving a mechanically propelled vehicle dangerously on a road called . . .* (name the road and location) *or in a certain public place called . . .* (name the public place and location). *Contrary to s 1, Road Traffic Act 1988 as amended by s 1, Road Traffic Act 1991.*

(b) **Dangerous driving (SO only, max pen 6 mths imp)**

Powers of arrest

General power of arrest under s 25, PACE see pages 17–18.

Charge

Did drive a mechanically propelled vehicle dangerously on a road called . . . (name the road and location) *or in a certain public place called . . .* (name the public place and location). *Contrary to s 2, Road Traffic Act 1988 as amended by s 1, Road Traffic Act 1991.*

(c) **Dangerous cycling (SO only)**

Powers of arrest

General power of arrest under s 25, PACE, see pages 17–18.

Charge

Did ride a cycle on a certain road called . . . (name the road and location) *dangerously. Contrary to s 28, Road Traffic Act 1988.*

Comments on dangerous driving and cycling

The offences of causing death by dangerous driving and the lesser offence of dangerous driving replace the old offences of reckless driving which appeared in the Road Traffic Act 1988 when it was first enacted.

Under the new s 2A of the 1988 Act, the test for dangerous driving will be where the driving falls far below what would be expected of a competent and careful driver and where it would be obvious to such a driver that driving in that way would be dangerous. Furthermore the section goes on to mention that a person may also be regarded as driving dangerously if it would be obvious to a competent and careful driver that driving a vehicle in its current state would be dangerous. In considering the state of the vehicle the court may have regard to anything attached to it, or on it, and in the manner in which, anything is attached or carried. Thus a vehicle being driven in a poorly maintained condition, or travelling with an insecure load, or unevenly distributed load could be used as evidence in a prosecution.

The word 'dangerous' in ss 1, 2 and 28 refers to danger either of injury to any person or of serious damage to property. In determining what would be expected of, or obvious to a competent and careful driver (or cyclist) in a particular case, regard shall be had not only of the circumstances of which he could be expected to be aware but also of any circumstances shown to have been within the knowledge of the person accused.

With regard to dangerous cycling, s 28(2) applies the same test as set out in s 2A above.

DANGER–CAUSING DANGER TO ROAD USERS
(Triable 'either way', max pen 7 yrs imp)

Powers of arrest

Full powers for 'arrestable offences', see pages 14–15.

Charges

(a) *Did intentionally and without lawful authority or reasonable cause, cause a certain thing, namely a . . .* (specify) *to be on* (or *over*) *a certain road called . . .* (name the road) *situate at . . .* (give location) *in such circumstances that it would be obvious to a reasonable person that to do so would be dangerous. Contrary to s 22 (A), Road Traffic Act 1988 as inserted by s 6, Road Traffic Act 1991.*

(b) *Did intentionally and without lawful authority or reasonable cause interfere with a certain motor vehicle* (or *a certain trailer*) (or *a certain cycle*) *namely a . . .* (specify) *owned by . . .* (give name of owner) *in such circumstances that it would be obvious to a reasonable person that to do so would be dangerous. Contrary to s 22 (A) Road Traffic Act 1988 as inserted by s 6, Road Traffic Act 1991.*

(c) *Did intentionally and without lawful authority or reasonable cause interfere with certain traffic equipment namely . . .* (specify) *and owned by . . .* (name and address of owner) *in such circumstances*

*that it would be obvious to a reasonable person that to do so would
be dangerous. Contrary to s 22A, Road Traffic Act 1988 as inserted
by s 6, Road Traffic Act 1991.*

Comments

In relation to all three offences, the word 'dangerous' refers to danger either
of injury to any person while on or near a road, or of serious damage to
property on or near a road. In determining what would be obvious to a
reasonable person in a particular case, the Act directs that regard shall be
had not only to the circumstances of which he would be expected to be
aware but also to any circumstances shown to have been within the
knowledge of the accused.

For the purpose of the offence under (3) above, traffic equipment means
anything lawfully placed on or near a road by a highway authority and
traffic signs lawfully placed on or near a road by persons other than a
highway authority (eg private construction engineers making or repairing
highway). Fences, barriers and lights lawfully placed will also fall within
the definition in the circumstances set out in s 22A.

CARELESS AND INCONSIDERATE DRIVING AND CYCLING
(a) Causing death by careless or inconsiderate driving when under the influence of drink or drugs (IO max pen 10 yrs imp SAO)

Powers of arrest

Full powers for 'arrestable offences', see pages 14–15.

Charges

(i)   *Did cause the death of* . . . (name the victim) *by driving a
      mechanically propelled vehicle on a certain road called* . . . (name
      the road and location) *without due care and attention* or *without
      reasonable consideration for other persons using the said road* (or
      *said public place), and at the time of driving you were unfit to drive
      through drink or drugs. Contrary to s 3A(1)(a), Road Traffic Act
      1988, as added by s 3 Road Traffic Act 1991.*

(ii) *Did cause the death of* . . . (name the victim) *by driving a
      mechanically propelled vehicle on a certain road called* . . . (name
      the road and location) (or *in a certain public place called* . . . (name
      the public place and location) *without due care and attention* or
      *without reasonable consideration for other persons using the said
      road* (or *said public place) and you having consumed so much
      alcohol that the proportion of it in your breath* (or *blood) (or urine)*

at that time exceeded the prescribed limit. Contrary to s 3A(1)(b), Road Traffic Act 1988.

(iii)   *Did cause the death of*... (name the victim) *by driving a mechanically propelled vehicle on a certain road called* ... (name the road and location) *or in a certain public place called* ... (name the public place and location) *without due care and attention* or *without reasonable consideration for other persons using the said road* (or *said public place*), *and you within 18 hours after that time having been required to provide a specimen in pursuance of s 7 of the Road Traffic Act 1988, did without reasonable excuse fail to provide the said specimen. Contrary to s 3A(1)(c), Road Traffic Act 1988.*

(b) Careless and inconsiderate driving (SO only)

Powers of arrest

General powers of arrest under s 25, PACE, see pages 17–18.

Charge

Did drive a mechanically propelled vehicle on a certain road called ... (name the road and location) *or in a certain public place called* ... (name the public place and location) *without due care and attention,* or *without reasonable consideration for other persons using the said road* (or *said public place*). *Contrary to s 3, Road Traffic Act 1988 as amended by s 2, Road Traffic Act 1991.*

(c) Careless and inconsiderate cycling (SO only)

Powers of arrest

General power of arrest under s 25, PACE, see pages 17–18.

Charge

Did ride a cycle on a certain road called ... (name the road and location) *without due care and attention* (or *without reasonable consideration for other persons using the road*). *Contrary to s 29, Road Traffic Act 1988 as amended.*

Comments

The offences of causing death by careless or inconsiderate driving whilst under the influence of drink or drugs are new to criminal law. Officers should note that within s 3A there are three different offences. An example of the offence under s 3A(1)(a) might be where an offender passes the road-side breath test, but there is still evidence that the driver's ability is impaired, possibly through drugs. Officers should not hesitate to use the power of arrest in such cases. The offence under s 3A(1)(b) will arise where the offender shows excess alcohol in the body as ascertained from the usual breath, blood or urine samples. Section 3A(1)(c) can be used in those cases where the offender fails without reasonable excuse to provide specimens under s 7 of the Act. Note that the request for specimens should be made within 18 hours of the time of driving without due care and attention for this offence to be complete.

In all three of the above offences the evidence must show the following:

(a)   That the accused had driven carelessly or without reasonable consideration for other road users. Such evidence, for example will be established by what is found at the scene of an accident, the account of witnesses and the explanations of the accused.

(b)   It must be shown that it was the careless or inconsiderate driving which caused the death of another. This of course will rest upon proper medical evidence following post mortem examination.

(c)   The offending driver must be shown to be under the influence of drink or drugs so that his ability to drive was impaired, or that analyses of samples shows that he was over the prescribed limit. Where a driver fails to provide samples a careful log should be made of the time at which requests were made within 18 hours of the time of careless driving, if it is necessary to establish the offence under s 3A(1)(c).

It is open for a jury to return alternative verdicts of careless driving under s 3 if they are unsure that the careless driving caused the death. Furthermore, a jury can also bring in a verdict under the relevant drink/driving laws if they are unsure that the accused drove carelessly or in an inconsiderate manner.

With regard to careless driving generally, the standard of driving in order to establish the offence under s 3 must be such that the accused departed from the standard of care and skill that would in the circumstances of the case have been exercised by a reasonable, prudent and competent driver. Each case will turn on its own facts and officers should always ensure that the evidence reflects the standard of driving exercised by the defendant.

DRINK AND DRIVING OFFENCES
(Road Traffic Act 1988)
(All are SO only–See Sch 2, Road Traffic Offenders Act 1988 for penalties, endorsement and disqualification)

1. Powers of arrest–unfit through drink or drugs

A constable may arrest a person without a warrant if he has reasonable cause to suspect that that person is or has been committing an offence of driving or attempting to drive or being in charge of a motor vehicle on a road or other public place while he is unfit to drive through drink or drugs (s 4(6)).

For the purpose of arresting a person under the above provisions, a constable may enter (if need be by force) any place where that person is or where the constable, with reasonable cause, suspects him to be (s 4(7)).

2. Police powers–breath tests

Where a constable in uniform has reasonable cause to suspect:

(a)   that a person driving or attempting to drive or in charge of a motor vehicle on a road or other public place has alcohol in his body or has committed a traffic offence whilst the vehicle was in motion (s 6(1)(a)); or

(b)   that a person has been driving or attempting to drive or been in charge of a motor vehicle on a road or other public place with alcohol in his body and that person still has alcohol in his body (s 6(1)(b)); or

(c)   that a person has been driving or attempting to drive or been in charge of a motor vehicle on a road or other public place and has committed a traffic offence whilst the vehicle was in motion (s 56(1)(c));

he may (subject to the provisions of s 9 which provides for protection of patients in hospital) require him to provide a specimen of breath for a breath test.

If an accident occurs owing to the presence of a motor vehicle on a road or other public place, a constable may require any person whom he has reasonable cause to believe was driving or attempting to drive or in charge of the vehicle at the time of the accident to provide a specimen of breath for a breath test (subject to the provisions of s 9) (s 6(2)).

3. Power of arrest–exceeding prescribed limit

A constable may arrest a person without a warrant if:

(a)   as a result of a breath test he has reasonable cause to suspect that the proportion of alcohol in that person's breath or blood exceeds the prescribed limit (s 6(5)(a)); or

(b)   that person has failed to provide a specimen of breath for a breath test when required to do so in pursuance of (2) above and the constable has reasonable cause to suspect that he has alcohol in his body (s 6(5)(b)).

(Note: a person shall not be arrested by virtue of 3(a) or (b) when he is at a hospital as a patient.)

For the purpose of requiring a person to provide a specimen of breath under 56(2) above (ie accident cases) in a case where he has reasonable cause to suspect that the accident involved injury to another person or of arresting him under 3(a) or (b) above, a constable may enter (if need be by force) any place where that person is or where the constable with reasonable cause suspects him to be (s 56(b)).

Follow-up procedures

In the course of an investigation into whether a person has committed an offence under ss 3A, 4 or 5 of the Road Traffic Act 1988 (see 'charges' below) a constable may (subject to s 9, hospital cases) require a person:

(a)   to provide two specimens of breath for analysis; or
(b)   to provide a specimen of blood or urine for a laboratory test.

On requiring any person to provide a specimen, a constable *shall* warn that person that a failure to provide it may render him liable to a prosecution (s 7(7)).

Once the above requirements have been made and the warning given, you must be guided by your own supervisory officers who will instruct on procedure in accordance with your own force orders and Home Office circulars. Of particular importance will be the division of any blood or urine sample provided, the supply of one part of it to the accused and the completion of certificates relating to the taking of samples.

Note:

(i)   A requirement *under s 7* to provide a specimen of breath can only be made at a *police station* (s 57(2)).
(ii)   A requirement *under s 7* to provide a specimen of blood or urine can only be made at a *police station or at a* hospital (but see (iii)) (s 7(3)).
(iii) A requirement under (ii) above *cannot* be made at a police station unless:

    (a)   the constable making the requirement has reasonable cause to believe that for medical reasons a specimen of breath cannot be provided or should not be required; or

(b) at the time the requirement is made an approved breath testing device is not available at the police station or it is not practicable to use the device there; or

(c) the suspected offence is one under s 3A or 4 of the Act and the constable making the requirement has been advised by a medical practitioner that the condition of the person required to provide the specimen might be due to some drug,

but may then be made notwithstanding that the person required to provide the specimen has already provided or been required to provide two specimens of breath (s 7(3)).

(iv) The question of whether a specimen of *blood or of urine* is to be provided shall be decided by the constable making the requirement. However, if a medical practitioner is of the opinion that for medical reasons a specimen of blood cannot or should not be taken, the specimen shall be one of urine (s 7(4)).

(v) In the case of the provision of a specimen of urine this should be provided within one hour of the requirement for its provision being made and after the provision of a previous specimen of urine (s 7(5)).

(vi) Of any two specimens of breath provided *under s 7*, that with the lower proportion of alcohol in the breath shall be used and the other shall be disregarded (but see note (vii)) (s 8(1)).

(vii) Where two specimens of breath are taken and the lower proportion of alcohol contains no more than 50 microgrammes of alcohol in 100 millilitres of breath, the person who provided it may claim that it should be replaced by the provision of a specimen of blood or urine. If he then does provide blood or urine, neither specimen of breath should be used (s 8(2)).

Protection for hospital patients (s 9)

While a person is at a hospital as a patient he shall not be required to provide a specimen of breath for a breath test or to provide a specimen for a laboratory test unless the medical practitioner in immediate charge of his case has been notified of the proposal to make the requirement; and

(a) if the requirement is then made it shall be for the provision of a specimen at the hospital, but

(b) if the medical practitioner objects on the ground that the requirement or the provision of a specimen or, in the case of a specimen of blood or urine the warning required under s 7(7) (see under 'Follow-up procedures', page 161) would be prejudicial to the proper care and treatment of the patient.

To conform to hospital procedures, any blood specimen taken must be obtained by the doctor called by the police, not the hospital doctor in charge of the patient. Breath or urine samples can be taken by the police but the presence of a doctor or nurse is obviously advisable.

Charge

1. Driving, etc, motor vehicles when unfit through drink or drug

Did drive (or *did attempt to drive* or *when in charge of) a motor vehicle, namely a* . . . (name the make and registration number of the motor vehicle) *on a certain road (*or *public place), called* . . . (name the location) *was unfit to drive through drink* (or *drugs).*
Contrary to s 4, Road Traffic Act 1988, as amended by the Road Traffic Act 1991.

2. Failing to provide a specimen of breath under s 6

(a) *Being a person who in pursuance of s 6 of the Road Traffic Act 1988* was required by* . . . (name the constable), *a constable in uniform, to provide a specimen of breath for a breath test, you did, without reasonable excuse, fail to do so. Contrary to s 6(4), Road Traffic Act 1988.*

(*Note: For the provisions of s 6 see under (2) and (3) of powers of arrest, etc, above.)

(b) *Being a person whom* . . . (name the constable), *a police constable, had reasonable cause to believe was driving* (or *attempting to drive* or *in charge of) a certain motor vehicle namely* . . . (name the make and registration mark of the motor vehicle) *at a time when an accident occurred owing to the presence of that motor vehicle on a certain road* (or *public place) called* . . . (name the location) *and having been required by the said constable to provide a specimen of breath for a breath test, you did, without reasonable excuse, fail to do so. Contrary to s 6(4), Road Traffic Act 1988.*

3. Driving etc, motor vehicles with blood/alcohol above limit

Did drive (or *did attempt to drive* or *when in charge of) a certain motor vehicle, namely a* . . . (name the make and registration number of the motor vehicle) *on a certain road* (or *public place) called* . . . (name the location), *having consumed so much alcohol that the proportion of it in his breath* (or *blood* or *urine) exceeded the prescribed limit. Contrary to s 5(1), Road Traffic Act 1988.*

4. Failure to provide a specimen under s 7, Road Traffic Act 1988

You being a person subject to an investigation whether you have committed an offence under s 3A (or s 4 or s 5), Road Traffic Act 1988, and having been required by . . . (name the officer making the requirement), *a constable of the . . .* (name the constabulary) *to provide two specimens of breath for analysis by means of a device of a type approved by the Secretary of State* (or *to provide a specimen of blood or urine for a laboratory test), you did, without reasonable excuse, fail to provide a specimen when required to do so. Contrary to s 7(6), Road Traffic Act 1988, as amended by the Road Traffic Act 1991.*

Comments

The law relating to drink/driving offences is contained in ss 3A to 11 of the Road Traffic Act 1988.

Where an officer makes a request for a person to take a breath test under s 6 (see 'powers' above), the requirement may be made either at or near the place where the requirement was made or in accident cases at a police station if the constable thinks fit.

The term 'traffic offence' mentioned in the power at (2) above means an offence under any of the provisions of the Road Traffic Act 1988 (except Part V), any provisions of Part II, Public Passenger Vehicles Act 1981, Road Traffic Regulation Act 1984 and the Road Traffic Offenders Act 1988 except Part III.

Section 10 relates to the detention of persons affected by alcohol or drugs and should be carefully noted by officers.

For the purpose of the Act a 'drug' is *any* intoxicant other than alcohol.

The word 'fail' includes 'refuse' and a person *does not* provide a specimen of breath for a test or for analysis unless the specimen is sufficient to enable the test or the analysis to be carried out and is provided in such a way as to enable the objective of the test or analysis to be satisfactorily achieved.

There is a statutory defence open to drivers in charge of vehicles. A person is deemed not to be in charge if he proves to the court that at the material time the circumstances were such that there was no likelihood of his driving the vehicle so long as he remained unfit to drive (ss 54(5) and 55(2)).

Although arrests will generally be made for offences under s 6 (see charge (3)), do not lose sight of the s 4 provisions (charge (1)) as this covers contingencies for which the 'exceeding the prescribed limit' offences do not cater. For example, when an arrest is deserved and the obviously unfit driver is affected by a combination of drink and drugs which while making him unfit, enables him to pass the breath test, or the unfit driver refuses blood and urine specimens. If s 4 is to be proceeded with, call the police doctor straight away so that he may provide the necessary evidence of the prisoner's condition. Also make your own detailed notes concerning the defendant's demeanour and behaviour.

With regard to the first breath test, remember that if a person refuses this, it is an offence in itself and should be charged in addition to any other charge of driving under the influence or above the prescribed limits etc. If the first test is refused an arrest should be made under power (3(b)) above. Following the arrest officers should carry on with the procedures laid down.

DRINK AND DRUGS–CYCLING UNDER THE INFLUENCE OF DRINK OR DRUGS
(SO only)

Powers of arrest

General power of arrest under s 25, PACE, see pages 17–18.

Charge

Being a person who, when riding a cycle, not being a motor vehicle, on a road, namely . . . (name the road or street) or *in a public place, namely . . .* (name the public place) *was unfit to ride through drink or drugs. Contrary to s 30(1), Road Traffic Act 1988, as amended by Road Traffic Act 1991.*

Comments

It should be noted that no provision is made for attempting to ride or being in charge of a cycle which is not a motor vehicle while unfit through drink or drugs.

With regard to motor assisted pedal cycles, all machines of this type are motor vehicles. This applies even if the machine is only being pedalled along (*Floyd v Bush* [1953] 1 All ER 265; *Lawrence v Howlett* [1952] 2 All ER 74). A person in charge of or attempting to ride such a machine while unfit through drink or drugs is therefore liable to prosecution under ss 4 to 12, Road Traffic Act 1988 (see 'Drink and driving offences', pages 160–165).

'Drunkenness' must be proved in respect of an individual in charge of a pedal cycle in a public place who is not seen to ride (see 'drunk in charge of a carriage etc', page 75).

A person charged under s 30, Road Traffic Act 1988 cannot be additionally charged with an offence under s 12, Licensing Act 1872 (drunk in charge of a carriage).

By virtue of s 30(1) a person is 'unfit to ride through drink or drugs' where he is under the influence to such an extent as to be incapable of having proper control of the cycle. Officers should therefore include in their evidence observations of the offender's demeanour, the way in which the cycle was being ridden and the inconvenience and danger he was causing to other road users.

DRIVING MOTOR VEHICLE WHILE DISQUALIFIED
(SO only–max pen 12 mths imp)

Powers of arrest

A constable **in uniform** may arrest any person driving a motor vehicle on a road whom he has reasonable cause to suspect is disqualified from holding or obtaining a driving licence (s 103(3), Road Traffic Act 1988), as amended by Road Traffic Act 1991.

Charge

Then being disqualified from holding or obtaining a licence to drive a motor vehicle by virtue of an order made by the ... (Magistrates') Court on the ... day of ..., 19 ... (or by virtue of ... (describe breach respecting some other disqualification factor) did drive a certain motor vehicle, namely a ... on a certain road called ..., contrary to s 103(1), Road Traffic Act 1988.

Comments

Remember that any driving licence produced must relate to the class or description of vehicle then being driven.

Disqualification for the purpose of this offence must be by a court or by reason of a statutory age limit (eg youth under 21 years, driving a motor coach (heavy motor car) (*R v Saddleworth Justices,* 1968)). Mere **revocation** of a licence by a Licensing Authority because of physical infirmity, defective eyesight, etc, **is not a disqualification** for this purpose.

Experience shows that criminals are prone to risk driving while disqualified–particularly when 'out on a job'. Be alert to avoid any attempt at a quick getaway when you suspect this applies. The likely prospect of imprisonment for the offence can prompt desperate action. Section 44, Powers of Criminal Courts Act 1973, empowers Crown Courts to disqualify from driving any person convicted of *any offence punishable on indictment with not less than two years imprisonment,* if satisfied that a motor vehicle was used by that person, or by anyone else, for the purpose of committing that offence or facilitating its commission.

If doubtful whether a licence produced relates to the driver producing, obtain a specimen of his signature and compare this with the one on the licence.

FAILING TO STOP AFTER ACCIDENT
(SO only)

Power of arrest

General power of arrest under s 25, PACE, see pages 17–18.

Charge

You being the driver of a mechanically propelled vehicle, namely a . . . (name the vehicle and registration number) *on a certain road called . . .* (name the road and location) *at a time where due to the presence of that vehicle on the said road an accident occurred whereby personal injury was caused to . . .* (name) (or *damage was caused to . . .* (give brief details of other vehicle, trailer, animal or other property) *you failed to stop and provide particulars as required by s 170, Road Traffic Act 1988*, as amended.

Comments

The absolute obligation placed upon drivers involved in accidents is firstly to stop and then supply details of name and address of both the driver and the owner of the vehicle and the identification marks of the vehicle to any person having reasonable grounds for requiring these details. In addition, there is also a duty for drivers to produce their driving licence, certificate of insurance and test certificate if the person requiring the details is a constable.

If for some reason the above details are not given after the driver has stopped, then there is an obligation to report the accident to a constable or at a police station as soon as practicable. In any event the accident must be reported within 24 hours of its occurrence.

After a driver has stopped at the scene of the accident, he must remain there sufficiently long enough for a person having reasonable grounds for obtaining details to obtain them. Persons having reasonable grounds would not only be the police officer attending but also people such as drivers of other vehicles involved, injured parties, owners of damaged roadside property and so forth.

Drivers who do not stop after accidents (even those minor non-injury accidents) may do so in order to escape the consequences of the drink/driving legislation. Officers should be aware of this and apply the breath test procedures in appropriate cases once the driver has been located. It is important that where offending drivers cannot be traced immediately that evidence is gathered at the scene of the accident and witnesses are interviewed as soon as possible. Magistrates are well aware that drivers who do not stop may have a good deal to hide. Penalties can be quite severe and include sentencing options of up to six months imprisonment, disqualification from driving and obligatory endorsement of between five and ten penalty points on the licence.

HIGHWAY–WILFUL OBSTRUCTION OF
(SO only)

Powers of arrest

General power of arrest under s 25, PACE, see pages 17–18.

Charge

Without lawful authority or excuse did wilfully obstruct the free passage along . . . a highway by . . . (state method of obstruction), *contrary to s 137, Highways Act, 1980.*

Comments

This power to arrest is useful when dealing with demonstrators, the defiant individual who is showing-off, itinerant street traders, musicians, public speakers and others, who obstruct the highway unreasonably.

The highway is provided primarily for the lawful passage of the public. Acts which unreasonably interrupt the passage of the highway–or, in certain circumstances, are likely to interrupt–are punishable under this section. (For motor vehicle obstructions see Reg 103, Road Vehicles (Construction and Use) Regulations 1986).

'Highway' means the whole or any part of a highway other than a ferry or waterway, and includes any bridge, tunnel, etc, over or through which the highway passes (s 328(1) and (2), Highways Act 1980).

Offences of obstruction of the highway sometimes arise in employment or industrial disputes. Section 16 of the Employment Act 1980 sets out the relevant legal requirements in respect of 'peaceful picketing'. Guidelines on police duties and responsibilities in dealing with picketing situations will be laid down in your force instructions and orders. Always act under the direction of senior officers when dealing with disputes of this type.

MOTOR RACING ON PUBLIC WAYS
(SO only)

Powers of arrest

General power of arrest under s 25, PACE, see pages 17–18.

Charge

Did promote (or *did take part in*) *a race or trial of speed between motor vehicles on a public way. Contrary to s 12, Road Traffic Act 1988 as amended by Road Traffic Act 1991.*

Comments

Under s 12(2), a 'public way' is defined as a highway, which in turn means a way over which all members of the public are entitled to pass and repass. The definition is therefore wide enough to cover all carriageways, footways bridleways and pavements. In the event of conviction, disqualification from driving is obligatory as is three to eleven penalty points on the driving licence.

VEHICLES–UNLAWFUL TAKING. TAKING MOTOR VEHICLE OR OTHER CONVEYANCE WITHOUT AUTHORITY
(SO only, max pen 6 mths imp)

Powers of arrest

Full powers for 'arrestable offences', see pages 14–15.

Charges

1. *Without having the consent of the owner or other lawful authority did take a certain conveyance, namely . . .* (specify) *for his own use* (or *for the use of . . .* (name)). *Contrary to s 12(1), Theft Act 1968.*
2. *Knowing that a certain conveyance, namely . . .* (specify) *had been taken without the consent of the owner or other lawful authority, did drive the said conveyance* (or *did allow himself to be carried in* (or *on*) *the said conveyance). Contrary to s 12(1), Theft Act 1968.*

Comments

A 'conveyance', means any conveyance constructed or adapted for the carriage of a person or persons whether by land, sea, or air, but it does not include any conveyance which is for use only under the control of a person not carried in or on it (s 12(7)(a)). When the conveyance involved is subject to a hiring or hire purchase agreement, the 'owner' is the person in possession under the agreement (s 12(7)(b)).

There is a defence open to a defendant in s 12(6) whereby if he does anything in the belief that he has lawful authority to do it or that he would have had the owner's consent if the owner knew of his doing it and the circumstances of it.

Quite clearly in appropriate cases the charge of theft should be used. However, in such cases the prosecution would need to show that there was an intent to permanently deprive the owner of the conveyance.

Officers should note that a 'conveyance' does not have to be a mechanically propelled vehicle but by virtue of s 12(6) it does not include pedal cycles. The taking of pedal cycles constitutes a separate charge under s 12(5), for which see below.

TAKING A PEDAL CYCLE WITHOUT AUTHORITY (SO only)

Power of arrest

General power of arrest under s 25, PACE, see pages 17–18.

Charge

Without having the consent of the owner or other lawful authority, did take a pedal cycle for his own use or *for the use of . . .* (name). *Contrary to s 12(5), Theft Act 1968.*

RIDING A PEDAL CYCLE TAKEN WITHOUT AUTHORITY (SO only)

Powers of arrest

General power of arrest under s 25, PACE, see pages 17–18.

Charge

Did ride a pedal cycle knowing that it had been taken without the consent of the owner or other lawful authority. Contrary to s 12(5), Theft Act 1968.

Comments

Note that officers will need to prove in the case of 'riding etc' the defendant had guilty knowledge that the cycle had been taken without consent. If the circumstances of 'appropriating' a pedal cycle were such that the intention was to permanently deprive the owner then a charge of theft should be used.

VEHICLE–AGGRAVATED TAKING
(Triable 'either way' max pen 2 yrs imp but if death occurs 5 yrs imp)

Powers of arrest

Full powers for 'arrestable offences' see pages 14–15.

Charges

1. *Without having the consent of the owner or other lawful authority did take a certain mechanically propelled vehicle namely . . . (specify) for his own use (or for the use of . . . (name)) and after the vehicle was so unlawfully taken and before it was recovered, the vehicle was driven dangerously on a road (or in a public place) [or . . . and after the vehicle was so unlawfully taken and before it was recovered and owing to the driving of the vehicle, an accident occurred by which injury was caused to . . . (name the injured person)] [or . . . and after the vehicle was so unlawfully taken and before it was recovered and owing to the driving of the vehicle, an accident occurred by which damage was caused to certain property, namely . . . (specify the property) belonging to . . . (name the owner) (or belonging to a person or persons unknown)] [or . . . and after the vehicle was so unlawfully taken and before it was recovered damage was caused to the said vehicle]. Contrary to s 12(A), Theft Act 1968, as inserted by the Aggravated Vehicle Taking Act 1992.*

2. *Knowing that a certain mechanically propelled vehicle namely . . . (specify) had been taken without the consent of the owner or other lawful authority you did drive the said vehicle (or you did allow yourself to be carried in (or on) it)* and after the vehicle was so unlawfully taken and before it was recovered the vehicle was driven dangerously on a road (or in a public place). Contrary to s 12(A), Theft Act 1968, as inserted by the Aggravated Vehicle Taking Act 1992.*

(Note: any of the alternative charges set out in charge (1) above can be used from the point shown by the asterisk.)

Comments

The above aggravated forms of unlawful vehicle taking should always be used where following the taking of the vehicle there is evidence of dangerous driving or injury to persons or property (including the vehicle itself). It is suggested that where the circumstances show both dangerous driving and injury or damage, separate charges should be brought in respect of each. Thus, for example, if a prosecution for the dangerous driving element fails, there could still be a conviction on the alternative charges.

Officers should note that the basic offence of taking without authority must firstly be proved and then in addition there must be firm evidence relating to the aggravated circumstances. The second charge above will provide for those offenders who do not themselves take the vehicle but drive it or are carried as passengers knowing that the vehicle has been unlawfully taken. Unlawful takers, drivers and passengers with guilty knowledge will all be guilty of this offence. In this respect it is important that evidence in relation to the guilty knowledge of each defendant is obtained.

With regard to the aggravated circumstances, the proof of injury or damage may be relatively straightforward but even here there must be appropriate evidence to show that it was the driving of the vehicle which caused the injury or damage.

As far as dangerous driving is concerned s 12(A)(7) states that for the purpose of the section a vehicle is driven dangerously if it is driven in a way which falls far below what would be expected of a competent and careful driver and it would be obvious to such a driver that driving the vehicle in that way would be dangerous.

There are defences open to an offender charged with the aggravated offence. The first arises if he can show that the driving, accident or damage occurred before he committed the basic offence and the second if he can show that he was neither in nor on, nor in the immediate vicinity of the vehicle when the driving accident or damage occurred. Officers should seek out appropriate evidence to rebut this defence should it arise.

The section makes it clear that a vehicle is recovered when it is restored to its owner or to other lawful possession or custody. It should also be noted that whereas the basic offence is concerned with the unlawful taking of conveyances (which embraces mechanically propelled vehicles), the aggravated offence mentions only mechanically propelled vehicles.

VEHICLES–INTERFERENCE WITH
(SO, max pen 3 mths imp)

Powers of arrest

General power of arrest under s 25, PACE see pages 17–18.

Charges

(a) *You did interfere with a certain motor vehicle, namely a . . .* (name the make and registration mark of the motor vehicle concerned); or

(b) *You did interfere with a certain trailer, namely . . .* (name the make or type of trailer and any number of it). (Note: Caravans would be classed as trailers for the purpose of this charge); or

(c) *You did interfere with a certain thing namely . . .*(name the thing interfered with) *carried in* (or *on) a certain motor vehicle namely . . .* (name the make and registration mark of the vehicle concerned) (or *a certain trailer, namely a . . .* (name the make or type of the trailer concerned and any number of it)).

Continue for each of the above charges with the following as appropriate:

. . . with the intention that an offence of theft of (1) *a motor vehicle* (or *trailer* or *part of a trailer)* or (2) *a certain thing namely . . . carried in* (or *on) a motor vehicle* (or *trailer)* or (3) *taking and driving away a motor vehicle without consent should be committed by yourself* (or *by . . .)* (name) or *by a person* (or *persons) unknown. Contrary to s 9, Criminal Attempts Act 1981.*

Comments

This statutory offence replaces the provisions of the controversial 'Sus' law contained in s 4 of the Vagrancy Act 1824. By virtue of s 8, Criminal Attempts Act 1981, so much of the said s 4 which applies to suspected persons or reputed thieves frequenting or loitering about in the places described in that section shall cease to have effect.

The following points will need to be proved if there is to be a successful prosecution:

1. The interference with a motor vehicle or trailer (eg a holiday caravan) or anything in or on the motor vehicle or trailer. Ill-disposed persons interfere with vehicles in various ways and the best type of evidence can be provided by witnesses or by officers maintaining observation. The types of interference envisaged are wide ranging and will include such acts as tampering with locks or vehicle mechanisms and rummaging through personal possessions or goods inside motor vehicles and caravans, etc.

2. It must be shown that the accused intended either to steal the motor vehicle or trailer or part of it or anything carried in or on the vehicle, etc (eg, personal possessions, shopping, vehicle parts, etc) or that he intended to take the vehicle without the owner's consent (s 12, Theft Act 1968, see page 169).

It will be appreciated that where a person is merely seen to interfere with a vehicle it may not provide sufficient evidence to arrest. The officer must at least have *reasonable cause to suspect a person guilty of the offence* as defined which will necessarily include the elements of both the physical act of interference and the intent. As a matter of practice, 'Intent' can best be shown by not acting too soon. A person merely trying car door handles could put forward a wealth of reasons for his behaviour. If, however, he opens a door and reaches in and starts to sort through goods or possessions or he tries to dismantle equipment such as a radio or cassette player he has a lot more explaining to do and his 'Intent' clearly becomes more obvious. The softly, softly approach is all important in cases of this sort. Where a theft occurs in such circumstances always make this the primary charge (see page 140).

PART FOUR

Codes of Practice and Procedure

THE CODES OF PRACTICE

The Police and Criminal Evidence Act 1984 requires the Home Secretary, with the approval of Parliament, to issue codes of practice for the guidance of the police and other agencies who have the responsibility of implementing the provisions of the Act. There are five codes in total and for the purpose and extent of this book three of those codes are set out in their entirety. They are as follows:

1. The code of practice for the exercise by police officers of statutory powers of stop and search (pages 177–184),
2. The code of practice for the searching of premises by police officers and the seizure of property found by police officers on persons or premises (pages 184–192).
3. The code of practice for the detention, treatment and questioning of persons by police officers (pages 192–226).

Section 67 of the Act states that any breach of the Codes by police officers is automatically a disciplinary offence but it does not render an officer liable to any criminal or civil proceedings. Any of the codes are admissible as evidence at a trial and judges may exclude evidence which has been obtained in breach of the codes. It is therefore essential that officers refer themselves frequently to the codes and comply with them. Officers should particularly note the provisions of s 76 of the Act. Here it is made clear that confessions of accused persons are admissible in evidence but where they are obtained by oppression or in circumstances which render them unreliable then the court may exclude such evidence. Section 78 goes even further and states that the court may exclude any evidence where the circumstances show it would have an adverse effect on the fairness of the trial. Provided that the codes are faithfully adhered to officers will be able to demonstrate that the evidence produced at trial is accurate and is fair to the accused and in the interests of justice.

(A) CODE OF PRACTICE FOR THE EXERCISE BY POLICE OFFICERS OF STATUTORY POWERS OF STOP AND SEARCH

1. General

1.1 This code of practice must be readily available at all police stations for consultation by police officers, detained persons and members of the public.

1.2 The notes for guidance included are not provisions of this code, but are guidance to police officers and others about its application and interpretation. Provisions in the annexes to the code are provisions of this code.

1.3 This code governs the exercise by police officers of statutory powers to search a person without first arresting him or to search a vehicle without making an arrest. The main stop and search powers in existence at the time when this code was prepared are set out in the Annex, but that list should not be regarded as definitive. 1.4 This code does not apply to the following powers of stop and search:

(i)   Aviation Security Act 1982, s 27(2);
(ii)   Police and Criminal Evidence Act 1984, s 6(1) (which relates specifically to powers of constables employed by statutory undertakers on the premises of the statutory undertakers).

1.5 The exercise of the powers to which this code applies requires reasonable grounds for suspicion that articles unlawfully obtained or possessed are being carried. Where a police officer has reasonable grounds to suspect that a person is in innocent possession of a stolen or prohibited article, the power of stop and search exists notwithstanding that there would be no power of arrest. However, every effort should be made to secure the voluntary production of the article before the power is resorted to.

1.6 Whether reasonable grounds for suspicion exist will depend on the circumstances in each case, but there must be some objective basis for it. An officer will need to consider the nature of the article suspected of being carried in the context of other factors such as the time and the place, and the behaviour of the person concerned or those with him. Reasonable suspicion may exist, for example, where information has been received such as a description of an article being carried or of a suspected offender; a person is seen acting covertly or warily or attempting to hide something; or a person is carrying a certain type of article at an unusual time or in a place where a number of burglaries or thefts are known to have taken place recently. But the decision to stop and search must be based on all the facts which bear on the likelihood that an article of a certain kind will be found.

1.7 Reasonable suspicion can never be supported on the basis of personal factors alone. For example, a person's colour, age, hairstyle or manner of dress, or the fact that he is known to have a previous conviction for possession of an unlawful article, cannot be used alone or in combination with each other as the sole basis on which to search that person. Nor may it be founded on the basis of stereotyped images of certain persons or groups as more likely to be committing offences.

The Notes for Guidance to this section state:

1A It is important to ensure that powers of stop and search are used responsibly. An officer should bear in mind that he may be required to justify the use of the powers to a senior officer and in court, and also that misuse of the powers is likely to be harmful to the police effort in the long term. This can lead to mistrust of the police by the community. It is also particularly important to ensure that any person searched is treated courteously and considerately.

1B This code does not affect the ability of an officer to speak to or question a person in the ordinary course of his duties (and in the absence of reasonable suspicion) without detaining him or exercising any element of compulsion. It is not the purpose of the code to prohibit such encounters between the police and the community with the co-operation of the person concerned and neither does it affect the principle that all citizens have a duty to help police officers to prevent crime and discover offenders.

1C The power of search under paragraph 4(2) of Schedule 5 to the Prevention of Terrorism (Temporary Provisions) Act 1989 which does not require reasonable grounds for suspicion is not a power of stop and search as defined in paragraph 1.3 and is not covered by this code, but searches carried out under paragraph 4(2) should follow the procedures laid down in this code as far as practicable.

1D Nothing in this code affects

(a) the routine searching of persons entering sports grounds or other premises with their consent, or as a condition of entry; or

(b) the ability of an officer to search a person in the street on a voluntary basis. In these circumstances, an officer should always make it clear that he is seeking the co-operation of the person concerned.

1E If an officer acts in an improper manner this will invalidate a voluntary search. Juveniles, persons suffering from a mental handicap or mental disorder and others who appear not to be capable of giving an informed consent should not be subject to a voluntary search.

2. Action before a search is carried out

2.1 Where an officer has the reasonable grounds for suspicion necessary to exercise a power of stop and search he may detain the person concerned for the purposes of and with a view to searching him. There is no power to stop or detain a person against his will in order to find grounds for a search.

2.2 Before carrying out a search the officer may question the person about his behaviour or his presence in circumstances which gave rise to the suspicion, since he may have a satisfactory explanation which will make a search unnecessary. If, as a result of any questioning preparatory to a search, or other circumstances which come to the attention of the officer, there cease to be reasonable grounds for suspecting that an article is being carried of a kind for which there is a power of stop and search, no search may take place.

2.3. The reasonable grounds for suspicion which are necessary for the exercise of the initial power to detain may be confirmed or eliminated as a result of the questioning of a person detained for the purposes of a search (or such questioning may reveal reasonable grounds to suspect the possession of a different kind of unlawful article from that originally suspected); but the reasonable grounds for suspicion without which any search or detention for the purposes of a search is unlawful cannot be retrospectively provided by such questioning during his detention or by his refusal to answer any question put to him.

2.4 Before any search of a detained person or attended vehicle takes place the officer must take reasonable steps to give the person to be searched or in charge of the vehicle the following information:

(i)   his name (except in the case of enquiries linked to the investigation of terrorism, in which case he shall give his warrant number) and the name of the police station to which he is attached;

(ii)   the object to the search; and

(iii)   his grounds for undertaking it.

2.5 If the officer is not in uniform he must show his warrant card. In doing so in the case of enquiries linked to the investigation of terrorism, the officer need not reveal his name.

2.6 Unless it appears to the officer that it will not be practicable to make a record of the search, he must also inform the person to be searched (or the owner or person in charge of a vehicle that is to be searched, as the case may be) that he is entitled to a copy of the record of the search if he asks for it within a year. If the person wishes to have a copy and is not given one on the spot, he should be advised to which police station he should apply.

2.7 If the person to be searched, or in charge of a vehicle to be searched, doe not understand what is being said, the officer must take reasonable steps to brings the information in paragraphs 2.4 to 2.6 to his attention. If the person has someone with him then the officer must try to establish whether that person can interpret.

The Note for Guidance to this section states:

2A In some circumstances preparatory questioning may be unnecessary, but in general a brief conversation or exchange will be desirable as a means of avoiding unsuccessful searches. Where a person is lawfully detained for the purpose of a search, but no search in the event takes place, the detention will not thereby have been rendered unlawful.

3. Conduct of the search

3.1 Every reasonable effort must be made to reduce to the minimum the embarrassment that a person being searched may experience.

3.2 The co-operation of the person to be searched should be sought in every case, even if he initially objects to the search. A forcible search may be made only if it has been established that the person is unwilling to co-operate (eg by opening a bag) or resists. Although force may only be used as a last resort, reasonable force may be used if necessary to conduct a search or to detain a person or vehicle for the purposes of a search.

3.3 The length of time for which a person or vehicle may be detained will depend on the circumstances, but must in all circumstances be reasonable and not extend beyond the time taken for the search. The thoroughness and extent of a search must depend on what is suspected of being carried, and by whom. If the suspicion relates to a particular article which is seen to be slipped into a person's pocket, then, in the absence of other grounds for suspicion or an opportunity for the article to be moved elsewhere, the search must be confined to that pocket. In the case of a small article which can readily be concealed, such as a drug, and which might be concealed anywhere on the person, a more extensive search may be necessary. [See note 3B.]

3.4 The search must be conducted at or nearby the place where the person or vehicle was first detained.

3.5 Searches in public must be restricted to superficial examination of outer clothing. There is no power to require a person to remove any clothing in public other than an outer coat, jacket or gloves. Where on reasonable grounds it is considered necessary to conduct a more thorough search (eg by requiring a person to take off a T-shirt or headgear), this should be done out of public view (eg in a police van or nearby police station if there is one). Any search involving the removal of more than an outer coat, jacket, gloves, headgear or footwear may only be made by an officer of the same sex as the person searched and may not be made in the presence of anyone of the opposite sex unless the person being searched specifically requests it. [See Note 3A].

The Notes for Guidance for this section state:

3A A search in the street itself should be regarded as being in public for the purposes of paragraph 3.5 above, even though it may be empty at the time a search begins. Although there is no power to require a person to do so, there is nothing to prevent an officer from asking a person to voluntarily remove more than an outer coat, jacket or gloves in public.

3B As a search of a person in public should be a superficial examination of outer clothing, such searches should be completed as soon as possible.

4. Action after a search is carried out

a) General

4.1 An officer who has carried out a search must make a written record unless it is not practicable to do so, on account of the numbers to be searched or for some other operational reason, eg in situations involving public disorder.

4.2 The record must be completed as soon as practicable – on the spot unless circumstances (eg other immediate duties or very bad weather) make this impracticable.

4.3 The record must be made on the form provided for this purpose (the national search record).

4.4 In order to complete the search record the officer should normally seek the name, address and date of birth of the person searched, but under the search procedures there is no obligation on a person to provide these details and no power to detain him if he is unwilling to do so.

4.5 The following information should always be included in the record of a search even if the person does not wish to identify himself or give his date of birth.

(i)   the name of the person searched, or (if he withholds it) a description of him;
(ii)   a note of the person's ethnic origin;
(iii)   when a vehicle is searched, a description of it, including its registration number; [See Note 4B]
(iv)   the object of the search;
(v)   the grounds for making it;
(vi)   the date and time it was made;
(vii)   the place where it was made;
(viii) its results;
(ix)   a note of any injury or damage to property resulting from it;
(x)   the identity of the officer making it (except in the case of enquiries linked to the investigation of terrorism, in which case the record shall state the officer's warrant number and duty station). [See Note 4A].

4.6 A record is required for each person and each vehicle searched. However, if a person is in a vehicle and both are searched, and the object and grounds of the search are the same, only one record need be completed.

4.7 The record of the grounds for making a search must, briefly but informatively, explain the reason for suspecting the person concerned, whether by reference to his behaviour or other circumstances.

b) Unattended vehicles

4.8 After searching an unattended vehicle, or anything in or on it, an officer must leave a notice in it (or on it, if things in or on it have been searched without opening it) recording the fact it has been searched.

4.9 The notice should include the name of the police station to which the officer concerned is attached and state where a copy of the record of the search may be obtained and where any application for compensation should be directed.

4.10 The vehicle must if practicable be left secure.

The Notes for Guidance for this section state:

4A Where a search is conducted by more than one officer the identity of all the officers engaged in the search must be recorded on the search record.

4B Where a vehicle has not been allocated a registration number (eg a rally car or a trials motorbike) that part of the requirement under 4.5 (iii) does not apply.

ANNEX A

SUMMARY OF MAIN STOP AND SEARCH POWERS (see paragraph 1.3)

Power	Object of search	Extent of search	Where exercisable
Unlawful articles general			
1.Public Stores Act 1875, s 6	HM Stores stolen or unlawfully obtained	Persons, vehicles and vessels	Anywhere where the constabulary powers are exercisable
2.Firearms Act 1968, s 47	Firearms	Persons and vehicles	A public place
3.Misuse of Drugs Act 1971, s 23	Controlled drugs	Persons and vehicles	Anywhere
4.Customs and Excise Management Act 1979, s 163	Goods: (a) on which duty has not been paid (b) being unlawfully removed, imported or exported; (c) otherwise liable to forfeiture to HM Customs and Excise	Vehicles and vessels only	Anywhere

Power	Object of search	Extent of search	Where exercisable
5.Aviation Security Act 1982, s 27(1)	Stolen or unlawfully obtained goods	Airport employees and vehicles carrying airport employees or aircraft or any vehicle in a cargo area whether or not carrying an employee	Any designated airport
6.Police and Criminal Evidence Act 1984, s 1	Stolen goods; articles for use in certain Theft Act offences; offensive weapons, including bladed or sharply-pointed articles (except folding pocket-knives with a bladed cutting edge not exceeding 3 inches)	Persons and vehicles	Where there is public access
Police and Criminal Evidence Act 1984, s 6(3) (by a constable of the United Kingdom Atomic Energy Authority Constabulary in respect of property owned or controlled by British Nuclear Fuels plc)	HM Stores (in the form of goods and chattels belonging to British Nuclear Fuels plc)	Persons, vehicles and vessels	Anywhere where the constabulary powers are exercisable
7.Sporting Events (Control of Alcohol etc) Act 1985, s 7	Intoxicating liquor	Persons, coaches and trains	Designated sports grounds or coaches and trains travelling to or from a designated sporting event
8.Crossbows Act 1987, s 4	Crossbows or parts of crossbows (except crossbows with a draw weight of less than 1.4 kilograms)	Persons and vehicles	Anywhere except dwellings
Evidence of game wildlife offences 9.Poaching Prevention Act 1862, s 2	Game or poaching equipment	Persons and vehicles	A public place
10.Deer Acts 1963, s 5 and 1980, s 4	Evidence of offences under the Act	Persons and vehicles	Anywhere except dwellings

Power	Object of search	Extent of search	Where exercisable
11.Conservation of Seals Act 1970, s 4	Seals or hunting equipment	Vehicles only	Anywhere
12.Badgers Act 1973, s 10	Evidence of offences under the Act	Persons and vehicles	Anywhere
13.Wildlife and Countryside Act 1981, s 19	Evidence of wildlife offences	Persons and vehicles	Anywhere except dwellings
Other			
14.Prevention of Terrorism (Temporary Provisions) Act 1989, s 15 (3)	Evidence of liability to arrest under s 14 of the Act	Persons and vehicles	Anywhere

(B) CODE OF PRACTICE FOR THE SEARCHING OF PREMISES BY POLICE OFFICERS AND THE SEIZURE OF PROPERTY FOUND BY POLICE OFFICERS ON PERSONS OR PREMISES

1. General

1.1 This code of practice must be readily available at all police stations for consultation by police officers, detained persons and members of the public.

1.2 The notes for guidance included are not provisions of this code, but are guidance to police officers and others about its application and interpretation.

1.3 This code applies to the following searches of premises:

(a)   searches of premises undertaken for the purposes of an investigation into an alleged offence, with the occupier's consent, other than routine scenes of crime searches and searches following the activation of fire or burglar alarms or bomb threat calls;

(b)   searches of premises under powers conferred by sections 17, 18 and 32 of the Police and Criminal Evidence Act 1984;

(c)   searches of premises undertaken in pursuance of a search warrant issued in accordance with section 15 of, or Schedule 1 to, that Act, or Schedule 7 to the Prevention of Terrorism (Temporary Provisions) Act 1989.

'Premises' for the purpose of this code is defined in section 23 of the Police and Criminal Evidence Act 1984. It includes any place and, in particular, any vehicle, vessel, aircraft, hovercraft, tent or movable structure. It also includes any offshore installation as defined in section 1 of the Mineral Workings (Offshore Installations) Act 1971.

2. Search warrants and production orders

a) Action to be taken before an application is made

2.1 Where information is received which appears to justify an application, the officer concerned must take reasonable steps to check that the information is accurate, recent and has not been provided maliciously or irresponsibly. An application may not be made on the basis of information from an anonymous source where corroboration has not been sought.

2.2 The officer shall ascertain as specifically as is possible in the circumstances the nature of the articles concerned and their location.

2.3 The officer shall also make reasonable enquiries to establish what, if anything, is known about the likely occupier of the premises and the nature of the premises themselves; and whether they have been previously searched and if so how recently; and to obtain any other information relevant to the application.

2.4 No application for a search warrant may be made without the authority of an officer of at least the rank of inspector (or, in a case of urgency where no officer of this rank is readily available, the senior officer on duty). No application for a production order or warrant under Schedule 1 to the Police and Criminal Evidence Act 1984, or under Schedule 7 to the Prevention of Terrorism (Temporary Provisions) Act 1989, may be made without the authority of an officer of at least the rank of superintendent.

2.5 Except in a case of urgency, if there is reason to believe that a search might have an adverse effect on relations between the police and the community then the local police community liaison officer shall be consulted before it takes place. In urgent cases, the local police community liaison officer should be informed of the search as soon as practicable after it has been made [See Note 2B].

b) Making an application

2.6 An application for a search warrant must be supported by an information in writing, stating:
(i)   the enactment under which the application is made;
(ii)   as specifically as is reasonably practicable the premises to be searched and the object of the search; and
(iii)   the grounds on which the application is made (including, where the purpose of the proposed search is to find evidence of an alleged offence, an indication of how the evidence relates to the investigation).

2.7 An application for a search warrant under paragraph 12(*a*) of Schedule 1 to the Police and Criminal Evidence Act 1984, or under Schedule 7 to the Prevention of Terrorism (Temporary Provisions) Act 1989, shall also, where appropriate, indicate why it is believed that service of notice of an application for a production order may seriously prejudice the investigation.

2.8 If an application is refused, no further application may be made for a warrant to search those premises unless supported by additional grounds.

The Notes for Guidance under this section state:

2A The identity of an informant need not be discussed when making an application but the officer concerned should be prepared to deal with any questions the magistrate or judge may have about the accuracy of pervious information provided by that source or other related matters.

2B The local police/community consultative group, where it exists, or its equivalent, should be informed as soon as practicable after a search has taken place where there is reason to believe that it might have had an adverse effect on relations between the police and the community.

3. Entry without warrant

a) Making an arrest etc

3.1 The conditions under which an officer may enter and search premises without a warrant are set out in section 17 of the Police and Criminal Evidence Act 1984.

b) Search after arrest of premises in which arrest takes place or in which the arrested person was present immediately prior to arrest

3.2 The powers of an officer to search premises in which he has arrested a person or where the person was immediately before he was arrested are as set out in section 32 of the Police and Criminal Evidence Act 1984.

c) Search after arrest of premises other than those in which arrest takes place

3.3 The specific powers of an officer to search premises occupied or controlled by a person who has been arrested for an arrestable offence are as set out in section 18 of the Police and Criminal Evidence Act 1984. They may not (unless subsection 5 of section 18 applies) be exercised unless an officer of the rank of inspector or above has given authority in writing. That authority should (unless wholly impracticable) be given on the Notice of Powers and Rights (see paragraph 5.7(i)). The record of the search required by section 18(7) of the Act shall be made in the custody record, where there is one.

4. Search with consent

4.1 Subject to paragraph 4.4 below, if it is proposed to search premises with the consent of a person entitled to grant entry to the premises the consent must, if practicable, be given in writing on the Notice of Powers and Rights before the search takes place. The officer must make enquiries to satisfy himself that the person is in a position to give such consent. [See Note 4B and paragraph 5.7(i).]

4.2 Before seeking consent the officer in charge of the search shall state the purpose of the proposed search and inform the person concerned that he is not obliged to consent and that anything seized may be produced in evidence. If at the time the person is not suspected of an offence, the officer shall tell him so when stating the purpose of the search.

4.3 An officer cannot enter and search premises or continue to search premises under 4.1 above if the consent has been given under duress or is withdrawn before the search is completed.

4.4 It is unnecessary to seek consent under paragraphs 4.1 and 4.2 above where in the circumstances this would cause disproportionate inconvenience to the person concerned [See Note 4C.]

The Notes for Guidance under this section state:

4A In the case of a lodging house or similar accommodation a search should not be made on the basis solely of the landlord's consent unless the tenant is unavailable and the matter is urgent.

4B Where it is intended to search premises under the authority of a warrant or a power of entry and search without warrant, and the co-operation of the occupier of the premises is obtained in accordance with paragraph 5.4 below, there is no additional requirement to obtain written consent as at paragraph 4.1 above.

4C Paragraph 4.4 is intended in particular to apply, for example, to circumstances where police have arrested someone in the night after a pursuit and it is necessary to make a brief check of gardens along the route of the pursuit to see whether stolen or incriminating articles have been discarded.

5. Searching of premises: general considerations

a) Time of searches

5.1 Searches made under warrant must be made within one calendar month from the date of issue of the warrant.

5.2 Searches must be made at a reasonable hour unless this might frustrate the purpose of the search. [See Note 5A.]

5.3 A warrant authorises an entry on one occasion only.

b) Entry other than with consent

5.4 The officer in charge shall first attempt to communicate with the occupier or any other person entitled to grant access to the premises by explaining the authority under which he seeks entry to the premises and ask the occupier to allow him to do so, unless:

(i)   the premises to be searched are known to be unoccupied;

(ii)   the occupier and any other person entitled to grant access are known to be absent; or

(iii)   there are reasonable grounds for believing that to alert the occupier or any other person entitled to grant access by attempting to communicate with him would frustrate the object of the search or endanger the officers concerned or other persons.

5.5 Where the premises are occupied the officer shall identify himself (by warrant number in the case of inquiries linked to the investigation of terrorism) and, if not in uniform, show his warrant card (but in so doing in the case of enquiries linked to the investigation of terrorism, the officer need not reveal his name); and state the purpose of the search and the grounds for undertaking it, before a search begins, unless sub-paragraph 5.4(iii) applies.

5.6 Reasonable force may be used if necessary to enter premises if the officer in charge is satisfied that the premises are those specified in any warrant, or in exercise of the powers described in 3.1 to 3.3 above, and where:

(i)   the occupier or any other person entitled to grant access has refused a request to allow entry to his premises;

(ii)   it is impossible to communicate with the occupier or any other person entitled to grant access; or

(iii)   any of the provisions of 5.4(i) to (iii) apply.

c) Notice of powers and rights

5.7 If an officer conducts a search to which this code applies he shall, unless it is impracticable to do so, provide the occupier with a copy of a notice in a standard format:

(i)   specifying whether the search is made under warrant, or with consent, or in the exercise of the powers described in 3.1 to 3.3 above (the format of the notice shall provide for authority or consent to be indicated where appropriate – see 3.3 and 4.1 above);

(ii)   summarising the extent of the powers of search and seizure conferred in the Act;

(iii)   explaining the rights of the occupier, and of the owner of property seized in accordance with the provisions of 6.1 to 6.5 below, set out in the Act and in this code;

(iv)   explaining that compensation may be payable in appropriate cases for damage caused in entering and searching premises, and giving the address to which an application for compensation should be directed; and

(v)   stating that a copy of this code is available to be consulted at any police station.

5.8 If the occupier is present, copies of the notice mentioned above, and of the warrant (if the search is made under warrant) should if practicable be given to the occupier before the search begins, unless the officer in charge of the search reasonably believes that to do so would frustrate the object of the search or endanger the officers concerned or other persons. If the occupier is not present, copies of the notice, and of the warrant where appropriate, should be left in a prominent place on the premises or appropriate part of the premises and endorsed with the name of the officer in charge of the search (except in the case of enquiries linked to the investigation of terrorism, in which case the officer's warrant number should be given), the name of the police station to which he is attached and the date and time of the search. The warrant itself should be endorsed to show that this has been done.

d) Conduct of searches

5.9 Premises may be searched only to the extent necessary to achieve the object of the search, having regard to the size and nature of whatever is sought. A search under warrant may not continue under the authority of that warrant once all the things specified in it have been found, or the officer in charge of the search is satisfied that they are not on the premises.

5.10 Searches must be conducted with due consideration for the property and privacy of the occupier of the premises searched, and with no more disturbance than necessary. Reasonable force may be used only where this is necessary because the co-operation of the occupier cannot be obtained or is insufficient for the purpose.

5.11 If the occupier wishes to ask a friend, neighbour or other person to witness the search then he must be allowed to do so, unless the officer in charge has reasonable grounds for believing that this would seriously hinder the investigation. A search need not be unreasonably delayed for this purpose.

e) Leaving premises

5.12 If premises have been entered by force the officer in charge shall, before leaving them, satisfy himself that they are secure either by arranging for the occupier or his agent to be present or by any other appropriate means.

f) Search under Schedule 1 to the Police and Criminal Evidence Act 1984

5.13 An officer of the rank of inspector or above shall take charge of and be present at any search made under a warrant issued under Schedule 1 to the Police and Criminal Evidence Act 1984 or under Schedule 7 to the Prevention of Terrorism (Temporary Provisions) Act 1989. He is responsible for ensuring that the search is conducted with discretion and in such a manner as to cause the least possible disruption to any business or other activities carried on in the premises.

5.14 After satisfying himself that material may not be taken from the premises without his knowledge, the officer in charge of the search shall ask for the documents or other records concerned to be produced. He may also, if he considers it to be necessary, ask to see the index to files held on the premises, if there is one; and the officers conducting the search may inspect any files which, according to the index, appear to contain any of the material sought. A more extensive search of the premises may be made only if the person responsible for them refuses to produce the material sought, or to allow access to the index; if it appears that the index is inaccurate or incomplete; or if for any other reason the officer in charge has reasonable grounds for believing that such a search is necessary in order to find the material sought. [See Note 5B].

The Notes for Guidance under this section state:

5A In determining at what time to make a search, the officer in charge should have regard, among other considerations, to the times of day at which the occupier of the premises is likely to be present, and should not search at a time when he, or any other person on the premises, is likely to be asleep unless not doing so is likely to frustrate the purpose of the search.

5B In asking for documents to be produced in accordance with paragraph 5.14 above, officers should direct the request to a person in authority and with responsibility for the documents.

5C If the wrong premises are searched by mistake, everything possible should be done at the earliest opportunity to allay ay sense of grievance. In appropriate cases assistance should be given to obtain compensation.

6. Seizure and retention of property

a) Seizure

6.1 Subject to paragraph 6.2 below, an officer who is searching any premises under any statutory power or with the consent of the occupier may seize:

(a)   anything covered by a warrant; and

(*b*)   anything which he has reasonable grounds for believing is evidence of an offence or has been obtained in consequence of the commission of an offence.

Items under (b) may only be seized where this is necessary to prevent their concealment, alteration, loss, damage or destruction.

6.2 No item may be seized which is subject to legal privilege (as defined in section 10 of the Police and Criminal Evidence Act 1984).

6.3 An officer who decides that it is not appropriate to seize property because of an explanation given by the person holding it, but who has reasonable grounds for believing that it has been obtained in consequence of the commission of an offence by some person, shall inform the holder of his suspicions and shall explain that, if he disposes of the property, he may be liable to civil or criminal proceedings.

6.4 An officer may photograph or copy, or have photographed or copied, any document or other article which he has power to seize in accordance with paragraph 6.1 above.

6.5 Where an officer considers that a computer may contain information that could be used in evidence, he may require the information to be produced in a form that can be taken away and in which it is visible and legible.

b) Retention

6.6 Subject to paragraph 6.7 below, anything which has been seized in accordance with the above provisions may be retained only for as long as is necessary in the circumstances. It may be retained, among other purposes:

(i)   for use as evidence at a trial for an offence;
(ii)   for forensic examination or for other investigation in connection with an offence; or
(iii)   where there are reasonable grounds for believing that it has been stolen or obtained by the commission of an offence, in order to establish its lawful owner.

6.7 Property shall not be retained in accordance with 6.6(i) and (ii) (ie for use as evidence or for the purposes of investigation) if a photograph or copy would suffice for those purposes.

c) Rights of owners etc

6.8 If property is retained the person who had custody or control of it immediately prior to its seizure must on request be provided with a list or description of the property within a reasonable time.

6.9 He or his representative must be allowed supervised access to the property to examine it or have it photographed or copied, or must be provided with a photograph or copy, in either case within a reasonable time of any request and at his own expense, unless the officer in charge of an investigation has reasonable grounds for believing that this would prejudice the investigation of an offence or any criminal proceedings. In this case a record on the grounds must be made.

The Note for Guidance for this section states:

6A Any person claiming property seized by the police may apply to a magistrates' court under the Police (Property) Act 1897 for its possession, and should, where appropriate, be advised of this procedure.

7. Action to be taken after searches

7.1 Where premises have been searched in circumstances to which this code applies, other than in the circumstances covered by paragraph 4.4 above, the officer in charge of the search shall, on arrival at a police station, make or have made a record of the search. The record shall include:

(i)   the address of the premises searched;

(ii)   the date, time and duration of the search;

(iii)   the authority under which the search was made. Where the search was made in the exercise of a statutory power to search premises without warrant, the record shall include the power under which the search was made; and where the search was made under warrant, or with written consent, a copy of the warrant or consent shall be appended to the record or kept in a place identified in the record;

(iv)   the names of all the officers who conducted the search (except in the case of enquiries linked to the investigation of terrorism, in which case the record shall state the warrant number and duty station of each officer concerned);

(v)   the names of any persons on the premises if they are known;

(vi)   either a list of any articles seized or a note of where such a list is kept and, if not covered by a warrant, the reason for their seizure;

(vii)   whether force was used, and, if so, the reason why it was used;

(viii)   details of any damage caused during the search, and the circumstances in which it was caused.

7.2 Where premises have been searched under warrant, the warrant shall be endorsed to show:

(i)   whether any articles specified in the warrant were found;

(ii)   whether any other articles were seized;

(iii)   the date and time at which it was executed;

(iv)   the names of the officers who executed it (except in the case of enquiries linked to the investigation of terrorism, in which case the warrant number and duty station of each officer concerned shall be shown);

(v)   whether a copy, together with a copy of the notice of powers and rights was handed to the occupier; or whether it was endorsed as required by paragraph 5.8, and left on the premises together with the copy notice and, if so, where.

7.3 Any warrant which has been executed or which has not been executed within one calendar month of its issue shall be returned, if it was issued by a justice of the peace, to the clerk to the justices for the petty sessions area concerned or, if issued by a judge, to the appropriate officer of the court from which he issued it.

8. Search registers

8.1 A search register shall be maintained at each sub-divisional police station. All records which are required to be made by this code shall be made, copied, or referred to in the register.

(C) CODE OF PRACTICE FOR THE DETENTION, TREATMENT AND QUESTIONING OF PERSONS BY POLICE OFFICERS

1. *General*

1.1 All persons in custody must be dealt with expeditiously, and released as soon as the need for detention has ceased to apply.

1.2 This code of practice must be readily available at all police stations for consultation by police officers, detained persons and members of the public.

1.3 The notes for guidance included are not provisions of this code, but are guidance to police officers and others about its application and interpretation. Provisions in the annexes to this code are provisions of this code.

1.4 If an officer has any suspicion, or is told in good faith, that a person of any age may be mentally disordered or mentally handicapped, or mentally incapable of understanding the significance of questions put to him or his replies, then that person shall be treated as a mentally disordered or mentally handicapped person for the purposes of this code. [See Note 1G.]

1.5 If anyone appears to be under the age of 17 then he shall be treated as a juvenile for the purposes of this code in the absence of clear evidence to show that he is older.

1.6 If a person appears to be blind or seriously visually handicapped, deaf, unable to read, unable to speak or has difficulty orally because of a speech impediment, he should be treated as such for the purposes of this code in the absence of clear evidence to the contrary.

1.7 In this code 'the appropriate adult' means:

(*a*)   in the case of a juvenile:

    (i)   his parent or guardian (or, if he is in care, the care authority or voluntary organisation);

    (ii)   a social worker; or

    (iii) failing either of the above, another responsible adult aged 18 or over who is not a police officer or employed by the police.

(*b*)   in the case of a person who is mentally disordered or mentally handicapped;

    (i)   a relative, guardian or other person responsible for his care or custody;

    (ii)   someone who has experience of dealing with mentally disordered or mentally handicapped persons but is not a police officer or employed by the police (such as an approved social worker as defined by the Mental Health Act 1983 or a specialist social worker); or

    (iii) failing either of the above, some other responsible adult aged 18 or over who is not a police officer or employed by the police. [See note 1E.]

1.8 Whenever this code requires a person to be given certain information he does not have to be given it if he is incapable at the time of understanding what is said to him or is violent or likely to become violent or is in urgent need of medical attention, but he must be given it as soon as practicable.

1.9 Any reference to a custody officer in this code includes an officer who is performing the functions of a custody officer.

1.10 This code applies to persons who are in custody at police stations whether or not they have been arrested for an offence and to those who have been removed to a police station as a place of safety under sections 135 and 136 of the Mental Health Act 1983. Section 15, however, applies solely to persons in police detention.

1.11 Persons in police detention include persons taken to a police station after being arrested under section 14 of the Prevention of Terrorism (Temporary Provisions) Act 1989 or under paragraph 6 of Schedule 5 to that Act by an examining officer who is a constable.

The Notes for Guidance for this section state:

1A Although certain sections of this code (eg section 9–treatment of detained persons) apply specifically to persons in custody at police stations, those there voluntarily to assist with an investigation should be treated with no less consideration (eg offered refreshments at appropriate times) and enjoy an absolute right to obtain legal advice or communicate with anyone outside the police station.

1B This code does not affect the principle that all citizens have a duty to help police officers to prevent crime and discover offenders. This is a civic rather than a legal duty; but when a police officer is trying to discover whether, or by whom, an offence has been committed he is entitled to question any person from whom he thinks useful information can be obtained, subject to restrictions imposed by this code. A person's declaration that he is unwilling to reply does not alter this entitlement.

1C The parent or guardian of a juvenile should be the appropriate adult unless he is suspected of involvement in the offence, is the victim, is a witness, is involved in the investigation or has received admissions. In such circumstances it will be desirable for the appropriate adult to be some other person. If the parent of a juvenile is estranged from the juvenile, he should not be asked to act as the appropriate adult if the juvenile expressly and specifically objects to his presence.

1D If a child in care admits an offence to a social worker, another social worker should be the appropriate adult in the interest of fairness.

1E In the case of persons who are mentally disordered or mentally handicapped, it may in certain circumstances be more satisfactory for all concerned if the appropriate adult is someone who has experience or training in their care rather than a relative lacking such qualifications. But if the person himself prefers a relative to a better qualified stranger his wishes should if practicable be respected.

1F A solicitor who is present at the station in a professional capacity may not act as the appropriate adult.

1G The generic term 'mental disorder' is used throughout this code. Mental disorder is defined by the Mental Health Act 1983 as mental illness, arrested or incomplete development of mind, psychopathic disorder and any other disorder or disability of mind. It should be noted that 'mental disorder' is different to 'mental handicap' although the two forms of disorder are dealt with similarly throughout this code.

2. Custody records

2.1 A separate custody record must be opened as soon as practicable for each person who is brought to a police station under arrest or is arrested at the police station having attended there voluntarily. All information which has to be recorded under this code must be recorded as soon as practicable, in the custody record unless otherwise specified.

2.2 In the case of any action requiring the authority of an officer of a specified rank, his name and rank must be noted in the custody record. The recording of names does not apply to officers dealing with persons detained under the Prevention of Terrorism (Temporary Provisions) Act 1989. Instead the record shall state the warrant number and duty station of such officers.

2.3 The custody officer is responsible for the accuracy and completeness of the custody record and for ensuring that the record or a copy of the record accompanies a detained person if he is transferred to another police station. The record shall show the time of and reason for transfer and the time a person is released from detention.

2.4 When a person leaves police detention or is taken before a court he or his legal representative or his appropriate adult shall be supplied on request with a copy of the custody record as soon as practicable. This entitlement lasts for 12 months after his release.

2.5 The person who has been detained, the appropriate adult, or legal representative who gives reasonable notice of a request to inspect the original custody record after the person has left police detention should be allowed to do so. A note of any such inspection should be made in the custody record.

2.6 All entries in custody records must be timed and signed by the maker. In the case of a record entered on a computer this should be timed and contain the operator's identification. Warrant numbers should be used rather than names in the case of detention under the Prevention of Terrorism (Temporary Provisions) Act 1989.

2.7 The fact and time of any refusal by a person to sign a custody record when asked to do so in accordance with the provisions of this code must itself be recorded.

3. Initial action

a) Detained persons: normal procedure

3.1 When a person is brought to a police station under arrest or is arrested at the police station having attended there voluntarily the custody officer must inform him clearly of the following rights and of the fact that they are continuing rights which may be exercised at any stage during the period in custody.

(i)   the right to have someone informed of his arrest in accordance with section 5 below;

(ii)   the right to consult privately with a solicitor in accordance with section 6 below, and the fact that independent legal advice is available free of charge; and

(iii)   the right to consult this and the other codes of practices. [See Note 3E]

3.2 The custody officer must give the person a written notice setting out the above three rights, the right to a copy of the custody record in accordance with paragraph 2.4 above and the caution in the terms prescribed in section 10 below. The notice must also explain the arrangements for obtaining legal advice. The custody officer must also give the person an additional written notice briefly setting out his entitlements while in custody. [See Notes 3A and 3B.] The custody officer shall ask the person to sign the custody record to acknowledge receipt of these notices and any refusal to sign must be recorded on the custody record.

3.3 A citizen of an independent Commonwealth country or a national of a foreign country (including the Republic of Ireland) must be informed as soon as practicable of his rights of communication with his High Commission, Embassy or Consulate (see Section 7).

3.4 If the custody officer authorises a person's detention he must inform him of the grounds as soon as practicable and in any case before that person is then questioned about any offence.

3.5 The person shall be asked to sign on the custody record to signify whether or not he wants legal advice at this point. The custody officer is responsible for ensuring that the person signs the custody record in the correct place to give effect to his decision. Where legal advice is requested (and unless Annex B applies) the custody officer must act without delay to secure the provision of such advice to the person concerned.

b) Detained persons: special groups

3.6 If the person appears to be *deaf* or there is doubt about his *hearing* or speaking ability or ability to understand English, and the custody officer cannot establish effective communication, the custody officer must as soon as practicable call an interpreter and ask him to provide the information required above. [See Section 13].

3.7 If the person is a juvenile, the custody officer must, if it is practicable, ascertain the identity of a person responsible for his welfare. That person may be his parent or guardian (or, if he is in care, the care authority or voluntary organisation) or any other person who has, for the time being, assumed responsibility for his welfare. That person must be informed as soon as practicable that the juvenile has been arrested, why he has been arrested and where he is detained. This right is in addition to the juvenile's right in section 5 of the code not to be held incommunicado [see Note 3C].

3.8 In the case of a juvenile who is known to be subject to a supervision order, reasonable steps must also be taken to notify the person supervising him.

3.9 If the person is a juvenile, is mentally handicapped or is suffering from a mental disorder, then the custody officer must, as soon as practicable, inform the appropriate adult (who in the case of a juvenile may or may not be a person responsible for his welfare, in accordance with paragraph 3.7 above) of the grounds for his detention and his whereabouts, and ask the adult to come to the police station to see the person.

3.10 It is imperative that a mentally disordered or mentally handicapped person who has been detained under section 136 of the Mental Health Act 1983 should be assessed as soon as possible. If that assessment is to take place at the police station, an approved social worker and a registered medical practitioner should be called to the police station as soon as possible in order to interview and examine the person. Once the person has been interviewed and examined and suitable arrangements have been made for his treatment or care, he can no longer be detained under section 136. The person should not be released until he has been seen by both the approved social worker and the registered medical practitioner.

3.11 If the appropriate adult is already at the police station when information is given to the person as required in paragraphs 3.1 to 3.4 above then the information must be given to the detained person in his presence. If the appropriate adult is not at the police station when the information is given then the information must be given to the detained person again in the presence of the appropriate adult once that person arrives.

3.12 The person should be advised by the custody officer that the appropriate adult (where applicable) is there to assist and advise him and that he can consult privately with the appropriate adult at any time.

3.13 If, having been informed of the right to legal advice under paragraph 3.11 above, the appropriate adult considers that legal advice should be taken, then the provisions of section 6 of this code apply. [See Note 3G.]

3.14 If the person is blind or seriously visually handicapped or is unable to read, the custody officer should ensure that his solicitor, relative, the appropriate adult or some other person likely to take an interest in him (and not involved in the investigation) is available to help in checking any documentation. Where this code requires written consent or signification, then the person who is assisting may be asked to sign instead if the detained person so wishes. [See Note 3F.]

c) Persons attending a police station voluntarily

3.15 Any person attending a police station voluntarily for the purpose of assisting with an investigation may leave at will unless placed under arrest. If it is decided that he should not be allowed to do so then he must be informed at once that he is under arrest and brought before the custody officer, who is responsible for ensuring that he is notified of his rights in the same way as other detained persons. If he is not placed under arrest but is cautioned in accordance with section 10 below, the officer who gives the caution must at the same time inform him that he is not under arrest, that he is not obliged to remain at the police station but that if he remains at the police station he may obtain free legal advice if he wishes.

3.16 If a person who is attending the police station voluntarily (in accordance with paragraph 3.15) asks about his entitlement to legal advice, he should be given a copy of the notice explaining the arrangements for obtaining legal advice. (See paragraph 3.2).

d) Documentation

3.17 The grounds for a person's detention shall be recorded, in his presence if practicable.

3.18 Action taken under paragraphs 3.6 to 3.14 shall be recorded.

The Notes for Guidance for this section state:

3A the notice of entitlements is intended to provide detained persons with brief details of their entitlements over and above the statutory rights which are set out in the notice of rights. The notice of entitlements should list the entitlements contained in this code, including visits and contact with outside parties (including special provisions for Commonwealth citizens and foreign nationals), reasonable standards of physical comfort, adequate food and drink, access to toilets and washing facilities, clothing, medical attention, and exercise where practicable. It should also mention the provisions relating to the conduct of interviews, the circumstances in which an appropriate adult should be available to assist the detained person and his statutory rights to make representation whenever the period of his detention is reviewed.

3B In addition to the notices in English, translations in Welsh, the main ethnic minority languages and the principal EC language should be available whenever they are likely to be helpful.

3C If the juvenile is in the care of a local authority or voluntary organisation but is living with his parents or other adults responsible for his welfare then, although there is no legal obligation on the police to inform them, they as well as the authority or organisation should normally be contacted unless suspected of involvement in the offence concerned. Even if a juvenile in care is not living with his parents, consideration should be given to informing them as well.

3D Most local authority Social Services Departments can supply a list of interpreters who have the necessary skills and experience to interpret for the deaf at police interviews. The local Community Relations Council may be able to provide similar information in cases where the person concerned does not understand English [See section 13].

3E The right to consult the codes of practice under paragraph 3.1 above does not entitle the person concerned to delay unreasonably any necessary investigative or administrative action while he does so. Procedures requiring the provision of breath, blood or urine specimens under the terms of the Road Traffic Act 1988 need not be delayed.

3F Blind or seriously visually handicapped persons may be unwilling to sign police documents. The alternative of their representative signing on their behalf seeks to protect the interests of both police and suspects.

3G The purpose of paragraph 3.13 is to protect the rights of a juvenile, mentally disordered or mentally handicapped person who may not understand the significance of what is being said to him. If such a person wishes to exercise the right to legal advice the appropriate action should be taken straightaway and not delayed until the appropriate adult arrives.

4. Detained persons' property

a) Action

4.1 The custody officer is responsible for:

(*a*)   ascertaining:

(i)   what property a detained person has with him when he comes to the police station (whether on arrest, re-detention on answering to bail, commitment to prison custody on the order or sentence of a court, lodgement at the police station with a view to his production in court from such custody, arrival at a police station on transfer from detention at another station or from hospital or on detention under section 135 or 136 of the Mental Health Act 1983);

(ii)   what property he might have acquired for an unlawful or harmful purpose while in custody.

(*b*)   the safekeeping of any property which is taken from him and which remains at the police station.

To these ends the custody officer may search him or authorise his being searched to the extent that he considers necessary (provided that a search of intimate parts of the body or involving the removal of more than outer clothing may only be made in accordance with Annex A to this code). A search may only be carried out by an officer of the same sex as the person searched. [See Note 4A.]

4.2   A detained person may retain clothing and personal effects at his own risk unless the custody officer considers that he may use them to cause harm to himself or others, interfere with evidence, damage property or effect an escape or they are needed as evidence. In this event the custody officer may withhold such articles as he considers necessary. If he does so he must tell the person why.

4.3   Personal effects are those items which a person may lawfully need or use or refer to while in detention but do not include cash and other items of value.

b) Documentation

4.4   The custody officer is responsible for recording all property brought to the police station that a detained person had with him, or had taken from him on arrest. The detained person shall be allowed to check and sign the record of property as correct. Any refusal to sign should be recorded.

4.5   If a detained person is not allowed to keep any article of clothing or personal effects the reason must be recorded.

The Notes for Guidance to this section state:

4A   Section 54(1) of PACE and paragraph 4.1 require a detained person to be searched where it is clear that the custody officer will have continuing duties in relation to that person or where that person's behaviour or offence makes an inventory appropriate. They do not require *every* detained person to be searched. Where, for example, it is clear that a person will only be detained for a short period and is not to be placed in a cell, the custody officer may decide not to search him. In such a case the custody record will be endorsed 'not searched', paragraph 4.4 will not apply, and the person will be invited to sign the entry. Where the person detained refuses to sign, the custody officer will be obliged to ascertain what property he has on him in accordance with paragraph 4.1.

4B   Paragraph 4.4 does not require the custody officer to record on the custody record property in the possession of the person on arrest, if by virtue of its nature, quantity or size, it is not practicable to remove it to the police station.

4C   Paragraph 4.4 above is not to be taken as requiring that items of clothing worn by the person be recorded unless withheld by the custody officer in accordance with paragraph 4.2.

5. Right not to be held incommunicado

a) Action

5.1 Any person arrested and held in custody at a police station or other premises may on request have one person known to him or who is likely to take an interest in his welfare informed at public expense as soon as practicable of his whereabouts. If the person cannot be contacted the person who has made the request may choose up to two alternatives. If they too cannot be contacted the person in charge of detention or of the investigation has discretion to allow further attempts until the information has been conveyed. [See Notes 5C and 5D.]

5.2 The exercise of the above right in respect of each of the persons nominated may be delayed only in accordance with Annex B to this code.

5.3 The above right may be exercised on each occasion that a person is taken to another police station.

5.4 The person may receive visits at the custody officer's discretion. [See Note 5B.]

5.5 Where an enquiry as to the whereabouts of the person is made by a friend, relative or person with an interest in his welfare, this information shall be given, if he agrees and if Annex B does not apply. [See Note 5D.]

5.6 Subject to the following condition, the person should be supplied with writing materials on request and allowed to speak on the telephone for a reasonable time to one person [see Note 5E]. Where an officer of the rank of inspector or above considers that the sending of a letter or the making of a telephone call may result in:

(*a*) any of the consequences set out in the first and second paragraphs of Annex B and the person is detained in connection with an arrestable or a serious arrestable offence; or

(*b*) either of the consequences set out in paragraph 8 of Annex B and the person is detained under the Prevention of Terrorism (Temporary Provisions) Act 1989,

that officer can deny or delay the exercise of either or both these privileges. However, nothing in this section permits the restriction or denial of the rights set out in sections 5.1 and 6.1.

5.7 Before any letter or message is sent, or telephone call made, the person shall be informed that what he says in any letter, call or message (other than in the case of a communication to a solicitor) may be read or listened to as appropriate and may be given in evidence. A telephone call may be terminated if it is being abused. The costs can be at public expense at the discretion of the custody officer.

b) Documentation

5.8 A record must be kept of:

(*a*) any request made under this section and the action taken on it;

(*b*) any letters, messages or telephone calls made or received or visits received;

and

(*c*)   any refusal on the part of the person to have information about himself or his whereabouts given to an outside enquirer. The person must be asked to countersign the record accordingly and any refusal to sign should be recorded.

The Notes for Guidance for this section state:

5A An interpreter may make a telephone call or write a letter on a person's behalf.

5B In the exercise of his discretion the custody officer should allow visits where possible in the light of the availability of sufficient manpower to supervise a visit and any possible hindrance to the investigation.

5C If the person does not know of anyone to contact for advice or support or cannot contact a friend or relative, the custody officer should bear in mind any local voluntary bodies or other organisations who might be able to offer help in such cases. But if it is specifically legal advice that is wanted, then paragraph 6.1 below will apply.

5D In some circumstances it may not be appropriate to use the telephone to disclose information under paragraphs 5.1 and 5.5 above.

5E The telephone call at paragraph 5.6 is in addition to any communication under paragraphs 5.1 and 6.1.

6. Right to legal advice

a) Action

6.1 Subject to paragraph 6.2, any person may at any time consult and communicate privately, whether in person, in writing or on the telephone with a solicitor. [See Note 6B.]

6.2 The exercise of the above right may be delayed only in accordance with Annex B to this code. Whenever legal advice is requested (and unless Annex B applies) the custody officer must act without delay to secure the provision of such advice to the person concerned.

6.3 A poster advertising the right to have legal advice must be prominently displayed in the charging area of every police station. [See Note 6H.]

6.4 No attempt should be made to dissuade the suspect from obtaining legal advice.

6.5 Reminders of the right to free legal advice must be given in accordance with paragraphs 11.2, 15.3 and paragraphs 2.5(ii) and 5.2 of code of practice D.

6.6 A person who wants legal advice may not be interviewed or continue to be interviewed until he has received it unless:

(*a*)   Annex B applies; or
(*b*)   an officer of the rank of superintendent or above has reasonable grounds for believing that:

   (i)   delay will involve an immediate risk of harm to persons or serious loss of, or damage to, property; or
   (ii)   where a solicitor, including a duty solicitor, has been contacted and has agreed to attend, awaiting his arrival would cause unreasonable delay to the process of investigation; or

(*c*)   the solicitor nominated by the person, or selected by him from a list:

(i)   cannot be contacted; or

(ii)   has previously indicated that he does not wish to be contacted; or

(iii)   having been contacted, has declined to attend;

and the person has been advised of the Duty Solicitor Scheme (where one is in operation) but has declined to ask for the duty solicitor, or the duty solicitor is unavailable. (In these circumstances the interview may be started or continued without further delay provided that an officer of the rank of inspector or above has given agreement for the interview to proceed in those circumstances - see Note 6B.)

(*d*)   the person who wanted legal advice changes his mind. In these circumstances the interview may be started or continued without further delay provided that the person has given his agreement in writing or on tape to being interviewed without receiving legal advice and that an officer of the rank of inspector or above has given agreement for the interview to proceed in those circumstances.

6.7   Where 6.6(*b*)(i) applies, once sufficient information to avert the risk has been obtained, questioning must cease until the person has received legal advice or 6.6(*a*), (*b*)(ii), (*c*) or (*d*) apply.

6.8   Where a person has been permitted to consult a solicitor and the solicitor is available (ie present at the station or on his way to the station or easily contactable by telephone) at the time the interview begins or is in progress, he must be allowed to have his solicitor present while he is interviewed.

6.9   The solicitor may only be required to leave the interview if his conduct is such that the investigating officer is unable properly to put questions to the suspect. [See Notes 6D and 6E.]

6.10   If the investigating officer considers that a solicitor is acting in such a way, he will stop the interview and consult an officer not below the rank of superintendent, if one is readily available, and otherwise an officer not below the rank of inspector who is not connected with the investigation. After speaking to the solicitor, the officer who has been consulted will decide whether or not the interview should continue in the presence of that solicitor. If he decides that it should not, the suspect will be given the opportunity to consult another solicitor before the interview continues and that solicitor will be given an opportunity to be present at the interview.

6.11   The removal of a solicitor from an interview is a serious step and, if it occurs, the officer of superintendent rank or above who took the decision will consider whether the incident should be reported to the Law Society. If the decision to remove the solicitor has been taken by an officer below the rank of superintendent, the facts must be reported to an officer of superintendent rank or above who will similarly consider whether a report to the Law Society would be appropriate. Where the solicitor concerned is a duty solicitor, the report should be both to the Law Society and to the Legal Aid Board.

6.12   In this code 'solicitor' means a solicitor qualified to practise in accordance with the Solicitors Act 1974. If a solicitor wishes to send a clerk or legal executive to provide advice on his behalf, then the clerk or legal executive shall be admitted to the police station for this purpose unless an officer of the rank of inspector or above considers that such a visit will hinder the investigation of crime and directs otherwise. Once admitted to the police station, the provisions of paragraphs 6.6 to 6.10 apply.

6.13 In exercising his discretion under paragraph 6.12, the officer should take into account in particular whether the identity and status of the clerk or legal executive have been satisfactorily established; whether he is of suitable character to provide legal advice (a person with a criminal record is unlikely to be suitable unless the conviction was for a minor offence and is not of recent date); and any other matters in any written letter of authorisation provided by the solicitor on whose behalf the clerk or legal executive is attending the police station. [See Note 6F.]

6.14 If the inspector refuses access to a clerk or legal executive or a decision is taken that such a person should not be permitted to remain at an interview he must forthwith notify the solicitor on whose behalf the clerk or legal executive was to have acted or was acting, and give him an opportunity of making alternative arrangements. The detained person must also be informed and the custody record noted.

6.15 If a solicitor arrives at the station to see a particular person, that person must (unless Annex B applies) be informed of the solicitor's arrival and asked whether he would like to see him. This applies even if the person concerned has already declined legal advice. The solicitor's attendance and the detained person's decision must be noted in the custody record.

b) Documentation

6.16 Any request for legal advice and the action taken on it shall be recorded.

6.17 If a person has asked for legal advice and an interview is begun in the absence of a solicitor or his representative (or the solicitor or his representative has been required to leave an interview), a record shall be made in the interview record.

The Notes for Guidance for this section state:

6A In considering whether paragraph 6.6(*b*) applies, the officer should where practicable ask the solicitor for an estimate of the time that he is likely to take in coming to the station, and relate this information to the time for which detention is permitted, the time of day (ie whether the period of rest required by paragraph 12.2 is imminent) and the requirements of other investigations in progress. If the solicitor says that he is on his way to the station or that he will set off immediately, it will not normally be appropriate to begin an interview before he arrives. If it appears that it will be necessary to begin an interview before the solicitor's arrival he should be given an indication of how long police would be able to wait before paragraph 6.6(*b*) applies so that he has an opportunity to make arrangements for legal advice to be provided by someone else.

6B A person who asks for legal advice should be given an opportunity to consult a specific solicitor (for example, his own solicitor or one known to him) or the duty solicitor where a Duty Solicitor Scheme is in operation. If advice is not available by these means, or he does not wish to consult the duty solicitor, the person should be given an opportunity to choose a solicitor from a list of those willing to provide legal advice. If his solicitor is unavailable, he may choose up to two alternatives. If these attempts to secure legal advice are unsuccessful, the custody officer has discretion to allow further attempts until a solicitor has been contacted and agrees to provide legal advice.

6C Procedures undertaken under section 7 of the Road Traffic Act 1988 do not constitute interviewing for the purposes of this code.

6D In considering whether paragraph 6.9 applies, a solicitor is not guilty of misconduct if he seeks to challenge an improper question to his client or the manner in which it is put or if he advises his client not to reply to particular questions or if he wishes to give his client further legal advice. It is the duty of a solicitor to look after the interests of his client and to advise him without obstructing the interview. He should not be required to leave an interview unless his interference with its conduct clearly goes beyond this. Examples of misconduct may include answering questions on the client's behalf, or providing written replies for the client to quote.

6E In a case where an officer takes the decision to exclude a solicitor, he must be in a position to satisfy the court that the decision was properly made. In order to do this he may need to witness what is happening himself.

6F If an officer of at least the rank of inspector considers that a particular solicitor or firm of solicitors is persistently sending as clerks or legal executives persons who are unsuited to provide legal advice, he should inform an officer of at least the rank of superintendent, who may wish to take the matter up with the Law Society.

6G Subject to the constraints of Annex B, a solicitor may advise more than one client in an investigation if he wishes. Any question of a conflict of interest is for the solicitor under his professional code of conduct. If, however, waiting for a solicitor to give advice to one client may lead to unreasonable delay to the interview with another, the provisions of paragraph 6.6(*b*) may apply.

6H In addition to the poster in English, a poster or posters containing translations in Welsh, the main ethnic minority languages and the principal EC languages should be displayed wherever they are likely to be helpful and it is practicable to do so.

7. *Citizens of independent Commonwealth countries or foreign nationals*

a) Action

7.1 A citizen of an independent Commonwealth country or a national of a foreign country (including the Republic of Ireland) may communicate at any time with his High Commission, Embassy or Consulate. He must be informed of this right as soon as practicable. He must also be informed as soon as practicable of his right to have his High Commission, Embassy or Consulate told of his whereabouts and the grounds for his detention.

7.2 If a citizen of an independent Commonwealth country or a national of a foreign country with which a consular convention is in force is detained, the appropriate High Commission, Embassy or Consulate shall be informed as soon as practicable, subject to paragraph 7.4 below. The countries to which this applies as at 20 April 1990 are listed in Annex F.

7.3 Consular officers may visit one of their nationals who is in police detention to talk to him and, if required, to arrange for legal advice. Such visits shall take place out of the hearing of a police officer.

7.4 Notwithstanding the provisions of consular conventions, where the person is a political refugee (whether for reasons of race, nationality, political opinion or religion) or is seeking political asylum, a consular officer shall not be informed of the arrest of one of his nationals or given access to or information about him except at the person's express request.

b) Documentation

7.5 A record shall be made when a person is informed of his rights under this section and of any communications with a High Commission, Embassy or Consulate.

The Note for Guidance for this section states:

7A The exercise of the rights in this section may not be interfered with even though Annex B applies.

8. *Conditions of detention*

a) Action

8.1 So far as is practicable, not more than one person shall be detained in each cell.

8.2 Cells in use must be adequately heated, cleaned and ventilated. They must be adequately lit, subject to such dimming as is compatible with safety and security to allow persons detained overnight to sleep. No additional restraints should be used within a locked cell unless absolutely necessary, and then only suitable handcuffs.

8.3 Blankets, mattresses, pillows and other bedding supplied should be of a reasonable standard and in a clean and sanitary condition. [See Note 8B.]

8.4 Access to toilet and washing facilities must be provided.

8.5 If it is necessary to remove a person's clothes for the purposes of investigation, for hygiene or health reasons or for cleaning, replacement clothing of a reasonable standard of comfort and cleanliness shall be provided. A person may not be interviewed unless adequate clothing has been offered to him.

8.6 At least two light meals and one main meal shall be offered in any period of 24 hours. Drinks should be provided at mealtimes and upon reasonable request between mealtimes. Whenever necessary, advice shall be sought from the police surgeon on medical or dietary matters. As far as practicable, meals provided shall offer a varied diet and meet any special dietary needs or religious beliefs that the person may have; he may also have meals supplied by his family or friends at his or their own expense. [See Note 8B.]

8.7 Brief outdoor exercise shall be offered daily if practicable.

8.8 A juvenile shall not be placed in a police cell unless no other secure accommodation is available and the custody officer considers that it is not practicable to supervise him if he is not placed in a cell. He may not be placed in a cell with a detained adult.

8.9 Reasonable force may be used if necessary for the following purposes:

(i)   to secure compliance with reasonable instructions, including instructions given in pursuance of the provisions of a code of practice; or

(ii) to prevent escape, injury, damage to property or the destruction of evidence.

8.10 Persons detained should be visited every hour, and those who are drunk, every half hour. [See Note 8A.]

b) Documentation

8.11 A record must be kept of replacement clothing and meals offered.

8.12 If a juvenile is placed in a cell, the reason must be recorded.

The Notes for Guidance for this section state:

8A Whenever possible juveniles and other persons at risk should be visited more regularly.

8B The provisions in paragraphs 8.3 and 8.6 respectively regarding bedding and a varied diet are of particular importance in the case of a person detained under the Prevention of Terrorism (Temporary Provisions) Act 1989. This is because such a person may well remain in custody for some time.

9. Treatment of detained persons

a) General

9.1 If a complaint is made by or on behalf of a detained person about his treatment since his arrest, or it comes to the notice of any officer that he may have been treated improperly, a report must be made as soon as practicable to an officer of the rank of inspector or above who is not connected with the investigation. If the matter concerns a possible assault or the possibility of the unnecessary or unreasonable use of force then the police surgeon must also be called as soon as practicable.

b) Medical treatment

9.2 The custody officer must immediately call the police surgeon (or, in urgent cases, send the person to hospital or call the nearest available medical practitioner) if a person brought to a police station or already detained there:

(*a*)   appears to be suffering from physical illness or a mental disorder; or

(*b*)   is injured; or

(*c*)   does not show signs of sensibility and awareness; or

(*d*)   fails to respond normally to questions or conversation (other than through drunkenness alone); or

(*e*)   otherwise appears to need medical attention.

This applies even if the person makes no request for medical attention and whether or not he had recently had medical treatment elsewhere (unless brought to the police station direct from hospital). It is not intended that the contents of this paragraph should delay the transfer of a person to a place of safety under section 136 of the Mental Health Act 1983 where that is applicable. Where an assessment under that Act is to take place at the police station, the custody officer has discretion not to call the police surgeon so long as he believes that the assessment by a registered medical practitioner can be undertaken without undue delay. [See Note 9A.]

9.3 If it appears to the custody officer, or he is told, that a person brought to the police station under arrest may be suffering from an infectious disease of any significance he must take steps to isolate the person and his property until he has obtained medical directions as to where the person should be taken, whether fumigation should take place and what precautions should be taken by officers who have been or will be in contact with him.

9.4 If a detained person requests a medical examination the police surgeon must be called as soon as practicable. He may in addition be examined by a medical practitioner of his own choice at his own expense.

9.5 If a person is required to take or apply any medication in compliance with medical directions, the custody officer is responsible for its safekeeping and for ensuring that he is given the opportunity to take or apply it at the appropriate time. No police officer may administer controlled drugs subject to the Misuse of Drugs Act 1971 for this purpose. A person may administer such drugs to himself only under the personal supervision of the police surgeon.

9.6 If a detained person has in his possession or claims to need medication relating to a heart condition, diabetes, epilepsy or a condition of comparable potential seriousness then, even though paragraph 9.2 may not apply, the advice of the police surgeon must be obtained.

c) Documentation

9.7 A record must be made of any arrangements made for an examination by a police surgeon under paragraph 9.1 above and of any complaint reported under that paragraph together with any relevant remarks by the custody officer.

9.8 A record must be kept of any request for a medical examination under paragraph 9.4, of the arrangements for any examination made, and of any medical directions to the police.

9.9 Subject to the requirements of section 4 above the custody record shall include not only a record of all medication that a detained person has in his possession on arrival at the police station but also a note of any such medication he claims he needs but does not have with him.

The Notes for Guidance for this section state:

9A The need to call a police surgeon need not apply to minor ailment or injuries which do not need attention. However, all such ailments must be recorded in the custody record and any doubt must be resolved in favour of calling the police surgeon.

9B It is important to remember that a person who appears to be drunk or behaving abnormally may be suffering from illness or the effects of drugs or may have sustained injury (particularly head injury) which is not apparent, and that someone needing or addicted to certain drugs may experience harmful effects within a short time of being deprived of their supply. Police should therefore always call the police surgeon when in any doubt, and act with all due speed.

9C If a medical practitioner does not record his clinical findings in the custody record, the record must show where they are recorded.

10. *Cautions*

a) *When a caution must be given*

10.1 A person whom there are grounds to suspect of an offence must be cautioned before any questions about it (or further questions if it is his answers to previous questions that provide grounds for suspicion) are put to him for the purpose of obtaining evidence which may be given to a court in a prosecution. He therefore need not be cautioned if questions are put for other purposes, for example, to establish his identity or his ownership of any vehicle or the need to search him in the exercise of powers of stop and search.

10.2 Whenever a person who is not under arrest is initially cautioned before or during an interview he must at the same time be told that he is not under arrest and is not obliged to remain with the officer (see paragraph 3.15).

10.3 A person must be cautioned upon arrest for an offence unless:

(a)   it is impracticable to do so by reason of his condition or behaviour at the time; or

(b)   he has already been cautioned immediately prior to arrest in accordance with paragraph 10.1 above.

b) *Action: general*

10.4 The caution shall be in the following terms:

'You do not have to say anything unless you wish to do so, but what you say may be given in evidence.'

Minor deviations do not constitute a breach of this requirement provided that the sense of the caution is preserved. [See Notes 10C and 10D.]

10.5 When there is a break in questioning under caution the interviewing officer must ensure that the person being questioned is aware that he remains under caution. If there is any doubt the caution should be given again in full when the interview resumes. [See Note 10A]

c) *Juveniles, the mentally disordered and the mentally handicapped*

10.6 If a juvenile or a person who is mentally disordered or mentally handicapped is cautioned in the absence of the appropriate adult, the caution must be repeated in the adult's presence.

d) *Documentation*

10.7 A record shall be made when a caution is given under this section, either in the officer's pocket book or in the interview record as appropriate.

The Notes for Guidance for this section state:

10A In considering whether or not to caution again after a break, the officer should bear in mind that he may have to satisfy a court that the person understood that he was still under caution when the interview resumed.

10B It is not necessary to give or repeat a caution when informing a person who is not under arrest that he may be prosecuted for an offence.

10C If it appears that a person does not understand what the caution means, the officer who has given it should go on to explain it in his own words.

10D In case anyone who is given a caution is unclear about its significance, the officer concerned should explain that the caution is given in pursuance of the general principle of English law that a person need not answer any questions or provide any information which might tend to incriminate him, and that no adverse inferences from this silence should be drawn at any trial that takes place. The person should not, however, be left with a false impression that non-cooperation will have no effect on his immediate treatment as, for example, his refusal to provide his name and address when charged with an offence may render him liable to detention.

11. *Interviews: general*

a) Action

11.1 Following a decision to arrest a suspect he must not be interviewed about the relevant offence except at a police station (or other authorised place of detention) unless the consequent delay would be likely:

(*a*)   to lead to interference with or harm to evidence connected with an offence or interference with or physical harm to other persons; or

(*b*)   to lead to the alerting of other persons suspected of having committed an offence but not yet arrested for it; or

(*c*)   to hinder the recovery of property obtained in consequence of the commission of an offence.

Interviewing in any of these circumstances should cease once the relevant risk has been averted or the necessary questions have been put in order to attempt to avert that risk. For the definition of an interview see Note 11A.

11.2 Immediately prior to the commencement or re-commencement of any interview at a police station or other authorised place of detention, the interviewing officer should remind the suspect of his entitlement to free legal advice. It is the responsibility of the interviewing officer to ensure that all such reminders are noted in the record of interview.

11.3 No police officer may try to obtain answers to questions or to elicit a statement by the use of oppression or shall indicate, except in answer to a direct question, what action will be taken on the part of the police if the person being interviewed answers questions, makes a statement or refuses to do either. If the person asks the officer directly what action will be taken in the event of his answering questions, making a statement or refusing to do either, then the officer may inform the person what action the police propose to take in that event provided that the action is itself proper and warranted.

11.4 As soon as a police officer who is making enquiries of any person about an offence believes that a prosecution should be brought against him and that there is sufficient evidence for it to succeed, he should ask the person if he has anything further to say. If the person indicates that he has nothing more to say the officer shall without delay cease to question him about that offence. This should not, however, be taken to prevent officers in revenue cases or acting under the confiscation provisions of the Criminal Justice Act 1988 or the Drug Trafficking

Offences Act 1986 from inviting suspects to complete a formal question and answer record after the interview is concluded.

b) *Interview records*

11.5

(*a*)   An accurate record must be made of each interview with a person suspected of an offence, whether or not the interview takes place at a police station.

(*b*)   The record must state the place of the interview, the time it begins and ends, the time the record is made (if different), any breaks in the interview and the names of all those present; and must be made on the forms provided for this purpose or in the officer's pocket-book or in accordance with the code of practice for the tape-recording of police interviews with suspects.

(*c*)   The record must be made during the course of the interview, unless the investigating officer's view this would not be practicable or would interfere with the conduct of the interview, and must constitute either a verbatim record of what has been said or, failing this, an account of the interview which adequately and accurately summarises it.

11.6   The requirement to record the names of all those present at an interview does not apply to police officers interviewing persons detained under the Prevention of Terrorism (Temporary Provisions) Act 1989. Instead the record shall state the warrant number and duty station of such officers.

11.7   If an interview record is not made during the course of the interview it must be made as soon as practicable after its completion.

11.8   Written interview records must be timed and signed by the maker.

11.9   If an interview record is not completed in the course of the interview the reason must be recorded in the officer's pocket book.

11.10   Unless it is impracticable the person interviewed shall be given the opportunity to read the interview record and to sign it as correct or to indicate the respects in which he considers it inaccurate. If the interview is tape-recorded the arrangements set out in the relevant code of practice apply. If the person concerned cannot read or refuses to read the record or to sign it, the senior police officer present shall read it over to him and ask him whether he would like to sign it as correct (or make his mark) or to indicate the respects in which he considers it inaccurate. The police officer shall then certify on the interview record itself what has occurred.

11.11   If the appropriate adult or the person's solicitor is present during the interview, he should also be given an opportunity to read and sign the interview record (or any written statement taken down by a police officer).

11.12   Any refusal by a person to sign an interview record when asked to do so in accordance with the provisions of the code must itself be recorded.

11.13   A written record should also be made of any comments made by a suspected person, including unsolicited comments, which are outside the context of an interview but which might be relevant to the offence. Any such record must be timed and signed by the maker. Where practicable the person shall be given the opportunity to read that record and to sign it as correct or to indicate the respects in which he considers it inaccurate. Any refusal to sign should be recorded.

c) Juveniles, the mentally disordered and the mentally handicapped

11.14 A juvenile or a person who is mentally disordered or mentally handicapped, whether suspected or not, must not be interviewed or asked to provide or sign a written statement in the absence of the appropriate adult unless Annex C applies.
11.15 Juveniles may only be interviewed at their places of education in exceptional circumstances and then only where the principal or his nominee agrees. Every effort should be made to notify both the parent(s) or other person responsible for the juvenile's welfare and the appropriate adult (if this is a different person) that the police want to interview the juvenile and reasonable time should be allowed to enable the appropriate adult to be present at the interview. Where awaiting the appropriate adult would cause unreasonable delay and unless the interviewee is suspected of an offence against the educational establishment, the principal or his nominee can act as the appropriate adult for the purposes of the interview.
11.16 Where the appropriate adult is present at an interview, he should be informed that he is not expected to act simply as an observer; and also that the purposes of his presence are, first, to advise the person being questioned and to observe whether or not the interview is being conducted properly and fairly, and, secondly, to facilitate communication with the person being interviewed.

The Notes for Guidance for this section state:
11A An interview is the questioning of a person regarding his involvement or suspected involvement in a criminal offence or offences. Questioning a person only to obtain information or his explanation of the facts or in the ordinary course of the officer's duties does not constitute an interview for the purpose of this code. Neither does questioning which is confined to the proper and effective conduct of a search.
11B It is important to bear in mind that, although juveniles or persons who are mentally disordered or mentally handicapped are often capable of providing reliable evidence, they may, without knowing or wishing to do so, be particularly prone in certain circumstances to provide information which is unreliable, misleading or self-incriminating. Special care should therefore always be exercised in questioning such a person, and the appropriate adult should be involved, if there is any doubt about a person' s age, mental state or capacity. Because of the risk of unreliable evidence it is also important to obtain corroboration of any facts admitted whenever possible.
11C A juvenile should not be arrested at his place of education unless this is unavoidable. In this case the principal or his nominee must be informed.

12. Interviews in police stations

a) Action

12.1 If a police officer wishes to interview, or conduct enquiries which require the presence of, a detained person the custody officer is responsible for deciding whether to deliver him into his custody.
12.2 In any period of 24 hours a detained person must be allowed a continuous period of at least 8 hours for rest, free from questioning, travel or any interruption arising out of the investigation concerned. This period should normally be at night.

The period of rest may not be interrupted or delayed unless there are reasonable grounds for believing that it would:

(i)   involve a risk of harm to persons or serious loss of, or damage to, property:
(ii)   delay unnecessarily the person's release from custody; or
(iii)   otherwise prejudice the outcome of the investigation.

If a person is arrested at a police station after going there voluntarily, the period of 24 hours runs from the time of his arrest and not the time of arrival at the police station.

12.3 A detained person may not be supplied with intoxicating liquor except on medical directions. No person who is unfit through drink or drugs to the extent that he is unable to appreciate the significance of questions put to him and his answers may be questioned about an alleged offence in that condition except in accordance with Annex C. [See Note 12B.]

12.4 As far as practicable interviews shall take place in interview rooms which must be adequately heated, lit and ventilated.

12.5 Persons being questioned or making statements shall not be required to stand.

12.6 Before the commencement of an interview each interviewing officer shall identify himself and any other officers present by name and rank to the person being interviewed, except in the case of persons detained under the Prevention of Terrorism (Temporary Provisions) Act 1989 when each officer shall identify himself by his warrant number and rank rather than his name.

12.7 Breaks from interviewing shall be made at recognised meal times. Short breaks for refreshment shall also be provided at intervals of approximately two hours, subject to the interviewing officer's discretion to delay a break if there are reasonable grounds for believing that it would:

(i)   involve a risk of harm to persons or serious loss of, or damage to, property;
(ii)   delay unnecessarily the person's release from custody; or
(iii)   otherwise prejudice the outcome of the investigation.

12.8 If in the course of the interview a complaint is made by the person being questioned or on his behalf concerning the provisions of this code then the interviewing officer shall:

(i)   record it in the interview record; and
(ii)   inform the custody officer, who is then responsible for dealing with it in accordance with section 9 of this code.

b) Documentation

12.9 A record must be made of the times at which a detained person is not in the custody of the custody officer, and why; and of the reason for any refusal to deliver him out of that custody.

12.10 A record must be made of any intoxicating liquor supplied to a detained person, in accordance with paragraph 12.3 above.

12.11 Any decision to delay a break in an interview must be recorded, with grounds, in the interview record.

12.12 All written statements made at police stations under caution shall be written on the forms provided for the purpose.

12.13 All written statements made under caution shall be taken in accordance with Annex D to this code.

The Notes for Guidance for this section state:

12A If the interview has been contemporaneously recorded and the record signed by the person interviewed in accordance with paragraph 11.10 above, or has been tape recorded, it is normally unnecessary to ask for a written statement. Statements under caution should normally be taken in these circumstances only at the person's express wish. An officer may, however, ask him whether or not he wants to make such a statement.

12B The police surgeon can give advice about whether or not a person is fit to be interviewed in accordance with paragraph 12.3 above.

13. Interpreters

a) General

13.1 Information on obtaining the services of a suitably qualified interpreter for the deaf or for persons who do not understand English is given in Note for Guidance 3D.

b) Foreign languages

13.2 Unless Annex C applies, a person must not be interviewed in the absence of a person capable of acting as interpreter if:

(*a*)   he has difficulty in understanding English;

(*b*)   the interviewing officer cannot himself speak the person's own language; and

(*c*)   the person wishes an interpreter to be present.

13.3 The interviewing officer shall ensure that the interpreter makes a note of the interview at the time in the language of the person being interviewed for use in the event of his being called to give evidence, and certifies its accuracy. He shall allow sufficient time for the interpreter to make a note of each question and answer after each has been put or given and interpreted. The person shall be given an opportunity to read it or have it read to him and sign it as correct or to indicate the respects in which he considers it inaccurate. If the interview is tape-recorded the arrangements set out in the relevant code of practice apply.

13.4 In the case of a person making a statement in a language other than English:

(*a*)   the interpreter shall take down the statement in the language in which it is made;

(*b*)   the person making the statement shall be invited to sign it; and

(*c*)   an official English translation shall be made in due course.

c) The deaf and speech handicapped

13.5 If a person appears to be deaf or there is doubt about his hearing or speaking ability, he must not be interviewed in the absence of an interpreter unless he agrees in writing to be interviewed without one or Annex C applies.

13.6 An interpreter should also be called if a juvenile is interviewed and the parent or guardian present as the appropriate adult appears to be deaf or there is doubt about his hearing or speaking ability, unless he agrees in writing that the interview should proceed without one or Annex C applies.

13.7 The interviewing officer shall ensure that the interpreter is given an opportunity to read the record of the interview and to certify its accuracy in the event of his being called to give evidence.

d) Additional rules for detained persons

13.8 All reasonable attempts should be made to make clear to the detained person that interpreters will be provided at public expense.

13.9 Where paragraph 6.1 applies and the person concerned cannot communicate with the solicitor, whether because of language hearing or speech difficulties, an interpreter must be called. The interpreter may not be a police officer when interpretation is needed for the purposes of obtaining legal advice. In all other cases a police officer may only interpret if he first obtains the detained person's (or the appropriate adult's) agreement in writing or if the interview is tape-recorded in accordance with the relevant code of practice.

13.10 When a person is charged with an offence who appears to be deaf or there is doubt about his hearing or speaking ability or ability to understand English, and the custody officer cannot establish effective communication, arrangements must be made for an interpreter to explain as soon as practicable the offence concerned and any other information given by the custody officer.

e) Documentation

13.11 Action taken to call an interpreter under this section and any agreement to be interviewed in the absence of an interpreter must be recorded.

The Note for Guidance for this section states:

13A If the interpreter is needed as a prosecution witness at the person's trial, a second interpreter must act as the court interpreter.

14. Questioning: special restrictions

14.1 If a person has been arrested by one police force on behalf of another and the lawful period of detention in respect of that offence has not yet commenced in accordance with section 41 of the Police and Criminal Evidence Act 1984 no questions may be put to him about the offence while he is in transit between the forces except in order to clarify any voluntary statement made by him.

14.2 If a person is in police detention at a hospital he may not be questioned without the agreement of a responsible doctor. [See Note 14A.]

The Note for Guidance for this section states:
14A If questioning takes place at a hospital under paragraph 14.2 (or on the way to or from a hospital) the period concerned counts towards the total period of detention permitted.

15. *Reviews and extensions of detention*

a) *Action*

15.1 The review officer is responsible under section 40 of the Police and Criminal Evidence Act 1984 (or, in terrorist cases, under Schedule 3 to the Prevention of Terrorism (Temporary Provisions) Act 1989) for determining whether or not a person's detention continues to be necessary. In reaching a decision he shall provide an opportunity to the detained person himself to make representations (unless he is unfit to do so because of his condition or behaviour) or to his solicitor or the appropriate adult if available at the time. Other persons having an interest in the person's welfare may make representations at the review officer's discretion.

15.2 The same persons may make representations to the officer determining whether further detention should be authorised under section 42 of the Act or under Schedule 3 to the 1989 Act. [See Note 15A.]

b) *Documentation*

15.3 Before conducting a review the review officer must ensure that the detained person is reminded of his entitlement to free legal advice. It is the responsibility of the review officer to ensure that all such reminders are noted in the custody record.

15.4 The grounds for and extent of any delay in conducting a review shall be recorded.

15.5 Any written representations shall be retained.

15.6 A record shall be made as soon as practicable of the outcome of each review and application for a warrant of further detention or its extension.

The Notes for Guidance for this section state:

15A If the detained person is likely to be asleep at the latest time when a review of detention or an authorisation of continued detention may take place, the appropriate officer should bring it forward so that the detained person may make representations without being woken up.

15B An application for a warrant of further detention or its extension should be made between 10am and 9pm, and if possible during normal court hours. It will not be practicable to arrange for a court to sit specially outside the hours of 10am to 9pm. If it appears possible that a special sitting may be needed (either at a weekend, Bank/Public Holiday or on a weekday outside normal court hours but between 10am and 9pm) then the clerk to the justices should be given notice and informed of this possibility, while the court is sitting if possible.

15C If in the circumstances the only practicable way of conducting a review is over the telephone then this is permissible, provided that the requirements of section 40 of the Police and Criminal Evidence Act 1984 or of Schedule 3 to the Prevention of Terrorism (Temporary Provisions) Act 1989 are observed. However, a review to decide whether to authorise a person's continued detention under section 42 of the Act must be done in person rather than over the telephone.

16. Charging of detained persons

a) Action

16.1 When an officer considers that there is sufficient evidence to prosecute a detained person, and that there is sufficient evidence for a prosecution to succeed, and that the person has said all that he wishes to say about the offence, he should without delay (and subject to the following qualification) bring him before the custody officer who shall then be responsible for considering whether or not he should be charged. When a person is detained in respect of more than one offence it is permissible to delay bringing him before the custody officer until the above conditions are satisfied in respect of all the offences (but see para 11.4). Any resulting action should be taken in the presence of the appropriate adult if the person is a juvenile or mentally disordered or mentally handicapped.

16.2 When a detained person is charged with or informed that he may be prosecuted for an offence he shall be cautioned in the terms of paragraph 10.4 above.

16.3 At the time a person is charged he shall be given a written notice showing particulars of the offence with which he is charged and including the name of the officer in the case (in terrorist cases the officer's warrant number instead), his police station and the reference number for the case. So far as possible the particulars of the charge shall be stated in simple terms, but they shall also show the precise offence in law with which he is charged. The notice shall begin with the following words:

'You are charged with the offence(s) shown below. You do not have to say anything unless you wish to do so, but what you say may be given in evidence.'

If the person is a juvenile or is mentally disordered or mentally handicapped the notice shall be given to the appropriate adult.

16.4 If at any time after a person has been charged with or informed he may be prosecuted for an offence a police officer wishes to bring to the notice of that person any written statement made by another person or the content of an interview with another person, he shall hand to that person a true copy of any such written statement or bring to his attention the content of the interview record, but shall say or do nothing to invite any reply or comment save to caution him in the terms of paragraph 10.4 above. If the person cannot read then the officer may read it to him. If the person is a juvenile or mentally disordered or mentally handicapped the copy shall also be given to, or the interview record brought to the attention of, the appropriate adult.

16.5 Questions relating to an offence may not be put to a person after he has been charged with that offence, or informed that he may be prosecuted for it, unless they are necessary for the purpose of preventing or minimising harm or loss to some other person or to the public or for clearing up an ambiguity in a previous answer or statement, or where it is in the interests of justice that the person should have put to him and have an opportunity to comment on information concerning the offence which has come to light since he was charged or informed that he might be prosecuted. Before any such questions are put he shall be cautioned in the terms of paragraph 10.4 above. [See Note 16A.]

16.6 Where a juvenile is charged with an offence and the custody officer authorises his continuing detention he must try to make arrangements for the juvenile to be taken into care of a local authority to be detained pending appearance in court unless he certifies that it is impracticable to do so in accordance with section 38(6) of the Police and Criminal Evidence Act 1984. [See Note 16B.]

b) Documentation

16.7 A record shall be made of anything a detained person says when charged.

16.8 Any questions put after charge and answers given relating to the offence shall be contemporaneously recorded in full on the forms provided and the record signed by that person or, if he refuses, by the interviewing officer and any third parties present. If the questions are tape-recorded the arrangements set out in the relevant code of practice apply.

16.9 If it is not practicable to make arrangements for the transfer of a juvenile into local authority care in accordance with paragraph 16.6 above the custody officer must record the reasons and make out a certificate to be produced before the court together with the juvenile.

The Notes for Guidance for this section state:

16A The service of the Notice of Intended Prosecution under sections 1 and 2 of the Road Traffic Offenders Act 1988 does not amount to informing a person that he may be prosecuted for an offence and so does not preclude further questioning in relation to that offence.

16B Neither a juvenile's behaviour nor the nature of the offence with which he is charged provides grounds for the custody officer to retain him in police custody rather than seek to arrange for his transfer to the care of the local authority.

ANNEX A
INTIMATE AND STRIP SEARCHES (See paragraph 4.1)

a) Action

1. Body orifices may be searched only if an officer of the rank of superintendent or above has reasonable grounds for believing:

(*a*)   that an article which could cause physical injury to a detained person or others at the police station has been concealed; or

(*b*)   that the person has concealed a Class A drug which he intended to supply to another or to export; and

(*c*)   that in either case an intimate search is the only practicable means of removing it.

The reasons why an intimate search is considered necessary shall be explained to the person before the search takes place.

2. An intimate search may only be carried out by a registered medical practitioner or registered nurse, unless an officer of at least the rank of superintendent considers that this is not practicable and the search is to take place under sub-paragraph 1(*a*) above.

3. An intimate search under sub-paragraph 1(*a*) above may take place only at a hospital, surgery, other medical premises or police station. A search under sub-paragraph 1(*b*) may take place only at a hospital, surgery or other medical premises.

4. An intimate search at a police station of a juvenile or a mentally disordered or mentally handicapped person may take place only in the presence of the appropriate adult of the same sex (unless the person specifically requests the presence of a particular adult of the opposite sex who is readily available). In the case of a juvenile the search may take place in the absence of the appropriate adult only if the juvenile signifies in the presence of the appropriate adult that he prefers the search to be done in his absence and the appropriate adult agrees. A record should be made of the juvenile's decision and signed by the appropriate adult.

5. A strip search (that is a search involving the removal of more than outer clothing) may take place only if the custody officer considers it to be necessary to remove an article which the detained person would not be allowed to keep.

6. Where an intimate search under sub-paragraph 1(*a*) above or a strip search is carried out by a police officer, the officer must be of the same sex as the person searched. Subject to paragraph 4 above, no person of the opposite sex who is not a medical practitioner or nurse shall be present, nor shall anyone whose presence is unnecessary.

b) Documentation

7. In the case of an intimate search the custody officer shall as soon as practicable record which parts of the person's body were searched, who carried out the search, who was present, the reasons for the search and its results.

8. In the case of a strip search he shall record the reasons for the search and its result.

9. If an intimate search is carried out by a police officer, the reason why it is impracticable for a suitably qualified person to conduct it must be recorded.

ANNEX B
DELAY IN NOTIFYING ARREST OR ALLOWING ACCESS TO
LEGAL ADVICE

A. *Persons detained under the Police and Criminal Evidence Act 1984*

a) Action

1. The rights set out in sections 5 or 6 of the code or both may be delayed if the person is in police detention in connection with a serious arrestable offence, has not yet been charged with an offence and an officer of the rank of superintendent or above has reasonable grounds for believing that the exercise of either right:

(i)   will lead to interference with or harm to evidence connected with a serious arrestable offence or interference with or physical injury to other persons; or

(ii)   will lead to the alerting of other persons suspected of having committed such an offence but not yet arrested for it; or

(iii)   will hinder the recovery of property obtained as a result of such an offence. [See Note B3.]

2.   These rights may also be delayed where the serious arrestable offence is either:

(i)   a drug trafficking offence and the officer has reasonable grounds for believing that the detained person has benefited from drug trafficking, and that the recovery of the value of that persons's proceeds of drug trafficking will be hindered by the exercise of either right or;

(ii)   an offence to which Part VI of the Criminal Justice Act 1988 (covering confiscation orders) applies and the officer has reasonable grounds for believing that the detained person has benefited from the offence, and that the recovery of the value of the property obtained by that person from or in connection with the offence or the pecuniary advantage derived by him from or in connection with it will be hindered by the exercise of either right.

3.   Access to a solicitor may not be delayed on the grounds that he might advise the person not to answer any questions or that the solicitor was initially asked to attend the police station by someone else, provided that the person himself then wishes to see the solicitor. In the latter case the detained person must be told that the solicitor has come to the police station at another person's request, and must be asked to sign the custody record to signify whether or not he wishes to see the solicitor.

4.   These rights may be delayed only for as long as is necessary and, subject to paragraph 9 below, in no case beyond 36 hours after the relevant time as defined in section 41 of the Police and Criminal Evidence Act 1984. If the above grounds cease to apply within this time, the person must as soon as practicable be asked if he wishes to exercise either right, the custody record must be noted accordingly, and action must be taken in accordance with the relevant section of the code.

5.   A detained person must be permitted to consult a solicitor for a reasonable time before any court hearing.

b) Documentation

6.   The grounds for action under this Annex shall be recorded and the person informed of them as soon as practicable.

7.   Any reply given by a person under paragraphs 4 or 9 must be recorded and the person asked to endorse the record in relation to whether he wishes to receive legal advice at this point.

B. Persons detained under the Prevention of Terrorism (Temporary Provisions) Act 1989

a) Action

8.   The rights set out in sections 5 or 6 of this code or both may be delayed if paragraph 1 above applies or if an officer of the rank of superintendent or above has reasonable grounds for believing that the exercise of either right:

(a)   will lead to interference with the gathering of information about the commission, preparation or instigation of acts of terrorism; or (*b*) by alerting any person, will make it more difficult to prevent an act of terrorism or to secure the apprehension, prosecution or conviction of any person in connection with the commission, preparation or instigation of an act of terrorism.

9. These rights may be delayed only for as long as is necessary and in no case beyond 48 hours from the time of arrest. If the above grounds cease to apply within this time, the person must as soon as practicable be asked if he wishes to exercise either right, the custody record must be noted accordingly, and action must be taken in accordance with the relevant section of this code.

10. Paragraphs 3 and 5 above apply.

b) Documentation

11. Paragraphs 6 and 7 above apply.

The Notes for Guidance for this Annex state:

B1 Even if Annex B applies in the case of a juvenile, or a person who is mentally disordered or mentally handicapped, action to inform the appropriate adult (and the person responsible for a juvenile's welfare, if that is a different person) must nevertheless be taken in accordance with paragraphs 3.7 and 3.9 of this code.

B2 In the case of Commonwealth citizens and foreign nationals see Note 7A.

B3 Police detention is defined in section 118(2) of the Police and Criminal Evidence Act 1984.

B4 The effect of paragraph 1 above is that the officer may authorise delaying access to a specific solicitor only if he has reasonable grounds to believe that the specific solicitor will, inadvertently or otherwise, pass on a message from the detained person or act in some other way which will lead to any of the three results in paragraph 1 coming about. In these circumstances the officer should offer the detained person access to a solicitor (who is not the specific solicitor referred to above) on the Duty Solicitor Scheme.

B5 The fact that the grounds for delaying notification of arrest under paragraph 1 above may be satisfied does not automatically mean that the grounds for delaying access to legal advice will also be satisfied.

ANNEX C
URGENT INTERVIEWS

1. If, and only if, an officer of the rank of superintendent or above considers that delay will involve an immediate risk of harm to persons or serious loss of or serious damage to property:

(*a*) a person heavily under the influence of drink or drugs may be interviewed in that state; or

(*b*) an arrested juvenile or a person who is mentally disordered or mentally handicapped may be interviewed in the absence of the appropriate adult; or

(*c*) a person who has difficulty in understanding English or who has a hearing disability may be interviewed in the absence of an interpreter.

2. Questioning in these circumstances may not continue once sufficient information to avert the immediate risk has been obtained.
3. A record shall be made of the grounds for any decision to interview a person under paragraph 1 above.

The Note for Guidance for this Annex states:
C1 The special groups referred to in Annex C are all particularly vulnerable. The provisions of the annex, which override safeguards designed to protect them and to minimise the risk of interviews producing unreliable evidence, should be applied only in exceptional cases of need.

ANNEX D
WRITTEN STATEMENTS UNDER CAUTION (See paragraph 12.13)

a) *Written by a person under caution*

1. A person shall always be invited to write down himself what he wants to say.
2. Where the person wishes to write it himself, he shall be asked to write out and sign before writing what he wants to say, the following:
'I make this statement of my own free will. I understand that I need not say anything unless I wish to do so and that what I say may be given in evidence.'
3. Any person writing his own statement shall be allowed to do so without any prompting except that a police officer may indicate to him which matters are material or question any ambiguity in the statement.

b) *Written by a police officer*

4. If a person says that he would like someone to write it for him, a police officer shall write the statement, but, before starting, he must ask him to sign, or make his mark, to the following:
'I . . . wish to make a statement. I want someone to write down what I say. I understand that I need not say anything unless I wish to do so and that what I say may be given in evidence.'
5. Where a police officer writes the statement, he must take down the exact words spoken by the person making it and he must not edit or paraphrase it. Any questions that are necessary (eg to make it more intelligible) and the answers given must be recorded contemporaneously on the statement form.
6. When the writing of a statement by a police officer is finished the person making it shall be asked to read it and to make any corrections, alterations or additions he wishes. When he has finished reading it he shall be asked to write and sign or make his mark on the following certificate at the end of the statement:
'I have read the above statement, and I have been able to correct, alter or add anything I wish. This statement is true. I have made it of my own free will.'
7. If the person making the statement cannot read, or refuses to read it, or to write the above mentioned certificate at the end of it or to sign it, the senior police officer present shall read it over to him and ask him whether he would like to correct, alter or add anything and to put his signature or make his mark at the end. The police officer shall then certify on the statement itself what has occurred.

ANNEX E
SUMMARY OF PROVISIONS RELATING TO MENTALLY DISORDERED
AND MENTALLY HANDICAPPED PERSONS

1. If an officer has any suspicion or is told in good faith that a person of any age, whether or not in custody, may be suffering from mental disorder or mental handicap, or cannot understand the significance of questions put to him or his replies, then he shall be treated as a mentally disordered or mentally handicapped person. (See paragraph 1.4).

2. In the case of a person who is mentally disordered or mentally handicapped, 'the appropriate adult' means:

(a) a relative, guardian or some other person responsible for his care or custody;

(b) someone who has experience of dealing with mentally disordered or mentally handicapped persons but is not a police officer or employed by the police; or

(c) failing either of the above, some other responsible adult aged 18 or over who is not a police officer or employed by the police. (See paragraph 1.7(b).)

3. If the custody officer authorises the detention of a person who is mentally handicapped or is suffering from a mental disorder he must as soon as practicable inform the appropriate adult of the grounds for the person's detention and his whereabouts, and ask the adult to come to the police station to see the person. If the appropriate adult is already at the police station when information is given as required in paragraphs 3.1 to 3.4 the information must be given to the detained person in his presence. If the appropriate adult is not at the police station when the information is given then the information must be given to the detained person again in the presence of the appropriate adult once that person arrives. (See paragraphs 3.9 and 3.11.)

4. If the appropriate adult, having been informed of the right to legal advice, considers that legal advice should be taken, the provisions of section 6 of the code apply as if the mentally disordered or mentally handicapped person had requested access to legal advice. (See paragraph 3.13.)

5. If a person brought to a police station appears to be suffering from mental disorder or is incoherent other than through drunkenness alone, or if a detained person subsequently appears to be mentally disordered, the custody officer must immediately call the police surgeon or, in urgent cases, send the person to hospital or call the nearest available medical practitioner. It is not intended that these provisions should delay the transfer of a person to a place of safety under section 136 of the Mental Health Act 1983 where that is applicable. Where an assessment under that Act is to take place at the police station, the custody officer had discretion not to call the police surgeon so long as he believes that the assessment by a registered medical practitioner can be undertaken without undue delay. (See paragraph 9.2.)

6. It is imperative that a mentally disordered or mentally handicapped person who has been detained under section 136 of the Mental Health Act 1983 should be assessed as soon as possible. If that assessment is to take place at the police station, an approved social worker and a registered medical practitioner should be called to the police station as soon as possible in order to interview and examine the

person. Once the person has been interviewed and examined and suitable arrangements have been made for his treatment or care, he can no longer be detained under section 136. The person should not be released until he has been seen by both the approved social worker and the registered medical practitioner (see paragraph 3.10).

7. If a mentally disordered or mentally handicapped person is cautioned in the absence of the appropriate adult, the caution must be repeated in the adult's presence. (See paragraph 10.6.)

8. A mentally disordered or mentally handicapped person must not be interviewed or asked to provide or sign a written statement in the absence of the appropriate adult unless an officer of the rank of superintendent or above considers that delay will involve an immediate risk of harm to persons or serious loss of or serious damage to property. Questioning in these circumstances may not continue in the absence of the appropriate adult once sufficient information to avert the risk has been obtained. A record shall be made of the grounds for any decision to begin an interview in these circumstances. (See paragraph 11.14 and Annex C.)

9. Where the appropriate adult is present at an interview, he should be informed that he is not expected to act simply as an observer; and also that the purposes of his presence are, first, to advise the person being interviewed and to observe whether or not the interview is being conducted properly and fairly, and, secondly, to facilitate communication with the person being interviewed. (See paragraph 11.16.)

10. If the detention of a mentally disordered or mentally handicapped person is reviewed by a review officer or a superintendent, the appropriate adult must, if available at the time, be given the opportunity to make representations to the officer about the need for continuing detention. (See paras 15.1 and 15.2.)

11. If the custody officer charges a mentally disordered or mentally handicapped person with an offence or takes such other action as is appropriate when there is sufficient evidence for a prosecution this must be done in the presence of the appropriate adult. The written notice embodying any charge must be given to the appropriate adult. (See paragraphs 16.1 to 16.3.)

12. An intimate search of a mentally disordered or mentally handicapped person may take place only in the presence of the appropriate adult of the same sex, unless the person specifically requests the presence of a particular adult of the opposite sex. (See Annex A, paragraph 5.)

The Notes for Guidance for this Annex state:

E1 In the case of persons who are mentally disordered or mentally handicapped, it may in certain circumstances be more satisfactory for all concerned if the appropriate adult is someone who has experience or training in their care rather than a relative lacking such qualifications. But if the person himself prefers a relative to a better qualified stranger his wishes should if practicable be respected (see Note 1E).

E2 The purpose of the provision at paragraph 3.13 is to protect the rights of a mentally disordered or mentally handicapped person who does not understand the significance of what is being said to him. It is not intended that, if such person wishes to exercise the right to legal advice, no action should be taken until the appropriate adult arrives. (See Note 3G.)

E3 It is important to bear in mind that although persons who are mentally disordered or mentally handicapped are often capable of providing reliable evidence, they may, without knowing or wishing to do so, be particularly prone in certain circumstances to provide information which is unreliable, misleading or self-incriminating. Special care should therefore always be exercised in questioning such a person, and the appropriate adult involved, if there is any doubt about a person's mental state or capacity. Because of the risk of unreliable evidence, it is important to obtain corroboration of any facts admitted whenever possible. (See Note 11B.)

E4 Because of the risks referred to in Note E3, which the presence of the appropriate adult is intended to minimise, officers of superintendent rank or above should exercise their discretion to authorise the commencement of an interview in the adult's absence only in exceptional cases, where it is necessary to avert an immediate risk of serious harm. (See Annex C, sub-paragraph 1(*b*) and Note C1.

ANNEX F
COUNTRIES WITH WHICH CONSULAR CONVENTIONS ARE IN FORCE AS AT 20 APRIL 1990

Algeria
Antigua and Barbuda
Argentina
Australia
Austria
Bahamas
Bangladesh
Belgium
Benin
Bhutan
Bolivia
Brazil
Bulgaria
Burkina Faso
Byelorussian SSR
Cameroon
Canada
Cape Verde
Central African Republic
Chile
China
Colombia
Congo
Costa Rica
Côte d'Ivoire
Cuba
Cyprus
Czechoslovakia

Democratic People's Republic of Korea
Denmark
Djibouti
Dominica
Dominican Republic
Ecuador
Egypt
El Salvador
Equatorial Guinea
Fiji
Finland
France
Gabon
German Democratic Republic
Germany, Federal Republic of
Ghana
Greece
Guatemala
Guinea
Guyana
Haiti
Holy See
Honduras
Hungary
Iceland
India
Indonesia
Iran (Islamic Republic of)
Iraq
Ireland
Israel
Italy
Jamaica
Japan
Jordan
Kenya
Kiribati
Lao People's Democratic Republic
Lebanon
Lesotho
Liberia
Liechtenstein
Luxembourg
Madagascar
Malawi
Mali
Mauritius
Mexico

Mongolia
Morocco
Mozambique
Nepal
Netherlands
New Zealand
Nicaragua
Niger
Nigeria
Norway
Oman
Pakistan
Panama
Papua New Guinea
Paraguay
Peru
Philippines
Poland
Portugal
Republic of Korea
Republic of South Vietnam
Romania
Rwanda
Saint Lucia
Samoa
Sao Tome and Principe
Saudi Arabia
Senegal
Seychelles
Somalia
South Africa
Soviet Union
Spain
Suriname
Sweden
Switzerland
Syrian Arab Republic
Togo
Tonga
Trinidad and Tobago
Tunisia
Turkey
Tuvalu
Ukrainian SSR
United Arab Emirates
United Kingdom
United Republic of Tanzania
United States of America

Uruguay
Vanuatu
Venezuela
Yemen
Yugoslavia
Zaire

Index